DATE DUE

NO 28 05			
FE 9 06			
MR 2 8 07			
AP 2 3 07			

DEMCO 38-296

MARLOW

Major Literary Characters

**THE ANCIENT WORLD THROUGH
THE SEVENTEENTH CENTURY**

ACHILLES
Homer, *Iliad*

CALIBAN
William Shakespeare, *The Tempest*
Robert Browning, *Caliban upon Setebos*

CLEOPATRA
William Shakespeare, *Antony and
    Cleopatra*
John Dryden, *All for Love*
George Bernard Shaw, *Caesar and
    Cleopatra*

DON QUIXOTE
Miguel de Cervantes, *Don Quixote*
Franz Kafka, *Parables*

FALSTAFF
William Shakespeare, *Henry IV, Part I,
    Henry IV, Part II, The Merry Wives
    of Windsor*

FAUST
Christopher Marlowe, *Doctor Faustus*
Johann Wolfgang von Goethe, *Faust*
Thomas Mann, *Doctor Faustus*

HAMLET
William Shakespeare, *Hamlet*

IAGO
William Shakespeare, *Othello*

JULIUS CAESAR
William Shakespeare, *Julius Caesar*
George Bernard Shaw, *Caesar and
    Cleopatra*

KING LEAR
William Shakespeare, *King Lear*

MACBETH
William Shakespeare, *Macbeth*

ODYSSEUS/ULYSSES
Homer, *Odyssey*
James Joyce, *Ulysses*

OEDIPUS
Sophocles, *Oedipus Rex, Oedipus
    at Colonus*

OTHELLO
William Shakespeare, *Othello*

ROSALIND
William Shakespeare, *As You Like It*

SANCHO PANZA
Miguel de Cervantes, *Don Quixote*
Franz Kafka, *Parables*

SATAN
The Book of Job
John Milton, *Paradise Lost*

SHYLOCK
William Shakespeare, *The Merchant
    of Venice*

THE WIFE OF BATH
Geoffrey Chaucer, *The Canterbury
    Tales*

**THE EIGHTEENTH AND
NINETEENTH CENTURIES**

AHAB
Herman Melville, *Moby-Dick*

ISABEL ARCHER
Henry James, *Portrait of a Lady*

EMMA BOVARY
Gustave Flaubert, *Madame Bovary*

DOROTHEA BROOKE
George Eliot, *Middlemarch*

CHELSEA HOUSE PUBLISHERS

Major Literary Characters

DAVID COPPERFIELD
Charles Dickens, *David Copperfield*

ROBINSON CRUSOE
Daniel Defoe, *Robinson Crusoe*

DON JUAN
Molière, *Don Juan*
Lord Byron, *Don Juan*

HUCK FINN
Mark Twain, *The Adventures of
    Tom Sawyer, Adventures of
    Huckleberry Finn*

CLARISSA HARLOWE
Samuel Richardson, *Clarissa*

HEATHCLIFF
Emily Brontë, *Wuthering Heights*

ANNA KARENINA
Leo Tolstoy, *Anna Karenina*

MR. PICKWICK
Charles Dickens, *The Pickwick Papers*

HESTER PRYNNE
Nathaniel Hawthorne, *The Scarlet Letter*

BECKY SHARP
William Makepeace Thackeray, *Vanity Fair*

LAMBERT STRETHER
Henry James, *The Ambassadors*

EUSTACIA VYE
Thomas Hardy, *The Return of the Native*

TWENTIETH CENTURY

ÁNTONIA
Willa Cather, *My Ántonia*

BRETT ASHLEY
Ernest Hemingway, *The Sun Also Rises*

HANS CASTORP
Thomas Mann, *The Magic Mountain*

HOLDEN CAULFIELD
J. D. Salinger, *The Catcher in the Rye*

CADDY COMPSON
William Faulkner, *The Sound and the Fury*

JANIE CRAWFORD
Zora Neale Hurston, *Their Eyes Were
    Watching God*

CLARISSA DALLOWAY
Virginia Woolf, *Mrs. Dalloway*

DILSEY
William Faulkner, *The Sound and the Fury*

GATSBY
F. Scott Fitzgerald, *The Great Gatsby*

HERZOG
Saul Bellow, *Herzog*

JOAN OF ARC
William Shakespeare, *Henry VI*
George Bernard Shaw, *Saint Joan*

LOLITA
Vladimir Nabokov, *Lolita*

WILLY LOMAN
Arthur Miller, *Death of a Salesman*

MARLOW
Joseph Conrad, *Lord Jim, Heart of
    Darkness, Youth, Chance*

PORTNOY
Philip Roth, *Portnoy's Complaint*

BIGGER THOMAS
Richard Wright, *Native Son*

CHELSEA HOUSE PUBLISHERS

Major Literary Characters

MARLOW

Edited and with an introduction by
HAROLD BLOOM

CHELSEA HOUSE PUBLISHERS
New York ◇ Philadelphia

Jacket illustration: Joseph Conrad in 1923 (UPI/Bettmann).

Chelsea House Publishers

Editor-in-Chief   Richard S. Papale
Managing Editor   Karyn Gullen Browne
Picture Editor   Adrian G. Allen
Art Director   Maria Epes
Manufacturing Manager   Gerald Levine

Major Literary Characters

Senior Editor   S. T. Joshi
Copy Chief   Philip Koslow
Designer   Maria Epes

Staff for MARLOW

Picture Researcher   Ellen Barrett
Assistant Art Director   Howard Brotman
Production Manager   Joseph Romano
Production Coordinator   Marie Claire Cebrián

First Printing

1   3   5   7   9   8   6   4   2

Library of Congress Cataloging-in-Publication Data

Marlow / edited and with an introduction by Harold Bloom.
        p.   cm.—(Major literary characters)
Includes bibliographical references and index.
ISBN 0-7910-0963-7.—ISBN 0-7910-1018-X (pbk.)
1. Conrad, Joseph, 1857–1927. Lord Jim.   2. Conrad, Joseph, 1857–1927.
Heart of Darkness.   3. Conrad, Joseph, 1857–1927—Characters—Marlow.
4. Marlow (Fictitious character). I. Bloom, Harold. II. Series.
PR6005.04L737   1992
823'.912-dc20
91-43981
CIP

CONTENTS

CONTENTS

THE ANALYSIS OF CHARACTER

Harold Bloom

"Character," according to our dictionaries, still has as a primary meaning a graphic symbol, such as a letter of the alphabet. This meaning reflects the word's apparent origin in the ancient Greek *charactēr,* a sharp stylus. *Charactēr* also meant the mark of the stylus' incisions. Recent fashions in literary criticism have reduced "character" in literature to a matter of marks upon a page. But our word "character" also has a very different meaning, matching that of the ancient Greek *ēthos,* "habitual way of life." Shall we say then that literary character is an imitation of human character, or is it just a grouping of marks? The issue is between a critic like Dr. Samuel Johnson, for whom words were as much like people as like things, and a critic like the late Roland Barthes, who told us that "the fact can only exist linguistically, as a term of discourse." Who is closer to our experience of reading literature, Johnson or Barthes? What difference does it make, if we side with one critic rather than the other?

Barthes is famous, like Foucault and other recent French theorists, for having added to Nietzsche's proclamation of the death of God a subsidiary demise, that of the literary author. If there are no authors, then there are no fictional personages, presumably because literature does not refer to a world outside language. Words indeed necessarily refer to other words in the first place, but the impact of words ultimately is drawn from a universe of fact. Stories, poems, and plays are recognizable as such because they are human utterances within traditions of utterances, and traditions, by achieving authority, become a kind of fact, or at least the sense of a fact. Our sense that literary characters, within the context of a fictive cosmos, indeed are fictional personages is also a kind of fact. The meaning and value of every character in a successful work of literary representation depend upon our ideas of persons in the factual reality of our lives.

Literary character is always an invention, and inventions generally are indebted to prior inventions. Shakespeare is the inventor of literary character as we know it; he reformed the universal human expectations for the verbal imitation of personality, and the reformation appears now to be permanent and uncannily inevitable. Remarkable as the Bible and Homer are at representing personages, their characters are relatively unchanging. They age within their stories, but their habitual modes of being do not develop. Jacob and Achilles unfold before us, but without metamorphoses. Lear and Macbeth, Hamlet and Othello severely modify themselves not only by their actions, but by their utterances, and most of all through *overhearing themselves,* whether they speak to themselves or to others. Pondering what they themselves have said, they will to change, and actually do change, sometimes extravagantly yet always persuasively. Or else they suffer change, without willing it, but in reaction not so much to their language as to their relation to that language.

I do not think it useful to say that Shakespeare successfully imitated elements in our characters. Rather, it could be argued that he compelled aspects of character to appear that previously were concealed, or not available to representation. This is not to say that Shakespeare is God, but to remind us that language is not God either. The mimesis of character in Shakespeare's dramas now seems to us normative, and indeed became the accepted mode almost immediately, as Ben Jonson shrewdly and somewhat grudgingly implied. And yet, Shakespearean representation has surprisingly little in common with the imitation of reality in Jonson or in Christopher Marlowe. The origins of Shakespeare's originality in the portrayal of men and women are to be found in the *Canterbury Tales* of Geoffrey Chaucer, insofar as they can be located anywhere before Shakespeare himself. Chaucer's savage and superb Pardoner overhears his own tale-telling, as well as his mocking rehearsal of his own spiel, and through this overhearing he is emboldened to forget himself, and enthusiastically urges all his fellow-pilgrims to come forward to be fleeced by him. His self-awareness, and apocalyptically rancid sense of spiritual fall, are preludes to the even grander abysses of the perverted will in Iago and in Edmund. What might be called the character trait of a negative charisma may be Chaucer's invention, but came to its perfection in Shakespearean mimesis.

The analysis of character is as much Shakespeare's invention as the representation of character is, since Iago and Edmund are adepts at analyzing both themselves and their victims. Hamlet, whose overwhelming charisma has many negative components, is certainly the most comprehensive of all literary characters, and so necessarily prophesies the labyrinthine complexities of the will in Iago and Edmund. Charisma, according to Max Weber, its first codifier, is primarily a natural endowment, and implies a primordial and idiosyncratic power over nature, and so finally over death. Hamlet's uncanniness is at its most suggestive in the scene of his long dying, where the audience, through the mediation of Horatio, itself is compelled to meditate upon suicide, if only because outliving the prince of Denmark scarcely seems an option.

Shakespearean representation has usurped not only our sense of literary character, but our sense of ourselves as characters, with Hamlet playing the part of the largest of these usurpations. Insofar as we have an idea of human disinterestedness, we tend to derive it from the Hamlet of Act V, whose quietism has about it a ghostly authority. Oscar Wilde, in his profound and profoundly witty dialogue, "The Decay of Lying," expressed a permanent insight when he insisted that art shaped every era, far more than any age formed art. Life imitates art, we imitate Shakespeare, because without Shakespeare we would perish for lack of images. Wilde's grandest audacity demystifies Shakespearean mimesis with a Shakespearean vivaciousness: "This unfortunate aphorism about art holding the mirror up to Nature is deliberately said by Hamlet in order to convince the bystanders of his absolute insanity in all art-matters." Of *Hamlet*'s influence upon the ages Wilde remarked that: "The world has grown sad because a puppet was once melancholy." "Puppet" is Wilde's own deconstruction, a brilliant reminder that Shakespeare's artistry of illusion has so mastered reality as to have changed reality, evidently forever.

The analysis of character, as a critical pursuit, seems to me as much a Shakespearean invention as literary character was, since much of what we know about how to analyze character necessarily follows Shakespearean procedures. His hero-villains, from Richard III through Iago, Edmund, and Macbeth, are shrewd and endless questers into their own self-motivations. If we could bear to see Hamlet, in his unwearied negations, as another hero-villain, then we would judge him the supreme analyst of the darker recalcitrances in the selfhood. Freud followed the pre-Socratic Empedocles, in arguing that character is fate, a frightening doctrine that maintains the fear that there are no accidents, that over-determination rules us all of our lives. Hamlet assumes the same, yet adds to this argument the terrible passivity he manifests in Act V. Throughout Shakespeare's tragedies, the most interesting personages seem doom-eager, reminding us again that a Shakespearean reading of Freud would be more illuminating than a Freudian exegesis of Shakespeare. We learn more when we discover Hamlet in the Freudian Death Drive, than when we read *Beyond the Pleasure Principle* into *Hamlet.*

In Shakespearean comedy, character achieves its true literary apotheosis, which is the representation of the inner freedom that can be created by great wit alone. Rosalind and Falstaff, perhaps alone among Shakespeare's personages, match Hamlet in wit, though hardly in the metaphysics of consciousness. Whether in the comic or the modern mode, Shakespeare has set the standard of measurement in the balance between character and passion.

In Shakespeare the self is more dramatized than theatricalized, which is why a Shakespearean reading of Freud works out so well. Character-formation after the passing of the Oedipal stage takes the place of fetishistic fragmentings of the self. Critics who now call literary character into question, and who proclaim also the death of the author, invariably also regard all notions, literary and human, of a stable character as being mere reductions of deeper pre-Oedipal desires. It becomes clear that the fortunes of literary character rise and fall with the prestige of normative conceptions of the ego. Shakespeare's Iago, who wars against being, may be the first deconstructionist of the self, with his proclamation of "I am not what I am." This constitutes the necessary prologue to any view that would regard a fixed ego as a virtual abnormality. But deconstructions of the self are no more modern than Modernism is. Like literary modernism, the decentered ego came out of the Hellenistic culture of ancient Alexandria. The Gnostic heretics believed that the psyche, like the body, was a fallen entity, mechanically fashioned by the Demiurge or false creator. They held however that each of us possessed also a spark or pneuma, which was a fragment of the original Abyss or true, alien God. The soul or psyche within every one of us was thus at war with the self or pneuma, and only that sparklike self could be saved.

Shakespeare, following after Chaucer in this respect, was the first and remains still the greatest master of representing character both as a stable soul and a wavering self. There is a substance that endures in Shakespeare's figures, and there is also a quicksilver rendition of the unsettling sparks. Racine and Tolstoy, Balzac and Dickens, follow in Shakespeare's wake by giving us some sense of pre-Oedipal sparks or drives, and considerably more sense of post-Oedipal character and personality, stabilizations or sublimations of the fetish-seeking drives. Critics like Leo Bersani and René Girard argue eloquently against our taking this mimesis as the only proper work of literature. I would suggest that strong fictions of the self, from the Bible through Samuel Beckett, necessarily participate in both modes, the sublimation of desire, and the persistence of a primordial desire. The mystery of Hamlet or of Lear is intimately invested in the tangled mixture of the two modes of representation.

Psychic mobility is proposed by Bersani as the ideal to which deconstructions of the literary self may yet guide us. The ideal has its pathos, but the realities of literary representation seem to me very different, perhaps destructively so. When a novelist like D. H. Lawrence sought to reduce his characters to Eros and the Death Drive, he still had to persuade us of his authority at mimesis by lavishing upon the figures of *The Rainbow* and *Women in Love* all of the vivid stigmata of normative personality. Birkin and Ursula may represent antithetical and uncanny drives, but they develop and change as characters pondering their own pronouncements and reactions to self and others. The cost of a non-Shakespearean representation is enormous. Pynchon, in *The Crying of Lot 49* and *Gravity's Rainbow*, evades the burden of the normative by resorting to something like Christopher Marlowe's art of caricature in *The Jew of Malta*. Marlowe's Barabas is a marvelous rhetorician, yet he is a cartoon alongside the troublingly equivocal Shylock. Pynchon's personages are deliberate cartoons also, as flat as comic strips. Marlowe's achievement, and Pynchon's, are beyond dispute, yet they are like the prelude and the postlude to Shakespearean reality. They do not wish to engage with our hunger for the empirical world and so they enter the problematic cosmos of literary fantasy.

No writer, not even Shakespeare or Proust, alters the available stock that we agree to call reality, but Shakespeare, more than any other, does show us how much of reality we could encounter if only we retained adequate desire. The strong literary representation of character is already an analysis of character, and is part of the healing work of a literary culture, which implicitly seeks to cure violence through a normative mimesis of ego, *as if it were stable,* whether in actuality it is or is not. I do not believe that this is a social quest taken on by literary culture, but rather that we confront here the aesthetic essence of what makes a culture *literary,* rather than metaphysical or ethical or religious. A culture becomes literary when its conceptual modes have failed it, which means when religion, philosophy, and science have begun to lose their authority. If they cannot heal violence, then literature attempts to do so, which may be only a turning inside out of the critical arguments of Girard and Bersani.

I conclude by offering a particular instance or special case as a paradigm for the healing enterprise that is at once the representation and the analysis of literary character. Let us call it the aesthetics of being outraged, or rather of successfully representing the state of being outraged. W. C. Fields was one modern master of such representation, and Nathanael West was another, as was Faulkner before him. Here also the greatest master remains Shakespeare, whose Macbeth, himself a bloody outrage, yet retains our imaginative sympathy precisely because he grows increasingly outraged as he experiences the equivocation of the fiend that lies like truth. The double-natured promises and the prophecies of the weird sisters finally induce in Macbeth an apocalyptic version of the stage actor's anxiety at missing cues, the horror of a phantasmagoric stage fright of missing one's time, of always reacting too late. Macbeth, a veritable monster of solipsistic inwardness but no intellectual, counters his dilemma by fresh murders, that prolong him in time yet provoke him only to a perpetually freshened sense of being outraged, as all his expectations become still worse confounded. We are moved by Macbeth, however estrangedly, because his terrible inwardness is a paradigm for our own solipsism, but also because none of us can resist a strong and successful representation of the human in a state of being outraged.

The ultimate outrage is the necessity of dying, an outrage concealed in a multitude of masks, including the tyrannical ambitions of Macbeth. I suspect that our outrage at being outraged is the most difficult of all our affects for us to represent to ourselves, which is why we are so inclined to imaginative sympathy for a character who strongly conveys that affect to us. The Shrike of West's *Miss Lonelyhearts* or Faulkner's Joe Christmas of *Light in August* are crucial modern instances, but such figures can be located in many other works, since the ability to represent this extreme emotion is one of the tests that strong writers are driven to set for themselves.

However a reader seeks to reduce literary character to a question of marks on a page, she will come at last to the impasse constituted by the thought of death, her death, and before that to all the stations of being outraged that memorialize her own drive towards death. In reading, she quests for evidences that are strong representations, whether of her desire or her despair. Such questings constitute the necessary basis for the analysis of literary character, an enterprise that always will survive every vagary of critical fashion.

EDITOR'S NOTE

This book gathers together a representative selection of the best criticism that has been devoted to Marlow, who appears as one of the narrators in four works of Joseph Conrad: "Youth," *Heart of Darkness, Lord Jim,* and *Chance.* I am indebted to S. T. Joshi for his skill and erudition in helping me to edit this volume.

My introduction centers upon Marlow's own Romanticism, with its exaltation of courage. The critical extracts, arranged like the critical essays in the chronological order of their original publication, begin with Henry James's rather negative reaction to Marlow and then continue through Conrad himself and Virginia Woolf on to noted modern scholar-critics, including Joseph Warren Beach, Albert J. Guérard, and Aaron Fogel.

Full-scale critical essays start with Alan Warren Friedman's charting of Marlow's quest from "Youth" through *Heart of Darkness* and *Lord Jim* on to its conclusion in *Chance.* Jacques Berthoud centers upon Marlow's "positive illusion" in *Heart of Darkness,* after which Ian Watt shrewdly outlines Henry James's attitude toward Conrad's "magical mariner."

The intricate dialectic of "lying" and "dying" in *Heart of Darkness* is set forth by Garrett Stewart, while Benita Parry considers the larger context of imperialism in *Lord Jim.*

Mark Conroy analyzes the relationship between Jim and Marlow as a study in the enigmatic nature of heroism, after which Kenneth Simons describes the properly ludic imagination of the young Marlow in "Youth."

We are returned to *Heart of Darkness* by Fred Madden, who sees Marlow as growing in "restraint" and compassion even as he confronts the "double horror" of societal and individual corruption. In this volume's final essay, Anthony Winner finds in the Marlow of *Lord Jim* a moralist who can bid an ironic farewell to the Romantic dream, a judgment somewhat at variance with the view of Marlow set forth in my Introduction.

INTRODUCTION

Marlow is one of the most curious and fascinating of modern literary characters, even though he is rather more a voice than an active being in all four Conradian narratives in which he appears: "Youth," *Heart of Darkness, Lord Jim, Chance.* Very little that is crucial about Marlow can be resolved; perhaps he represents, against Conrad's conscious designs, what is most enigmatic or reserved or even repressed in Conrad himself. The life of Conrad, until he quit his sea career at the age of thirty-six, is High Romantic to an almost sublimely absurd degree, and may have helped set the Byronic standard that Hemingway strenuously sought to attain. At five, Conrad was taken into Russian exile by his father, an heroic Polish nationalist. Losing his mother when he was eight, and his father four years later, the orphaned Conrad left Poland at seventeen, bound for Marseilles and a sailor's career. Eighteen years at sea included gunrunning, voyages as extensive as those to India and the Congo, a desperate love affair ending in attempted suicide, and ultimate ascension to command. By 1886, Conrad was a British subject, and by 1895 a published novelist in English. This is not exactly the life of Henry James, who was to become the prime influence upon Conrad's matured narrative art. Marlow is the mark of Conrad's difference from James, and one can surmise that Marlow originated as a Conradian defense against James, lest the disciple yield up too much of his own authorial self to the lesson of the master.

Conrad's James is the Middle James of *The Spoils of Poynton* and *What Maisie Knew,* masterpieces in which the narrative is firmly held within the viewpoint of a single crucial character. Early Conrad, much influenced by Flaubert and Maupassant, is narrated in the supposed impersonal mode, in the third person. But by October 1898, Conrad and James were friends and neighbors, and Conrad was about to write *Heart of Darkness.* Critics agree that Marlow is a response to what can be called James's "Impressionism," but Ian Watt is clearly accurate when he charts the difference between the two degress of impressionism that are involved here:

> . . . whereas James as author selects and orders the "meaning" of what happens . . . Conrad lets his protagonist muddle out the meaning of his own experiences as best he can.

Marlow, admirable fellow as he certainly is, is very much a muddler. Conrad's ironies are highly operative in Marlow's misapprehensions, and yet Conrad's stance towards Marlow is hardly ironic in itself. Henry James regarded Marlow with inevitable irony, dismissing him, in conversation, as "that preposterous magic mariner," who emulated Coleridge's Ancient Mariner by "mixing himself up with the narrative." But that indeed is Marlow's function; he is not *the* narrator, but another narrator, sometimes antiphonal but more often antithetical to the narrator's voice. Ian Watt amiably points out how unrealistic Marlow is as a character; we are given a British sea officer whose mind and heart essentially are the Polish Conrad's, and we are ventured no background or context that could explain Marlow's anomalies of spirit. Yet Marlow does not need to convince us of his authenticity as a representation, because his voice persuades us, indeed obsesses us, just as Kurtz's voice obsesses and almost persuades Marlow. What we hear in Marlow, in all four of his narratives, is the accent of the initiate, of the *man who knows,* not by or through mere experience, but by having reflected upon the secrets of a now lost reality, a more primal mode of existence than our own.

Like Conrad, Marlow is a spiritual knower rather than a believer, and therefore also a moralist detached from Christianity. The line of descent from Conrad to some of the principal modern novelists—Faulkner, Fitzgerald, Hemingway—is clear and direct. Their narrators owe much to Marlow, including the rhetoric of elitism, of knowing always who is or isn't "one of us." I would not go so far as some critics, who have located a Gnosticism in Conrad, and in *Heart of Darkness* in particular, but certainly there are Gnostic elements in Marlow's modes of knowing, and there is a link between Conrad's mystic mariner and Ishmael in *Moby-Dick*. Martin Price suggestively compares the Marlow of *Lord Jim* to the narrator of Byron's *Don Juan:* both storytellers are content to be beyond certitudes, but each goes on studying the nostalgias of romance. I think we hover here very close to the center of Marlow's appeal for Conrad's readers. In Marlow, we hear renewed the tones of the Romantic age, of all those wanderers who have outlasted illusions and yet still long for the vision of something that calls everyday existence into question.

Kurtz and Jim are belated versions of the Romantic hero, far more estranged from transcendental yearnings than are the protagonists of Byron and of Melville. Marlow, as Martin Price gently puts it, "has unfinished business with romantic dreams." But Conrad has declined to give us any knowledge of what those dreams could be. We know that Marlow was immensely vulnerable to Kurtz's dream of power, but not as vulnerable as ever to have yielded to its equivalent. More strikingly, we can see Marlow becoming a kind of father to Jim, and a brother to Stein, insofar as Stein is an almost Jamesian artist, gazing at his butterflies in much the same way that James contemplates his characters. Stein might be called an *artist of courage,* and courage is Marlow's hidden talisman about which he is not prepared to be ironic. Perhaps we can say that Conrad is a Romantic skeptic, while his Marlow is a skeptic Romantic, closer to Conrad's own father than to Conrad himself.

One way of understanding Marlow is to ask what his presence would do to

Conrad's masterpiece, *Nostromo*, which has no figure like him. The answer would depend upon *which* Marlow, for the intensely likeable mariner of *Youth*, *Heart of Darkness*, and *Lord Jim*, turns very tiresome in the late *Chance*, a decade after *Nostromo*. The earlier Marlow is an ascetic, but immensely appreciative of women, whereas the Marlow of *Chance* resents and fears women, and seems driven by this aversion to a rather desperate repetitiveness. But if the Marlow so moved by Kurtz and by Jim could have entered the pages of *Nostromo*, then *Nostromo* himself would have been celebrated as the authentic Romantic hero he truly constitutes. Conrad defends himself against his own creation here with a wavering rhetorical irony, one that would have been set aside by the Romantic, Marlow. Without Marlow, Conrad has no firm defense against his own skepticism of romance, his own awareness that he lives in the age of Henry James, and not that of Lord Byron.

One can concede to James that Marlow muddles his stories by mixing himself up so much into them, but Kurtz and Jim are not Hamlets to Marlow's Horatio. Horatio mediates the charismatic Hamlet for us; without Horatio the play would evade us, but we enter the play with Horatio, who reminds us that, even at the end, Hamlet needs us, if only as mute audience. Neither Kurtz nor Jim are beyond us, and so Marlow's function necessarily is more modest. There are no victories in Conrad, whether transcendent or immanent, not even in *Victory* itself. Marlow exists partly to show us that there are no total defeats in Conrad, or perhaps that the contest in Conrad is perpetually renewable. Courage may be the only indubitable moral virtue that imaginative literature can celebrate; kindness becomes either banal or sentimental in fiction. The magic in Marlow is more than rhetorical, if only because quest, or purposefulness without purpose, always seems to break through the limits of rhetoric. *Lord Jim* is a much better book, in my judgment, than *Heart of Darkness*, but whenever I think of Marlow I recall first his concluding words in the story of Kurtz: "It would have been too dark—too dark altogether . . ." In that we hear a permanent credo of Romanticism, however wounded by skepticism. If the truth is too dark altogether, then we turn to a fiction, not to evade the truth entirely, but to pay some final tribute to the courage of our broken idealism.

—H. B.

CRITICAL EXTRACTS

HENRY JAMES

Mr. Conrad's first care *Chance* is expressly to posit or set up a reciter, a definite responsible intervening first person singular, possessed of infinite sources of reference, who immediately proceeds to set up another, to the end that this other may conform again to the practice, and that even at that point the bridge over to the creature, or in other words to the situation or the subject, the thing "produced," shall, if the fancy takes it, once more and yet once more glory in a gap. It is easy to see how heroic the undertaking of an effective fusion becomes on these terms, fusion between what we are to know and that prodigy of our knowing which is ever half the very beauty of the atmosphere of authenticity; from the moment the reporters are thus multiplied from pitch to pitch the tone of each, especially as "rendered" by his precursor in the series, becomes for the prime poet of all an immense question—these circumferential tones having not only to be such individually separate notes, but to keep so clear of the others, the central, the numerous and various voices of the agents proper, those expressive of the action itself and in whom the objectivity resides. We usually escape the worst of this difficulty of a tone *about* the tone of our characters, our projected performers, by keeping it single, keeping it "down" and thereby comparatively impersonal or, as we may say, inscrutable; which is what a creative force, in its blest fatuity, likes to be. But the omniscience, remaining indeed nameless, though constantly active, which sets Marlow's omniscience in motion from the very first page, insisting on a reciprocity with it throughout, this original omniscience invites consideration of itself only in a degree less than that in which Marlow's own invites it; and Marlow's own is a prolonged hovering flight of the subjective over the outstretched ground of the case exposed. We make out this ground but through the shadow cast by the flight, clarify it though the real author visibly reminds himself again and again that he must—all the more that, as if by some tremendous forecast of future applied science, the upper aeroplane causes another, as we have said, to depend from it and that one still another; these dropping shadow after shadow, to the no small menace of intrinsic colour and form and whatever, upon the passive expanse. What shall we most call Mr. Conrad's method accordingly but his attempt to clarify *quand même*—ridden as he has been, we perceive at the end of fifty pages of *Chance* by such a danger of steeping his matter in perfect eventual obscuration as we recall no other artist's consenting to with an equal grace. This grace, which presently comes over us as the sign of the whole business, is Mr. Conrad's gallantry itself, and the shortest account of the rest of the connection for our present purpose is that his gallantry is thus his success. It literally strikes us that his volume sets in motion more than anything else a drama in which his own system and his combined eccentricities of recital represent the protagonist in face of powers leagued against it, and of which the dénouement gives us the system fighting in triumph, though with its back desperately to the wall, and laying the powers piled up at its feet. This frankly has been *our* spectacle, our suspense and our thrill; with the one flaw on the roundness of it all the fact that the predicament was not imposed rather than invoked, was not the effect of a challenge from without, but that of a mystic impulse from within.

—HENRY JAMES, "The New Novel," *Notes on Novelists* (New York: Scribner's, 1914), pp. 347–49

JOHN COWPER POWYS

Except for a few insignificant passages when that sly old mariner Marlowe, of whom Conrad seems perhaps unduly fond, lights his pipe and passes the beer and utters breezy and bracing sentiments, I can enjoy with unmitigated delight all the convolutions and overlappings of his inverted method of narration—of those rambling "advances," as Mr. Follet calls them, to already consummated "conclusions." In the few occasional passages where Marlowe assumes a moralising tone and becomes bracing and strenuous I fancy I detect the influence of certain muscular, healthy-minded, worthy men, among our modern writers, who I daresay appeal to the Slavonic soul of this great Pole as something quite wonderfully and pathetically English.

—JOHN COWPER POWYS, "Joseph Conrad," *Suspended Judgments: Essays on Books and Sensations* (New York: G. Arnold Shaw, 1916), p. 355

HUGH WALPOLE

Conrad, having discovered his subject ⟨in *Lord Jim*⟩, must, for the satisfaction of that honour which is his most deeply cherished virtue, prove to us his authenticity. "I was not there myself," he tells us, "but I can show you someone who was." He introduces us to a first-hand witness, Marlowe or another. "Now tell your story." He has at once the atmosphere in which he is happiest, and so, having his audience clustered about him, unlimited time at everyone's disposal, whiskies and cigars without stint, he lets himself go. He is bothered now by no question but the thorough investigation of his discovery. What had Jim done that he should be in such a case? We must have the story of the loss of the *Patna,* that marvellous journey across the waters, all the world of the pilgrims, the obscene captain and Jim's fine, chivalrous soul. Marlowe is inexhaustible. He has so much to say and so many fine words in which to say it. At present, so absorbed are we, so successful is he, that we are completely held. The illusion is perfect. We come to the inquiry. One of the judges is Captain Brierly. "What! not know Captain Brierly! Ah! but I must tell you! Most extraordinary thing!"

The world grows around us; a world that can contain the captain of the *Patna,* Brierly and Jim at the same time! The subject before us seems now so rich that we are expecting to see it burst, at any moment, in the author's hands, but so long as that first visualised scene is the centre of the episode, so long as the experience hovers round that inquiry and the Esplanade outside it, we are held, breathless and believing. We believe even in the eloquent Marlowe. Then the moment passes. Every possible probe into its heart has been made. We are satisfied.

There follows then the sequel, and here at once the weakness of the method is apparent. The author having created his narrator must continue with him. Marlowe is there, untired, eager, waiting to begin again. But the trouble is that we are no longer assured now of the truth and reality of his story. He saw—we cannot for an instant doubt it—that group on the Esplanade; all that he could tell us about that we, breathlessly, awaited. But now we are uncertain whether he is not inventing a romantic sequel. He must go on—that is the truly terrible thing about Marlowe— and at the moment when we question his authenticity we are suspicious of his very existence, ready to be irritated by his flow of words demanding something more authentic than that voice that is now only dimly heard. The author himself perhaps feels this; he duplicates, he even trebles his narrators and with each fresh agent raises a fresh crop of facts, contrasts, habits and histories. That then is the peril of the method. Whilst we believe we are completely held, but let the authenticity waver for a moment and the danger of disaster is more excessive than with any other possible form of narration. Create your authority and we have at once someone at whom we may throw stones if we are not beguiled. Marlowe has certainly been compelled to face, at moments in his career, an angry, irritated audience.

—HUGH WALPOLE, "The Novelist," *Joseph Conrad* (London: Nisbet, 1916
[rev. ed. 1924]), pp. 45–48

JOSEPH CONRAD

'Youth' was not my first contribution to *Maga* ⟨*Blackwood's Edinburgh Magazine*⟩. It was the second. But that story marks the first appearance in the world of the man Marlow, with whom my relations have grown very intimate in the course of years. The origins of that gentleman (nobody as far as I know had ever hinted that he was anything but that)—his origins have been the subject of some literary speculation of, I am glad to say, a friendly nature.

One would think that I am the proper person to throw a light on the matter; but in truth I find that it isn't so easy. It is pleasant to remember that nobody had charged him with fraudulent purposes or looked down on him as a charlatan; but apart from that he was supposed to be all sorts of things: a clever screen, a mere device, a 'personator,' a familiar spirit, a whispering 'daemon.' I myself have been suspected of a meditated plan for his capture.

That is not so. I made no plans. The man Marlow and I came together in the casual manner of those health-resort acquaintances which sometimes ripen into friendships. This one has ripened. For all his assertiveness in matters of opinion he is not an intrusive person. He haunts my hours of solitude, when, in silence, we lay our heads together in great comfort and harmony; but as we part at the end of a tale I am never sure that it may not be for the last time. Yet I don't think that either of us would care much to survive the other. In his case, at any rate, his occupation would be gone and he would suffer from that extinction, because I suspect him of some vanity. I don't mean vanity in the Solomonian sense. Of all my people he's the one that has never been a vexation to my spirit. A most discreet, understanding man. . . . ⟨. . .⟩

Heart of Darkness also received a certain amount of notice from the first; and of its origins this much may be said: it is well known that curious men go prying into all sorts of places (where they have no business) and come out of them with all kinds of spoil. This story, and one other, not in this volume, are all the spoil I brought out from the centre of Africa, where, really, I had no sort of business. More ambitious in its scope and longer in the telling, *Heart of Darkness* is quite as authentic in fundamentals as 'Youth.' It is, obviously, written in another mood, I won't characterize the mood precisely, but anybody can see that it is anything but the mood of wistful regret, of reminiscent tenderness.

—JOSEPH CONRAD, Introduction to Youth [1917], Conrad's Prefaces
to His Works (London: J. M. Dent, 1937), pp. 71–73

JOSEPH CONRAD

When this novel ⟨*Lord Jim*⟩ first appeared in book form a notion got about that I had been bolted away with. Some reviewers maintained that the work starting as a short story had got beyond the writer's control. One or two discovered internal evidence of the fact, which seemed to amuse them. They pointed out the limitations of the narrative form. They argued that no man could have been expected to talk all that time, and other men to listen so long. It was not, they said, very credible.

After thinking it over for something like sixteen years I am not so sure about that. Men have been known, both in the tropics and in the temperate zone, to sit up half the night 'swapping yarns.' This, however, is but one yarn, yet with interruptions affording some measure of relief; and in regard to the listeners' endurance, the postulate must be accepted that the story *was* interesting. It is the necessary preliminary assumption. If I hadn't believed that it *was* interesting I could never have begun to write it. As to the mere physical possibility we all know that some speeches in Parliament have taken nearer six than three hours in delivery; whereas all that part of the book which is Marlow's narrative can be read through aloud, I should say, in less than three hours. Besides—though I have kept strictly all such insignificant details out of the tale—we may presume that there must have been refreshments on that night, a glass of mineral water of some sort to help the narrator on.

—JOSEPH CONRAD, Introduction to *Lord Jim* [1917], *Conrad's Prefaces to His Works* (London: J. M. Dent, 1937), p. 65

FRANCES WENTWORTH CUTLER

"Truth, illusive, obscure, half submerged, floats in the silent, still waters of mystery." In that sea echo is the motive of this seaman's tale. Only by such a teller can we be drawn into the mystery of those tales. The "*I*" of Poe's tales would convince us of the reality of unearthly mysteries and inhuman horrors; Marlow would quicken us to the mystery of forgotten lives, would share with us his and our own questionings. And how could such tales be told save as Marlow tells them,—chance incidents, scraps of speech, interwoven, interpreted?

But the meaning of Marlow goes yet deeper. These tales woven of accident and coincidence mean just this: that real understanding, that "resonant" truth which alone is life and gives life, comes to us most directly through rumors, hearsays, echoes of long-spoken words. So Marlow's maxim, "The science of life consists in seizing every chance that presents itself," unlocks the method of his art,—the seizing and re-creating of chance human contacts. So only can we, onlookers, tale-tellers, snatch from the encircling mystery "that subtle but invincible conviction of solidarity that knits together the loneliness of innumerable hearts." ⟨. . .⟩

But we cannot dismiss Marlow without becoming aware of some implications of his method. We have seen him ignoring the rules of narration: that a story should have but one teller, to whom nothing in his tale is unknown; that the psychological story in particular demands the omniscient author-narrator. But Marlow's method not only defies the text-books: it insistently questions some basal assumptions of the critics of fiction. They have declared that the novelist, by eliminating the accidental and irrelevant and revealing the causal, simplifies life. Yet here is a writer who deliberately complicates life, who, instead of putting his characters under the microscope, surrounds them with their reflections in the mirroring minds of tellers and listeners. In so doing he has, we have seen, obeyed a higher law than that of text-books,—the law of his vision of reality created of human contact. And in so doing he has verily suggested another law and type for fiction. The older novel, the simplification of life, gave us the creative process achieved, the decision handed down. From the verdict on Becky Sharp or on Rosamond Lydgate there is no appeal. But with Conrad we actually enter into the creative process: we grope with him through blinding mists, we catch at fleeting glimpses and thrill with sudden illuminations. For the art of Conrad is literally a *social* art—the collaboration of many tellers and of many listeners:—

"In time the story shaped itself before me out of the listless answers to my questions, out of the indifferent words heard in wayside inns. . . . People confirmed and completed the story."

Thus we, the listeners, not only share in the creation, but verily "confirm and complete" these stories, whose aim is the search itself and not its ending. For the verdict on Jim and on Flora rests with us at last.

—FRANCES WENTWORTH CUTLER, "Why Marlow?," *Sewanee Review* 26, No. 1
(January 1918): 33–34, 37–38

FORD MADOX HUEFFER

He ⟨Conrad⟩ was conquering—conquering, truly—a foreign language. And that language was particularly unsuited to our joint purpose, in that its more polite forms, through centuries of literary usage, have become absolutely unsuited to direct statement. You cannot make a statement in Literary English. And Conrad came to it by way of Miss Braddon and the English Bible. . . .

In the end, of course, he achieved both a Form and a habit of language: he invented the figure of Marlow. To Henry James, whose eye for other people's work was, strangely, too literary, Marlow was always a fabulous Master Mariner. James refused to believe in him any more than he would believe in any other mechanical device. It was useless to argue with him: he used to groan over the matter and, if I persisted at all, would end by saying that Conrad—or Marlow, that old Man of the Sea, that incredible but enduring Vampire—was ruining my prospects.

He was wrong. Marlow is a natural, simple and not at all unusual, peasant type. He is wise as to human vicissitudes as the simple or the merely poor are so frequently wise: but he is not over-read in the book-lore that is so inevitably destructive of wisdom. If I go up the hill from where I sit, on the fifty-foot contour line, or thereabouts, I shall find an old shepherd. He will be just as wise as Marlow. And, gradually, from this old man I am learning the history of a fabulous farmer, Mr. Cummings. I know already that in 1892 Mr. Cummings married his third wife. Till 1870 he still bred the old, horned, Wiltshire sheep that has not disappeared. About 1880 he ate five-pound notes between thin bread and butter—to annoy the Income Tax Authorities. In 1879 he married the first Mrs. Cummings; she was still living when he married No. II, and No. III. Apparently all three ladies lived together in the great old farm till 1900. He was a little, terrible, swearing man, with a pimply face and no teeth. He was the first man to use a steam-plough in these parts, and his eldest son went to America because he didn't hold with it. That would be about 1894. In 1869 Annie Meggott drowned herself in the Arun: Mr. Cummings never got over that. It was why he was like what he was. For, in 1902, on his deathbed, he sent for the old shepherd and said: "That Annie Meggot she was terrible pernickety. But upstanding and with red cheeks." He had lost the use of one eye by then.

You perceive that that is how Marlow gets hold of and tells the stories of exceptional men. And it is in that way that life really presents itself to us: not as a rattling narrative beginning at a hero's birth and progressing to his not very carefully machined but predestined glory—but dallying backwards and forwards, now in 1890, now in 1869; in 1902—and then again in 1869—as forgotten episodes came up in the minds of simple narrators. And, if you put your Affair into the mouth of such a narrator your phraseology will be the Real thing in *mots justes,* for just so long as they remain within his probably vocabulary. There will be no jewels five words long, nor, for that matter, will the narrator say that Mr. Cummings ever hailed a hansom.

—FORD MADOX HUEFFER, "Thus to Revisit . . .: Some Reminiscences"
(Part II), *English Review* 31, No. 2 (August 1920): 116–17

VIRGINIA WOOLF

Marlow was one of those born observers who are happiest in retirement. Marlow liked nothing better than to sit on deck in some obscure creek of the Thames, smoking and recollecting; smoking and speculating; sending after his smoke beautiful rings of words until all the summer's night became a little clouded with tobacco smoke. Marlow, too, had a profound respect for the men with whom he had sailed; but he saw the humour of them. He nosed out and described in masterly fashion those livid creatures who prey successfully upon the clumsy veterans. He had a flair for human deformity; his humour was sardonic. Nor did Marlow live entirely wreathed in the smoke of his own cigars. He had a habit of opening his eyes suddenly and looking—at a rubbish heap, at a port, at a shop counter—and then complete in its burning ring of light that thing is flashed bright upon the mysterious background. Introspective and analytical, Marlow was aware of this peculiarity. He said the power came to him suddenly. He might, for instance, overhear a French officer murmur 'Mon Dieu, how the time passes!'

> Nothing [he comments] could have been more commonplace than this remark; but its utterance coincided for me with a moment of vision. It's extraordinary how we go through life with eyes half shut, with dull ears, with dormant thoughts. . . . Nevertheless, there can be but few of us who had never known one of these rare moments of awakening, when we see, hear, understand, ever so much—everything—in a flash, before we fall back again into our agreeable somnolence. I raised my eyes when he spoke, and I saw him as though I had never seen him before.

Picture after picture he painted thus upon the dark background; ships first and foremost, ships at anchor, ships flying before the storm, ships in harbour; he painted sunsets and dawns; he painted the night; he painted the sea in every aspect; he painted the gaudy brilliance of Eastern ports, and men and women, their houses and their attitudes, He was an accurate and unflinching observer, schooled to that 'absolute loyalty towards his feelings and sensations', which, Conrad wrote, 'an author should keep hold of in his most exalted moments of creation'. And very quietly and compassionately Marlow sometimes lets fall a few words of epitaph which remind us, with all that beauty and brilliance before our eyes, of the darkness of the background.

Thus a rough-and-ready distinction would make us say that it is Marlow who comments, Conrad who creates. It would lead us, aware that we are on dangerous ground, to account for that change which, Conrad tells us, took place when he had finished the last story in the *Typhoon* volume—'a subtle change in the nature of the inspiration'—by some alteration in the relationship of the two old friends. '. . . . it seemed somehow that there was nothing more in the world to write about.' It was Conrad, let us suppose, Conrad the creator, who said that, looking back with sorrowful satisfaction upon the stories he had told; feeling as he well might that he could never better the storm in *The Nigger of the 'Narcissus',* or render more faithful tribute to the qualities of British seamen than he had done already in 'Youth' and *Lord Jim.* It was then that Marlow, the commentator, reminded him how, in the course of nature, one must grow old, sit smoking on deck, and give up seafaring. But, he reminded him, those strenuous years had deposited their memories; and he even went so far perhaps as to hint that, though the last word might have been said about Captain Whalley and his relation to the universe, there remained on shore a number of men and women whose relationships, though of a more personal kind, might be worth looking into. If we further suppose that there was a volume of Henry James on board and that Marlow gave his friend the book to take to bed with him, we may seek support in the fact that it was in 1905 that Conrad wrote a very fine essay upon that master.

—VIRGINIA WOOLF, "Joseph Conrad" [1924], *Collected Essays* (New York: Harcourt, Brace & World, 1967), Vol. I, pp. 304–6

GERALD BULLETT

⟨. . .⟩ "Youth" is one of the many narratives put into the mouth of Marlow; and it provides a convenient example of the value of this technical device, which has been the subject of a good deal of rather peevish criticism. What is the good, we are asked, of this Marlow? Why cannot we have the story direct from the author himself? But one has only to read again such a piece as this to find the sufficient answer to these questions. Marlow, in late middle life, is telling a story of his rapturous youth, which has for us, as for him, a delicate quality of remoteness, a wistful charm as of some lost Eden. The sight of this mature, weatherbeaten man dreaming of his lusty past, quickens in us at once a sense of that beauty, at once magical and impermanent, which is the very soul of the theme. The tale is enriched, its emotional values heightened, by this flavour of reminiscence; it is delicately tinged throughout with the coulours of this mature personality. It is of the adventure of a young man that he is telling us, and we are fascinated and touched when we remember, at intervals in the narration, that he himself was once that young man. The two are separate, and yet are the same: the one mysteriously contains the other; and the intervening years have but added to the springtime glamour a poignantly autumnal tinge. And as Marlow talks we are conscious not only of his emotion and our own but of the response in the hearts of those others who are listening, "the man of finance, the man of accounts, the man of law," and that other who is called "myself." The effect is to give to what might have been a simple melody a symphonic quality, a depth and subtlety of coulour, a haunting and persuasive charm. They are drinking, these men; especially Marlow himself, who punctuates the latter part of his tale with the reiterated request, "Pass the bottle." He becomes, as no sensitive reader can fail to perceive, a little exhilarated. Not, in general, a man of facile emotions, certainly not given to the habit of sentimental ejaculation, he beings to lose his reserve and to cry out at intervals, "Ah, youth! youth! The good old time. Youth and the sea. Glamour and the sea!" From the author such interpolations would be intolerable, but coming from a man stirred by memories and stimulated by wine they are fitting and acceptable.

This defence of the Marlow device, though it touches only the fringe of an inviting subject, may perhaps be sufficient to suggest the spirit in which such things can be most usefully approached. And, though it has special reference to a particular work, much of it applies with equal force to longer and more elaborate creations such as *Chance* and *Lord Jim.* These works possess, in addition to their primary qualities, a deceptive air of haphazard or hearsay that peculiarly stimulates the reader by seeming to invite his collaboration. So about the given story there hovers, while it is yet in the making, a luminous and penetrable mist of conjecture delicately colouring the whole. And Conrad, despite this habit of filtering his stories through alien personalities and so rendering them one degree more remote from us than they need have been, succeeds, as few others have succeeded, in suggesting what he himself calls the "life-sensation," the flavour and the inexpressible meaning of events. To communicate this reality; to salute with a devotion almost mystical the idea of fidelity; and to shew the human spirit, naked, alone, and majestic in its capacity for striving and for suffering—this was his aim and his achievement.

—GERALD BULLETT, "Joseph Conrad," *Modern English Fiction: A Personal View*
(London: Herbert Jenkins, 1926), pp. 66–69

R. L. MÉGROZ

Making proper allowances, then, for that simple soul, Charlie Marlow, who so often takes the story out of his creator's mouth, we may examine indulgently the Marlowesque philosophy. Mr. Marlow has such a good fling in *Chance,* that nearly everything he had to say on the subject of Woman can be found in that novel. Her irrelevancy, more fantastic than 'sober humdrum Imagination'. And 'the secret scorn of women for the capacity to consider judiciously and to express profoundly a meditated conclusion'. He admits that 'if women are not rational they are indeed acute', because, as he saw the strange story of Flora de Barral and her friends the Fynes, Mrs. Fyne was acute. Marlow, on behalf of Conrad, in his whimsical sarcasm, explains that Mrs. Fyne wanted to make use of him to convince her very male and stupid husband, because 'she had scented in him that small portion of "femininity", that drop of superior essence of which I am myself aware'. Lest we misunderstand, he adds: 'Observe that I say "femininity", a privilege—not "feminism", an attitude. I am not a feminist. It was Fyne who on certain solemn grounds had adopted that mental attitude.' And the maleness of the attitude of the feminist becomes later in the story the ground of the terrible misunderstanding which Captain Anthony, by the excessive idealism of his self-sacrifice, brings into existence as a barrier between himself and his wife, the unlucky Flora. The question has often been asked, why *Chance* should have turned the commercial tide for its author, and indubitably the right answer is that it appeals to the intelligence and feelings of women readers. The pathetic Flora, her terrifying governess, and Mrs. Fyne the civil servant's wife, are living women, and express their common womanhood so diversely, that *Chance* alone is enough to establish Conrad among the successful creators of women characters. Marlow's half-facetious generalizations must not be taken too seriously, of course. Partly they are the expression of Marlow, whose personality and tone as narrator are an ingredient of the story, which would be less convincing and more painful without him.

—R. L. MÉGROZ, " 'True to Life,' " Joseph Conrad's Mind and Art: A Study
of Personality in Art (London: Faber & Faber, 1931), pp. 192–93

JOSEPH WARREN BEACH

One of the most interesting features of Conrad's Malay stories is the light thrown upon the character of the whites by the natives—the native comment on the folly, greed, cruelty, treachery, and indomitable power of the white race. But while there is a good deal of life in these stories, a great loss of force is sustained through the interference of one point of view with another and the more frequent indeterminateness of the point of view.

Conrad's problem was to secure the advantage of the many points of view without losing that of coherence. It was to make a real composite of these many pictures taken from so many diverse angles, to make a *synthesis* of material so disparate. And he solved that problem most successfully through the help of Captain Marlow.

This person he had created in the short story "Youth," and also used in "Heart of Darkness" before the completion of *Lord Jim* (1900). *Lord Jim* was intended to be likewise a short story, but was apparently begun without the idea of introducing

Marlow. The first three chapters are told in the ordinary manner of third-person omniscience. They give a general account of Jim in the days when he was a water-clerk in Eastern ports, then return to his childhood home and training, and sketch his voyage as chief mate on the *Patna* in the Indian Ocean up to the time of the collision. Then, in Chapter IV, Marlow is introduced as one of those later attending the trial of Jim and his fellow-officers for deserting their ship. From that time on to Chapter XXXVI, the story is represented as being related by Marlow to friends in moments of relaxation after dinner. The concluding chapters were read later, in the form of documents under his London reading-lamp, by one of the party of Marlow's auditors. But the documents are mainly written in the hand of Marlow, one of them a letter, and one a long narrative of the later events while Jim was living in Patusan.

Virtually the whole of the story therefore comes to us from one who knew Lord Jim and was deeply interested in letting us know the truth about him, but who was not a professional writer. By far the largest portion comes not from his pen but from his mouth, in the form of a story told aloud over the after-dinner cigars. And this at once has the most magical effect upon the style and tone. The Oriental style, in this word-of-mouth narrative, gives place largely to a natural, anecdotal manner, the manner of one speaking with authority of things of which he knows, and yet—in such a strange story—striving for plausibility, striving to convert his audience to sympathy with his point of view, arguing with them over the character of his hero, producing evidence for his knowledge of this or that episode. All this gives to the narrative an amazing air of authenticity; puts it in a class with that extraordinary feat of Defoe's in "The Apparition of Mrs. Veal."

But this is only a beginning of what Marlow does for *Lord Jim*. This character is, seemingly, much more a sheer creation of the imagination than Almayer, Willems, Lingard, or Doña Rita. And yet Lord Jim is more vividly realized than any of them, perhaps the most vividly realized of all Conrad's characters.

His motivation is subtle, paradoxical, obscure, and a matter of speculation. But that is one reason why he is such a good subject for Conrad's—and Marlow's—hand: this young Englishman who had, in a crisis, forfeited his honor as a seaman and an officer, who was haunted for years by the sense of his disgrace and driven from one inferior occupation to another, from one port to another, by his desire to escape his ill fame; and who then, among the savages of a remote trading-post, "made good," "mastered his fate," and so won back his honor and his self-respect. Marlow befriended him, sympathized with him, understood him in fleeting intuitions from time to time, but never really "knew" him. At the time when Marlow went back home after Stein had sent Jim to Patusan, he says:

> "I cannot say I had ever seen him distinctly—not even to this day, after I had my last view of him; but it seemed to me that the less I understood the more I was bound to him in the name of that doubt which is the inseparable part of our knowledge. I did not know so much more about myself."

Marlow himself is well motivated, and his interest in Jim. He is interested in Jim, just as Captain Brierly is, the judge at his trial, and the French lieutenant who took charge of the *Patna* after Jim's desertion. They have all faced the doubt of how they would have acted in a similar crisis, whether their honor was strong enough to stand the test. "I did not know so much more about myself." Marlow wishes most devoutly to believe in Jim, in order that he may believe in himself, in human nature in general, in the possibility of the ideal in this world. It is most important to him that Jim should maintain his illusion of being somehow not damned, or find some momentary flash of revelation in the midst of a world of illusion.

One reason why Jim is so vivid a character is precisely because Marlow found him so elusive, because he was forever trying so hard to "see him distinctly." This is what leads to the sharp isolation of this or that scene.

It is also what leads Marlow to his frequent change of the angle of vision. The truth about Jim, as about any human being, he seems to think, is something which can be approximated only by regarding him from many different points of view. Much of this story comes to Marlow from the lips of Jim, much from other witnesses: the French lieutenant, the trader Stein, Jim's native wife Jewel, the pirate Brown, and others still. For much of the story Marlow is himself an eye-witness. Thus there is brought to bear upon Jim's case the light of every variety of temperament and of attitude toward Jim determined by every variety of interest and motive. This book is streaked and spotted with colors as brilliant and variegated as any futurist painting. The thing has a splendor and vibrancy of life not conceivable on the sober canvas of the well-made novel.

And yet it has the steady progression, the steady concentration on a single subject, of a novel by Wharton or James. It is Marlow who is responsible for this. He it is who directs and controls this restless and ranging exploration, always having in mind just what dark corner we are seeking to illuminate. It is he who receives on the lens of his speculative mind light-rays coming from every conceivable direction and focuses them all so rigorously upon the one point which he wishes to make visible to our imagination.

—JOSEPH WARREN BEACH, "Impressionism: Conrad," *The Twentieth Century Novel: Studies in Technique* (New York: Appleton-Century-Crofts, 1932), pp. 353–56

LEONARD F. DEAN

The conclusion of "The Heart of Darkness" produces a far different effect, although the intention is the same. The symbolism is melodramatic. The Intended has not earned the quality which she is meant to represent, and her effect is further weakened by the Hollywood set in which she is placed. When she extends her arms, the pose and the calculated manipulation of light, shadow, and black drapery recall too obviously the earlier mechanical symbol of the savage queen on the banks of the Congo. These lapses may be explained in part by reference to limitations in

Conrad's artistic resources. The conclusion of the story, unlike the Congo experiences, was probably invented. Conrad's weakness in invention has often been
noticed. It is implied by his preoccupation with the importance of reading symbolic
meaning into actual experience. A wider explanation, however, is to be reached
through a study of his use of Marlow. This fictitious narrator is usually explained as
a device for securing aesthetic distance between the reader and the plot, thus
reducing the impact of Conrad's romantic material. In "The Heart of Darkness"
Marlow does serve to interest us in meaning rather than in brute action, but he also
prevents Conrad and the reader from fully experiencing the final tragic effect. It is
Marlow rather than Kurtz who returns to affirm his faith in the Intended. This is
unsatisfactory because Marlow has only observed Kurtz's horror. His somewhat
parallel sickness is an inadequate substitute for Kurtz's complete disillusionment. In
fact, Marlow's moral insight appears to be nearly as penetrating at the beginning of
his journey as at the end. It was perhaps inevitable, given his artistic function, that
he should be a static character.

—LEONARD F. DEAN, "Tragic Pattern in Conrad's 'The Heart of Darkness,'"
College English 6, No. 2 (November 1944): 103–4

ALBERT J. GUÉRARD

⟨. . .⟩ it is time to recognize that the story *Heart of Darkness* is not primarily about
Kurtz or about the brutality of Belgian officials but about Marlow its narrator. To
what extent it also expresses the Joseph Conrad a biographer might conceivably
recover, who in 1898 still felt a debt must be paid for his Congo journey and who
paid it by the writing of this story, is doubtless an insoluble question. I suspect two
facts (of a possible several hundred) are important. First, that going to the Congo
was the enactment of a childhood wish associated with the disapproved childhood
ambition to go to sea, and that this belated enactment was itself profoundly disapproved, in 1890, by the uncle and guardian. It was another gesture of a man bent
on throwing his life away. But even more important may be the guilt of complicity,
just such a guilt as many novelists of the Second World War have been obliged to
work off. What Conrad thought of the expedition of the Katanga Company of
1890–1892 is accurately reflected in his remarks on the "Eldorado Exploring Expedition" of "Heart of Darkness": "It was reckless without hardihood, greedy without audacity, and cruel without courage . . . with no more moral purpose at the
back of it than there is in burglars breaking into a safe." Yet Conrad hoped to obtain
command of the expedition's ship even after he had returned from the initiatory
voyage dramatized in his novel. Thus the adventurous Conrad and Conrad the
moralist may have experienced collision. But the collision, again as with so many
novelists of the second war, could well have been deferred and retrospective, not
felt intensely at the time.

So much for the elusive Conrad of the biographers and of the "Congo Diary."
Substantially and in its central emphasis "Heart of Darkness" concerns Marlow

(projection to whatever great or small degree of a more irrecoverable Conrad) and his journey toward and through certain facets or potentialities of self. F. R. Leavis seems to regard him as a narrator only, providing a "specific and concretely realized point of view." But Marlow reiterates often enough that he is recounting a spiritual voyage of self-discovery. He remarks casually but crucially that he did not know himself before setting out, and that he likes work for the chance it provides to "find yourself . . . what no other man can ever know." The Inner Station "was the farthest point of navigation and the culminating point of my experience." At a material and rather superficial level, the journey is through the temptation of atavism. It is a record of "remote kinship" with the "wild and passionate uproar," of a "trace of a response" to it, of a final rejection of the "fascination of the abomination." And why should there not be the trace of a response? "The mind of man is capable of anything—because everything is in it, all the past as well as all the future." Marlow's temptation is made concrete through his exposure to Kurtz, a white man and sometime idealist who had fully responded to the wilderness: a potential and fallen self. "I had turned to the wilderness really, not to Mr. Kurtz." At the climax Marlow follows Kurtz ashore, confounds the beat of the drum with the beating of his heart, goes through the ordeal of looking into Kurtz's "mad soul," and brings him back to the ship. He returns to Europe a changed and more knowing man. Ordinary people are now "intruders whose knowledge of life was to me an irritating pretence, because I felt so sure they could not possibly know the things I knew."

On this literal plane, and when the events are so abstracted from the dream-sensation conveying them, it is hard to take Marlow's plight very seriously. Will he, the busy captain and moralizing narrator, also revert to savagery, go ashore for a howl and a dance, indulge unspeakable lusts? The late Victorian reader (and possibly Conrad himself) could take this more seriously than we; could literally believe not merely in a Kurtz's deterioration through months of solitude but also in the sudden reversions to the "beast" of naturalistic fiction. Insofar as Conrad does want us to take it seriously and literally, we must admit the nominal triumph of a currently accepted but false psychology over his own truer intuitions. But the triumph is only nominal. For the personal narrative is unmistakably authentic, which means that it explores something truer, more fundamental, and distinctly less material: the night journey into the unconscious, and confrontation of an entity within the self. "I flung one shoe overboard, and became aware that that was exactly what I had been looking forward to—a talk with Kurtz." It little matters what, in terms of psychological symbolism, we call this double or say he represents: whether the Freudian id or the Jungian shadow or more vaguely the outlaw. And I am afraid it is impossible to say where Conrad's conscious understanding of his story began and ended. The important thing is that the introspective plunge and powerful dream seem true; and are therefore inevitably moving.

Certain circumstances of Marlow's voyage, looked at in these terms, take on a new importance. The true night journey can occur (except during analysis) only in sleep or in the waking dream of a profoundly intuitive mind. Marlow insists more than is necessary on the dreamlike quality of his narrative. "It seems to me I am trying to tell you a dream—making a vain attempt, because no relation of a dream can convey the dream-sensation, the commingling of absurdity, surprise, and bewilderment in a tremor of struggling revolt . . ." Even before leaving Brussels Marlow felt as though he "were about to set off for the center of the earth," not the center of a continent. The introspective voyager leaves his familiar rational world, is "cut off from the comprehension" of his surroundings; his steamer toils "along slowly on the edge of a black and incomprehensible frenzy." As the crisis approaches, the dreamer and his ship move through a silence that "seemed unnatural, like a state of trance"; then enter (a few miles below the Inner Station) a deep fog. "The approach to this Kurtz grubbing for ivory in the wretched bush was beset by as many dangers as though he had been an enchanted princess sleeping in a fabulous castle." Later, Marlow's task is to try "to break the spell" of the wilderness that holds Kurtz entranced.

The approach to the unconscious and primitive may be aided by a savage or half-savage guide, and may require the token removal of civilized trappings or aids; both conceptions are beautifully dramatized in Faulkner's "The Bear." In "Heart of Darkness" the token "relinquishment" and the death of the half-savage guide are connected. The helmsman falling at Marlow's feet casts blood on his shoes, which he is "morbidly anxious" to change and in fact throws overboard. (The rescue of Wait in The Nigger of the "Narcissus" shows a similar pattern.) Here we have presumably entered an area of unconscious creation; the dream is true but the teller may have no idea why it is. So too, possibly, a psychic need as well as literary tact compelled Conrad to defer the meeting between Marlow and Kurtz for some three thousand words after announcing that it took place. We think we are about to meet Kurtz at last. But instead Marlow leaps ahead to his meeting with the "Intended"; comments on Kurtz's megalomania and assumption of his place among the devils of the land; reports on the seventeen-page pamphlet; relates his meeting and conversation with Kurtz's harlequin disciple—and only then tells of seeing through his binoculars the heads on the stakes surrounding Kurtz's house. This is the "evasive" Conrad in full play, deferring what we most want to know and see; perhaps compelled to defer climax in this way. The tactic is dramatically effective, though possibly carried to excess: we are told on the authority of completed knowledge certain things we would have found hard to believe had they been presented through a slow consecutive realistic discovery. But also it can be argued that it was psychologically impossible for Marlow to go at once to Kurtz's house with the others. The double must be brought on board the ship, and the first confrontation must occur there. We are reminded of Leggatt in the narrator's cabin, of the trapped Wait on the Narcissus. The incorporation and alliance between the two becomes material, and the identification of "selves."

Hence the shock Marlow experiences when he discovers that Kurtz's cabin is empty and his secret sharer gone; a part of himself has vanished. "What made this emotion so overpowering was—how shall I define it?—the moral shock I received, as if something altogether monstrous, intolerable to thought and odious to the soul, had been thrust upon me unexpectedly." And now he must risk the ultimate confrontation in a true solitude and must do so on shore. "I was anxious to deal with this shadow by myself alone—and to this day I don't know why I was so jealous of sharing with anyone the peculiar blackness of that experience." He follows the crawling Kurtz through the grass; comes upon him "long, pale, indistinct, like a vapor exhaled by the earth." ("I had cut him off cleverly ...") We are told very little of what Kurtz said in the moments that follow; and little of his incoherent discourses after he is brought back to the ship. "His was an impenetrable darkness. I looked at him as you peer down at a man who is lying at the bottom of a precipice where the sun never shines"—a comment less vague and rhetorical, in terms of psychic geography, than it may seem at a first reading. And then Kurtz is dead, taken off the ship, his body buried in a "muddy hole." With the confrontation over, Marlow must still emerge from environing darkness, and does so through that other deep fog of sickness. The identification is not yet completely broken. "And it is not my own extremity I remember best—a vision of grayness without form filled with physical pain, and a careless contempt for the evanescence of all things—even of this pain itself. No! It is his extremity that I seem to have lived through." Only in the atonement of his lie to Kurtz's "Intended," back in the sepulchral city, does the experience come truly to an end. "I laid the ghost of his gifts at last with a lie ... "

Such seems to be the content of the dream. If my summary has even a partial validity it should explain and to an extent justify some of the "adjectival and worse than supererogatory insistence" to which F. R. Leavis (who sees only the travelogue and the portrait of Kurtz) objects. I am willing to grant that the unspeakable rites and unspeakable secrets become wearisome, but the fact—at once literary and psychological—is that they must remain *unspoken*. A confrontation with such a double and facet of the unconscious cannot be reported through realistic dialogue; the conversations must remain as shadowy as the narrator's conversations with Leggatt. So too when Marlow finds it hard to define the moral shock he received on seeing the empty cabin, or when he says he doesn't know why he was jealous of sharing his experience, I think we can take him literally ... and in a sense even be thankful for his uncertainty. The greater tautness and economy of "The Secret Sharer" comes from its larger conscious awareness of the psychological process it describes; from its more deliberate use of the double as symbol. And of the two stories I happen to prefer it. But it may be the groping, fumbling "Heart of Darkness" takes us into a deeper region of the mind. If the story is not about this deeper region, and not about Marlow himself, its length is quite indefensible. But even if one were to allow that the final section is about Kurtz (which I think simply absurd), a vivid pictorial record of his unspeakable lusts and gratifications would surely have been ludicrous. I share Mr. Leavis' admiration for the heads on the stakes. But not even Kurtz could have supported many such particulars.

—ALBERT J. GUÉRARD, "The Journey Within," Conrad the Novelist
(Cambridge, MA: Harvard University Press, 1958), pp. 37–43

HAROLD KAPLAN

In "Heart of Darkness" Conrad conceives the human enterprise as a kind of cardboard reality against the background of nature. The Europeans represent the pathos of civilization, mocked for its ingenuity as when we see the rusting carcasses of machinery in the Congo jungle, and mocked for its aggressions as the guns of the white men's ships point and go "pop" into the darkness. Their cause is only an "imbecile rapacity"; they are led by the "flabby weakeyed devil of commerce." The characteristic moral somberness of Conrad here stresses the triviality, meanness and inconsequence of the human adventure in the natural world.

Yet the ironic theme finds a contrasting quality in its own extremes. Such an extreme is expressed by the bookkeeper, who as Marlow finds him in the midst of the heat and lassitude of general defeat, wears his immaculate collars and keeps the uniform and gestures of his trade. The bookkeeper sits on his stool, sharing his hut with a dying man brought in from the wilderness, and he complains for the distraction which makes him commit errors in his accounts. This grotesquerie, if it isn't madness, is admirable for its unimaginative persistence in living, defined as an occupation, so to speak, a humble and routine task. Certainly the posture is not heroic. The manager of the jungle outpost, it is observed, has come to lead the enterprise not because of his ability but because he survived whereas others died. His commonplace health was the secret of his success, and Marlow adds, "perhaps he survived because there was nothing in him." Nature rewards neither intelligence nor great faculties, but simply a vulgar talent for survival.

Marlow, and Kurtz before him, has voyaged past a margin of intelligible values, into a darkness where the human genius founders and nothing has use except the capacity for endurance. The search for innermost and outermost reality which is the dramatic frame of this story, reaches an abyss which tells men nothing but shows them the shape of their own illusions. The ultimate reality is "an implacable force brooding over an inscrutable intention." That is why Kurtz, lost before him in the darkness, has become chiefly a voice for Marlow, remembered for an idealistic eloquence which is now heard simply as rhetoric.

We feel, as we respond to Conrad's own verbal music, a melancholy which communicates the illusionary effect of language. When we hear the words in the long ruminative accents of Marlow, for instance, we also feel the encircling silence. His periods roll against their own echoes, as though the world were an empty space filled only with the human voice, disembodied in the end like Kurtz's voice. In this sense Marlow is an indispensable agent in this story, as he is elsewhere in Conrad's work, for he plays the crucial role of a consciousness in a field of action which resists meaning. We find this stress on the ruminative spectatorial figure significant for our theme. Knowledge takes precedence over action, though knowledge is the on-looker, and the true protagonist is implicitly the analytical modern intelligence.

Marlow's search is in symbiotic relationship to Kurtz' more extreme ordeal which has ended in silence. The search is to find Kurtz and thereby know himself, as he goes further and further beyond institutional or "rhetorical" supports, past the "monkey tricks of civilization" into the wilderness which is dark. The darkness is a metaphysical and moral incoherence and it is here that the ultimate ordeal of consciousness takes place. It is an ultimate ordeal because the supports of meaning are gone; the reality he faces here is empty.

Despite some of the atmospheric hints and allusions, the corruption of the white men and of Kurtz in the wilderness is not complexly demonic or exotically immoral. Kurtz is not a Dr. Faust who has sold himself to anti-human rites and experiences; though he has participated in the practices of savagery, that is not the chief aspect of his degeneration. We know from observing the white men along the route toward Kurtz that their major afflictions are disease and a monstrous apathy which has made them shadows. Kurtz has gone further, to the limit of self-knowledge, and his death is an expression of final awareness as he exclaims, "the Horror, the Horror." But the Horror, which can be only obscurely communicated to Marlow, is really the compact revelation of a vision which is utterly nihilistic. "He was alone, he had kicked the earth to pieces." Being alone, he had looked into himself and into reality and had gone mad. Marlow speculates at one point that Kurtz had surrendered because there was something missing in him. Looking into himself he had found he was really hollow at the core and looking into natural reality he had found it a corresponding blank. At this point Conrad sets the ground for his moral theme, when Marlow observes, "he did not have what saves you, what brings a man back up."

To know what is missing in Kurtz we look to Marlow, who comes back from the wilderness, having gone almost as far as Kurtz. Marlow says, a man (stressing a manly courage and endurance) does not collapse in the face of Kurtz's revelation, nor does he let himself go so far as to embrace it. A man knows or guesses what Kurtz knows and restores himself with something. What is it? We very much need to know in this story; it arouses a demand for moral insight. Marlow says in his own voice, a speech which takes up Kurtz's lost rhetoric, that what saves a man and brings him back up is the "idea at whose shrine one worships."

There is nothing grandiose about Marlow's idea; no moral sublimity is expressed in it. Reduced to its essence it might be seen as his occupation, significantly the navigating of a ship in difficult water. The tattered book on navigation which Marlow finds in the wilderness is the key. Read and cherished by its owner, the mad Russian outcast, it is really the bible of civilization, plain, pragmatic, expressing the labor of survival. The ultimate concern is with survival, but not in the reductive terms expressed by the company manager, whose health is his blind natural luck. Rather the principle of survival is morally sophisticated, like Marlow himself. To navigate the ship involves labor and sacrifice, it embodies a definition of character. What a true man falls back upon there in the darkness, where the structure and the certainties of life have disappeared, is a capacity for faithfulness to the occupation of a man, that is, the craft, the discipline in nature which defines a man. The loyalty is not to a transcendent vision or command, but as Marlow says, "the devotion to an obscure, back-breaking business."

Stripped to its basis, this is a conscience without ideas at all really, without structure or pretense. The concept is that of a moral first choice, made before values themselves are defined, and its essence is a loyalty to man in the condition we find him, in his illusionary enterprises, obscurely formed and even more obscurely destined. In this sense Marlow navigates his ship loyal to an enterprise which is mysterious, surrounded by an unexplored wilderness, in search of a man whose identity is a deeper mystery and whose moral value is not merely ambiguous but suggestively monstrous. The idea of loyalty is a distillation of the conservative instinct, a sober, obstinate affirmation without reasons, expressed by devotion to one's metier, tradition and social commitment. It is a morally sensible conservatism, not complacent or obscurantist, which has emerged from the ordeal of disbelief. Realistically what has been affirmed in the wilderness is that human values have only themselves upon which to depend. At the last outpost of the voyage into reality, when human knowledge and belief are stripped bare like the decaying litter of the trading post, a choice remains. This is the choice of loyalty, the sense of honor which pulls a man up—and back to the human community which claims him.

It is evident that loyalty receives its severe test and is itself exhibited nobly not in the context of a faith but that of severe doubt. The moral order in its last crisis requires an affirmation which is not supported by images of belief but by a tenderness for images which have become apparitions in an empty world. In "Heart of Darkness," for instance, Kurtz has become a shadow in the knowledge of everyone in whose life he played a role, particularly his fiancée. That young woman, called with stress the "Intended," is perfectly innocent and illusioned, and it is evident that for her the real Kurtz is absolutely unknowable and cannot exist without changing her own essence completely. The close of the story, as Marlow visits her at her home in the setting of a western European city, is not an irrelevance nor an embellishment of pathos. The girl's illusions are grotesque, but irony is not the chief point of the scene, nor does Marlow make any effort to share the truth with her. Marlow pays his respect to her illusions, not in themselves as substance, but in the aspect of the life-giving capacity for illusion. The "Intended" has filled a void with resonant images; these are not as important (to Marlow) for what they reflect of Kurtz's reality as for what they reflect of her own. Marlow refuses to disillusion the girl for a profounder reason than its obvious and useless cruelty. He occupies an elevated moral stance in the end, far higher than that of the girl herself, and it would seem that his role is to protect her innocence. But in a sense he is protecting his own or all human innocence, as though affirming that the voyage into the darkness is a universal fate, the test of faith is universal and the decision to return and be loyal to what the human light provides is crucial. In this story, so immensely significant for understanding Conrad's work, what is suggested is not that the function of the enlightened man is to protect specific human illusions, but rather the task of making them "real" by accepting them as motives. Values are intended values, reality is an intended reality; the function of life is to work for them. That perhaps would have been the role of a returned Kurtz, if he had been able to return, like Marlow, redeemed from his vision of the Horror. We understand this better if we refer ourselves at this point to other work by Conrad, "The Secret Sharer," for instance, where the task of Captain Leggatt is to purge himself of ambiguities and contra-dictions and define himself finally (we might say create himself) in the form that the world needs and in which he *wills* to know himself. In "Heart of Darkness" because of the roles assigned to Kurtz and his fiancée, and the spectatorial role of Marlow, we see a stress upon the faculty of illusion as such in its aspect of innocence and vulnerability. In *Victory,* a later work where the theme carries itself forward, it is seen rather as a great strength.

—HAROLD KAPLAN, "Character as Reality: Joseph Conrad," The Passive Voice:
An Approach to Modern Fiction (Athens: Ohio University Press, 1966),
pp. 131–37

J. W. JOHNSON

By correlating the scattered data in the four pieces of fiction, the reader can construct a rudimentary biography for Charles Marlow. At twenty, he shipped off on the *Judea* and wound up after a mock-heroic voyage in the Orient, where he got "a regular dose of the East—six years or so." He then returned to London and, through the kind offices of his aunt, got a job with the Brussels firm that carried on an export trade in the Congo. His age at this time was probably near thirty. When he talked on board the *Nellie* in the London dusk, he still followed the sea but had begun to cultivate his ties with the shipping officers on the shore. Since his Congo venture preyed on his mind strongly, he probably was not more than five or six years away from it. In any case, the trial of Jim found Marlow a world traveler but more a man of business and affairs than an adventurer. The Marlow of the Jim story, which covers a period of perhaps five years, may be placed in his late thirties. In "Youth," Marlow is forty-two, and has stopped shipping out; he is beginning to be affluent, like the other professional men he spends a drinking evening with. And it is after his retirement from the sea that he commences the country holidays that lead him to the acquaintance of the Fynes and Flora de Barral. The period of time covered by the events in *Chance* is fourteen years. So Marlow is about fifty-six years old—"lanky, loose, quietly composed in varied shades of brown . . . with a predisposition to congestion of the liver"—when he meets Powell in the restaurant and begins to piece together the sage of the Damsel and the Knight that is *Chance.*

Clearly, to speak of a Marlovian "point of view" is impractical in light of the varying ages and positions Marlow occupies in the four works; rather, Marlow's "perspectives" are suited to the specific themes and subjects of the works and are modified by Conrad's use of a primary narrator who circumscribes Marlow and relates him to the totality of the work. At twenty, Marlow's view of himself and the world is the youthful one of adventuresome idealism; in literary terms, Marlow's perspective is that of the heroic—or the epic or romantic—mode. Since Marlow is never that age when he serves as a secondary narrator and character, Conrad does not use him to serve as a secondary narrator and character, Conrad does not use him to serve the heroic point of view. In *Heart of Darkness,* however, the character-Marlow starts out as a young, idealistic man, bent on an epic odyssey up the Congo; but his collision with the "truth" about Kurtz alters his perspective to the tragic. *Heart of Darkness* may not be pure tragedy in the literary sense; but it comes as close as anything Conrad every wrote, and it can be argued that Kurtz is a genuinely tragic protagonist. It is the double vision of the narrator-Marlow at thirty-five, relating the discoveries of himself at twenty-eight or twenty-nine, that keeps the work from being pure tragedy. The older Marlow is steadily in counterpoint with his youthful, idealistic self in its manifestations (the character-Marlow, the young Russian, Kurtz). And even as the younger Marlow meets Kurtz and disillusionment, seeing tragedy in the heart of darkness, the older Marlow, recounting the discovery, has plainly survived and been strengthened by the experience. The narrator-Marlow has gained emotional distance from the events he tells of; time, geography, age permit him a perspective that goes beyond the tragic catastrophe.

In turn, *Lord Jim* shows a Marlow whose heroic vision has become lost in ambiguities and whose tragic sense is fading. As Marlow views Jim's career, he no longer makes the simplistic disjunction between Good and Evil so apparent in *Heart of Darkness*. Jim himself makes this disjunction, of course. Like the boy Marlow, the young Russian, the glamour-hungry young Kurtz, Jim holds to the heroic ideal of conduct; he wants his life to be a chivalric romance. When he stares across the creek at Brown, he first sees himself as Good and Brown as Evil; when Brown equates himself with Jim, Jim comes to identify the heart of darkness in Brown with himself and then backs down, preparing his fate. This, at least, is the interpretation of Marlow, whose conjecture reflects his own confrontation with Kurtz. But whereas Marlow judged himself severely, even savagely, in his youth, he is tolerant of Jim, recognizing degrees of good and evil separating Jim and Brown (or Brierly and the captain of the *Patna*, Stein and old Robinson). Marlow no longer sees a sharp line separating hero from villain, Good from Evil. He therefore must lose that state of tragic awareness dependent on the conquest of Good by Evil. Marlow finds some elements of tragedy in Jim's life, just as there are elements of the chivalric "romance," but they are diffused and Marlow's emotions are mixed as he tries to define Jim's nature and the meaning of his life. Marlow in his maturity has come to see life as something far more complex, more confused than the heroic and tragic perspectives admit.

—J. W. JOHNSON, "Marlow and *Chance:* A Reappraisal," *Texas Studies in Literature and Language* 10, No. 1 (Spring 1968): 93–95

NORMAN SHERRY

Conrad's basic material for *Heart of Darkness* was a short personal experience of conditions on the Congo in 1890–1, and on the face of it this experience was a personal disaster. Disease, hardship, the pettiness of the activity and of the prevailing attitudes of the colonisers, the evidences of cruelty and exploitation and finally the active hostility of the Delcommunes and their refusal to allow him even his rights as a fully qualified sea-captain—all of these must have made it an exasperating, frustrating and humiliating experience. The 'loot' he brought out of Africa was certainly in part sickness and a sense of failure, and he must have brooded over what there was in it that was not simply a personal account of failure or a view of a contemporary abuse. And yet, if we consider the matter closely, we can see that the whole of *Heart of Darkness* lies in a dormant form within that unsatisfactory experience, and Conrad, as he considered it, must have been conscious that the 'features and character' did exist there if they could be brought out.

The essential development at that early stage was for Conrad to be able to see that his personal *emotional* development through his Congo experience could be related to a central truth of human nature, with regard to the exploitation of the Congo and with regard to the colonising activity generally. The development for Conrad was obviously from a strong idealism to an intense disillusionment. His comments upon the Congo outside the story suggest the strong desire he had to go there, as do the efforts he made to get a job there, and the nature of the desire is hinted also in the pleasure he felt at the prospect of being one of an exploring party. He later referred to his African trip as the end to 'the idealized realities of a boy's daydreams'. It was to have been part of the adventure of African exploration, of geographical discovery, and it must have been linked in his mind with the exploits of Henry Morton Stanley.

In 'Geography and Some Explorers', Conrad refers to Livingstone, with his 'unappeased desire for the sources of the Nile' which had 'changed him in his last days from a great explorer into a restless wanderer refusing to go home any more'. He does not refer to Stanley in this context, but it was Stanley who in 1871 searched out Livingstone, and who in 1888 found Emin Pasha (a man equally reluctant to leave Africa). It was Stanley whose prayer on Livingstone's death was the he might be allowed to open up Africa to the light of Christianity and whose exploration filled up the blank spaces on the map that Conrad had gazed at as a boy. It was Stanley who founded the Congo Free State and the trading-stations on the river for King Leopold of the Belgians. It must have been with these achievements in mind that Conrad went to the Congo only to find that it was all 'the vilest scramble for loot that ever disfigured the history of human conscience and geographical exploration', 'a prosaic newspaper "stunt"'. It is the movement from idealism to knowledge and disillusionment which is suggested by the movement within the story from the narrator's comments on the famous men who had sailed from the Thames—'What greatness had not floated on the ebb of that river into the mystery of an unknown earth! ... The dreams of men, the seed of commonwealths, the germs of empires'—to Marlow's comment on the Roman occupation of Britain that it was 'men going at it blind—as is very proper for those who tackle a darkness'.

Because he had been aware of the truth underlying the pretensions of men in a certain field of endeavour, Conrad was able to move his story from the area of mere personal disappointment: 'I don't want to bother you much with what happened to me personally', Marlow says, for it is 'the effect of it' on him that was important, just as it was in the case of Conrad. Considering the matter later, the personal disappointment and suffering became insignificant compared with the wider understanding that had been opened to him.

It must have been apparent to Conrad that he had material in plenty to demonstrate the process of 'men going at it blind', the ignorance, cruelty and grasping nature of the general run of the colonists. But these were men who had not voiced 'high ideals', who did not claim to see themselves as 'bearers of a spark from the sacred fire' yet, after all, this suggestion of idealism had been a significant part of the whole, both in Conrad's experience and in the propaganda of colonisation. Such a historical process with its marked fracture between man's stated intentions and the results of those intentions had to be presented concretely and individually.

Hodister's story, a part of all of Conrad's Congo experience, must have appeared to him as the right vehicle, an actual and strong example of that movement from idealism to the grotesque actuality. Hodister shared with Stanley an intense egoism, prodigious energy, idealism, and unwavering purpose. Like Stanley, he obtained the maximum publicity. And Hodister was obviously overcome by treachery on the part of envious men and by his own egoism which forced him to venture too far. It is an aspect of Conrad's genius that he was further able to see Hodister in the light of an earlier and more generally applicable myth—he was not only a colonist, he was also a Faust who, in a particularly dangerous field, had allowed 'his unlawful soul' to be beguiled 'beyond the bounds of permitted aspirations'.

Conrad's perception of the 'inner truth' of his material—not of his personal experience but what that experience had allowed him to perceive—and his obtaining of the right example, enforced upon him all the necessary further steps in the moulding of his own material. Conrad was fortunate here in two respects. His experience had partaken of the archetypal one for Stanley and indeed for the area generally—the journey up-river to bring off a man who was in some kind of danger. And on this journey Conrad was intimately connected with a traditional figure of some importance in that situation—the man who was in charge of the steamer making the journey. For the rest, in order to bring out the 'sombre theme' two major changes were necessary in moulding his source material.

The first was the necessity to take back several years the Congo he had known. The Hodister story, Stanley's explorations, the theme of the possible corruption of a man of high ideals, all required the isolation of the primitive to be possible. The Congo that Conrad knew was just a little too close to the idea of the 'two good addresses' and a policemen round the corner. And so large settlements disappear, to be replaced by native villages and small, lost trading-posts. Navigation is a matter of discovering the right channel, feeling one's way through an unknown waterway. The Inner Station became not a Stanley Falls but an isolated trading-post. For the same reason the fate of Freiesleben became the fate of a man involved with the natives at an isolated village, his body left to rot, and no European, let alone a military expedition, coming near until Marlow made his difficult journey up the same isolated stretch of water.

Conrad has gone to some trouble to recreate the story of Freiesleben in a form suited to Marlow's narrative by going beyond the events to give that 'sinister resonance' he desired. To begin with, the story deftly illustrates in advance the kind of human activity we are to find on Marlow's river, and it becomes a revelation in little of what happens to Kurtz on a much greater scale. Fresleven 'was the gentlest, quietest creature that ever walked on two legs', but two years there 'engaged in the noble cause' had changed the 'supernatural being' 'and he probably felt the need at last of asserting his self-respect in some way'. This reconstruction of the captain's character makes him an image in miniature of Kurtz. Moreover, Conrad fixes on the most trivial cause for the incident—provisions—enhancing and particularising this by stating that it was 'two black hens'. And given the conditions he wishes to establish on Marlow's river, he omits the punitive force of 370 soldiers and six white officers, which would be fatal to the sense of isolation he wishes to create. By ignoring the official burial of the remains, and particularly by substituting the more primitive spear for the gun actually used, he is enhancing those particular aspects of primitive isolation, of chance cruelty and neglect in the relations between white and black, which are a significant part of his story.

In spite of his encounters with corpses, Conrad's journey did not, I believe, bring him face to face with the cruelty that was traditionally part of the history of the Congo. One of his lasting impressions must have been rather that which he brings out in such figures as the manager of the Central Station, the brick-maker and the company's chief accountant, of a great deal of bureaucratic activity and posturing, operating incongruously in the midst of the jungle. But mainly, he was following the thin and uncertain line of civilisation up the Congo. The bureaucratic attitude was necessary to his theme—it was the alternative nightmare to Kurtz's, but the impression of the primitive had to be enhanced by an inclusion of the cruelty he knew existed in the history of the Congo. Thus what he had personally seen and heard had to be transformed by re-grouping and by the addition of material outside his experience which was, nevertheless, 'true' to that experience. His treatment of his rather uneventful stay at Matadi is interesting here since, following the necessities of his theme, Conrad re-works it to form Marlow's experience of the Company Station. Marlow's first close encounter with the 'devil' that exists in the heart of darkness is made dramatic and impressive, as it must be, because Conrad finds a forceful and representative image for the cruelty he knew existed. The cumulative effect of the 'grove of death' achieves more of the 'resonance' he desired than a mere recording of scattered and factual examples. The Company Station is Conrad's imaginative working over of those impressions of cruelty, waste, and selfish hypocrisy which must have been general during his stay but which are here clustered about three particular aspects—the railway, the loss of life, and the figure of the accountant—of what he observed in the area.

A further example of this 'distortion' of his material in the direction of an 'inner truth' can be seen by comparing the manuscript and the completed text.

Conrad writes in *Heart of Darkness:* 'I avoided a vast artificial hole somebody had been digging on the slope, the purpose of which I found it impossible to divine'. This appears in the manuscript first as 'I avoided an hole somebody evidently had been digging and the purpose of which I could not divine.' The addition of the adjectives 'vast' and 'artificial' transform a simple situation into a bizarre and extraordinary one.

The second development of Conrad's source material was in relation to the pattern of Marlow's experience. Conrad's experience of the Congo does not appear to have had a culmination in the sense of an illuminating point of climax, though one of its features had been a process of gradual enlightenment—he did say that before the Congo episode he was a mere animal. The process was maturing for him; not a maturing through exertion, growth, the satisfaction of a job well done and one's confidence in oneself justified (as in *The Shadow-Line*), but a maturing through disillusionment, insight into and recognition of the malice, the pettiness, the cruelty and the evil of which mankind is capable in certain circumstances. This general illuminating process, the increase of perception and understanding, becomes Marlow's, paralleling, as it did in Conrad's case, the movement up-river. To this extent, Conrad's experience underlines Marlow's and is the shape of its 'inner truth'.

The choice of nightmares given to Marlow existed also in Conrad's experience, although he did not meet personally with the nightmare of his particular choice. Like Marlow, Conrad rejected the petty corruption of the 'pilgrims', because he had shared, to some extent, the idealistic vision of a Hodister. He had sacrificed a good deal to make it materialise, and the materialisation had been, in a different way, equally disastrous for him.

But Conrad must have realised that that process of maturing, that journey into disillusionment and understanding, must, dramatically, have a 'culminating point' for Marlow, so that the whole effect of his own experience could be represented in a definite and climactic way. Kurtz's death could not come to Marlow by hearsay as Hodister's came to Conrad. Kurtz had to be present as an example, an example in its terminal stages, an example capable of being aware of what had happened, in order that the theme might be concretely presented in its movement from idealism to corruption, and in order that Marlow might experience the full 'effect'. Conrad's much less significant experience of Klein came in most appropriately as a part of the plot. To bring out the final clarification and maturing process for Marlow, therefore, the imaginative accretion of his meeting with the Hodister figure, Kurtz, was essential, the 'culminating point' of his experience.

But for the 'effect' of the whole experience upon Marlow to be brought out significantly, he could not have the minor and frustrating role that was assigned to Conrad by the Delcommunes, and so a major change to Conrad's experience comes about in the development of the figure of Marlow. Marlow is given the legacy of Conrad's hard-gained insight—he is sceptical from the first. Brussels is 'sepulchral', the two women concierges are fates at the door of hell, he is suspicious of the jargon that is applied to him, given the insignificance of the part he is to play—'an emissary of light', 'a lower sort of apostle'. Conrad is taking his revenge upon his own gullibility, and at the same time making his hero a man not easily gulled by the heroics of colonisation. Marlow, again unlike Conrad, is given considerable status within the world of the story, a status at once functional and moral, but on both these levels his status depends upon actions and events which are, in the main, imaginative additions to Conrad's own experience. Marlow is comparatively un-important as skipper of a steamboat, and yet much depends upon him in that capacity. He is the man with skill in seamanship who alone can salvage the vessel that is essential to the saving of Kurtz, he is the only man who can safely take her up to the Inner Station and back. On the moral level, Marlow is the man from the outer world, secure in his beliefs and his job. Ultimately, Marlow is the only one sensitive enough to appreciate the forces at work in the jungle, the nature of the two nightmares that are open to Kurtz and the pilgrims—the blindness of greed and self-deception, or the high but empty ideals that make one vulnerable in face of savagery and the lure of the primitive. Marlow alone forces Kurtz back ultimately from his nightmare into the real world of sickness, disillusionment and death. And in other smaller ways, we can see Conrad bending his experiences to enhance Marlow. Conrad had no part in the tragedy of Freiesleben, but he no doubt saw the ruins of Tchumbiri; and in making Marlow the person who attempted to recover Freiesleben's remains he is enlarging Marlow's stature in the story as one of the few who retain their humanity on the river, and contributing to the idea of Marlow's limited but moral victory over circumstances.

Yet, because of his superiority, Marlow is rejected by the pilgrims as Conrad was rejected by the Delcommunes. Conrad's own rejection therefore becomes the essence of Marlow's right-mindedness amidst the 'squeeze'. Like Conrad, he is not of the wrong party. We might conclude, therefore, that in Marlow Conrad is compensating for his own failure, and doing it very skilfully, for Marlow still remains merely the steamboat skipper, a modest, practical man, with a devotion to his craft.

Most interesting with regard to Marlow's significance in the story is the ele-vation of the homely river-steamboat. Conrad had eulogised ships before—the *Otago* is a case in point. But there he did have a command and the ship had her own beauty and courage. The steamer is a different matter, but it is an essential part of the theme of the story and of Marlow's role. It is the weapon Conrad ought to have had in face of his experience and was denied. It represents honest work and effort as opposed to the rapacious indolence of the pilgrims or the loudly acclaimed brilliance and ideals of Kurtz. While the 'pilgrims' intrigue and slander in order to be appointed to a lucrative trading-post, Marlow is at work on the 'battered, twisted, ruined tin-pot steamboat', which is nevertheless his 'influential friend', which gives him the chance to find himself in work. And the steamboat also is linked with the sombre theme of the river and the jungle, of whose threat only Marlow is aware, for Marlow has hauled the steamer out of the river 'like the carcass of some big river animal', smelling of 'primeval mud'. Given the truth of Conrad's slender actual responsibility for a river-steamer on the Congo, one must see this as a good example of Conrad moulding his experience to fit the 'inner truth'.

There is a further aspect of Conrad's experience which he introduces successfully into the story in order to bring out the 'resonance'. Part of the nightmare that Marlow rejects is the determination in the midst of the jungle to stick to the forms of European society, however irrelevant, in terms of status. And so there is an emphasis upon titles—'manager', 'chief accountant', 'brick-maker'. That this was part of Conrad's experience is suggested by the emphasis laid in the *Mouvement Géographique* on such status-indicating labels. Conrad, of course, twists them ironically, and adds his own 'pilgrims' equally ironically. Appropriate forms of expression are used by the manager after Kurtz has been found and are evidence of the need for self-deception (and for self-protection) from the actualities of their situation, on the part of the 'pilgrims'. For even in the face of the horrors that have been discovered the aim is to conceal the truth, denying its existence. References to minor issues, but issues which can equally well serve the purpose of damning Kurtz, are safer: 'the time was not ripe for vigorous action'; 'the district is closed'; the 'ivory—mostly fossil'; 'the method is unsound'. And when Marlow suggests 'no method at all', the manager seizes upon this as a better approach, indicating 'complete want of judgement'—very useful for a damning and face-saving report. These were the kind of criticisms that were levelled at Hodister after his death, and the attitude must have been common among the people Conrad met. It is an attitude he consciously develops, as we can see by his alterations to the manuscript. His comment that the touch of insanity 'was not dissipated by somebody on board assuring me earnestly that there was a camp of natives—he called them enemies!—hidden out of sight somewhere' was initially in the manuscript: 'which was not dissipated by somebody telling me there was a camp of "niggers" '. 'Niggers' has been crossed out and the word 'natives' substituted, followed by the interpolation 'he called them "enemies" '. It is most likely that 'niggers' was the term Conrad heard used, and for which he substituted the less objectionable 'natives', and then brought in his own development of the idea, 'enemies'. This introduces the theme of self-deceptive 'definitions' used by the colonists to give justification to their actions. Later, the natives become 'criminals', and the skulls on poles round Kurtz's home belonged to former 'rebels'; 'Rebels! What would be the next definition I was to hear? There had been enemies, criminals, workers—and these were rebels'. To Marlow, the nightmare of full self-realisation is preferable to the nightmare of self-deception.

Conrad had had a direct personal experience in the Congo of what lay behind the elevation of colonisation there. He was fortunate in that he was able to go beyond the apparent truth of that activity to the 'inner truth' and achieve an awareness which allowed his characteristically ironic approach to man's activity to permeate 'truthfully' his account of Marlow's journey. And Conrad is being quite honest when he borrows a metaphor from the conception of *Heart of Darkness* and speaks of the 'loot' he brought out of the Congo, for this story depends not upon his personal experience so much as upon impressions and ideas related to the area, a view which was permitted to him of man's activity there. The distinction is between 'adventures' in the sense of personally acted and felt incidents and 'experiences' which include a wider area of activity—a personal view of the adventures of others, impressions of a place and a people.

—NORMAN SHERRY, "Conclusion," *Conrad's Western World* (Cambridge: Cambridge University Press, 1971), pp. 339–50

WILLIAM W. BONNEY

Much has been written about the importance of the character of Marlow, Conrad's most famous first-person narrator, and perhaps the best work in this area has been done by John Palmer, who writes persuasively that only with the development of Marlow was Conrad able "for the first time to draw attention to the primary object of interest in his early fiction—the processes of moral discovery and self-exploration." That is, "Marlow's meditation is itself the hard fact of the story," which I feel is quite correct. However, Palmer goes on to make what I consider to be somewhat exaggerated claims about Marlow's importance as a character whose perception Conrad intends the reader to trust thoroughly: "all the Marlow tales involve such a variety of artifices tending to 'justify' Marlow as a choral voice that the reader must suppose Conrad to have been deeply concerned in gaining the reader's trust. . . ." Palmer feels that these tales "hold their narrator out as a trustworthy spiritual guide, one whose judgment about his own experience is likely to be both subtle and sound. . . ." I feel that Palmer's discussion of Marlow's function as a normative voice or choral figure, whose attitudes are basically congruent with Conrad's own, needs to be qualified somewhat; and the problem of the function of narrative inconsistency can be approached from a different direction by a brief demonstration of Marlow's subjective fallibility, for it is precisely such human perceptual limitations that the third-person narrative voice reveals and censures in those of Conrad's works in which the two narrative modes clash.

However much Conrad may sympathize (or even agree) with Marlow's philosophical meditations, it is indisputable that Marlow is repeatedly presented as a character whose personality is warped and whose vision is colored by subjective biases just like other of Conrad's characters, and as such Marlow's voice cannot be accepted unquestioningly by the reader. In "Heart of Darkness," for instance, Marlow's attitude toward women is openly scornful of what he considers to be their innate inability to cope with adversity; yet, when the steamer is departing at the end of the tale and Marlow blows the whistle, in the face of the shrieking of the whistle and the crashing of the pilgrims' rifles (what to her must have been a disorienting "darkness") only "the barbarous and superb woman did not so much as flinch" while the men of the tribe flee in terror, a detail which clearly undercuts Marlow's understanding. Similarly, in spite of the awed tones often assumed by critics when they write of Marlow's deep wisdom as displayed in "Heart of Darkness," the profundity of Marlow's deep wisdom is supposedly emphasized by the anonymous narrator's comparisons of Marlow to a Buddha, these critics overlook the important fact that Marlow is described as having "the pose of a Buddha preaching in European clothes and without a lotos-flower." Although the connotations of the Buddha pose suggest that Marlow is about to begin an introspective meditation the profundity of which cannot be denied, the fact that the Buddha is devoid of a lotos-flower (which, when present, symbolizes the flowering of a human spirit) requires that we understand Marlow's psyche has not attained the clear-sighted state of being which the presence of the lotos denotes in the iconography of the Far East as far as the mind of the anonymous narrator can discern.

But let us step away from Marlow in order to explore briefly the shifting narrative perspective as manifested in the volume in which Marlow makes perhaps his most memorable appearance. It is important to realize that "Heart of Darkness" is the second story in a volume consisting of a series of three tales ("Youth," "Heart of Darkness," and "The End of the Tether") which Conrad insists must be read as a unified work of art. In a letter dated February 7, 1924, and addressed to F. N. Doubleday, Conrad remarks "I told you that in my view every volume of my short stories has a unity of artistic purpose. . . ." In the same letter Conrad goes on to say that the "volume of *Youth* . . . presents the three ages of man (for that is what it really is, and I knew very well what I was doing when I wrote 'The End of the Tether' to be the last of the trio). I can't somehow imagine any of those stories taken out of it and bound cheek and jowl with a story from another volume. It is in fact unthinkable." And in another letter, addressed to Alfred A. Knopf, Conrad remarks, more generally, that "I don't shovel together my stories in a haphazard fashion." Thus, if we can trust Conrad's word in these instances, there should be several important principles of unity operant in the *Youth, and Two Other Stories* (1902) volume, perhaps the most significant of which is the modification of narrative perspective as the series of tales progresses.

In "Youth," a relatively congenial situation is established: the anonymous narrator agrees implicitly with the disturbingly maudlin Marlow, who bewails the departure of the state of being (youth) which he has endowed, somewhat foolishly, with almost transcendental value, exclaiming, for instance, " 'Oh, the glamour of youth! Oh, the fire of it, more dazzling than the flames of the burning ship, throwing a magic light on the wide earth . . .' " Certainly Palmer's assertion that we are meant to accept Marlow "as a trustworthy spiritual guide . . . whose judgment . . . is . . . both subtle and sound" must be qualified in view of this story, for Marlow is so overwhelmed by the prospect of his vanished youth that he, most depressingly, must buffer his feelings repeatedly with alcohol while sentimentally lamenting " 'O Youth!' " The most blatant sign of Marlow's intellectual inadequacy, however, is the fact that, even at a great chronological remove from his youth, he still takes seriously the pathetic and inept Captain Beard, who leaps into a painter without oars to save his equally inept wife when his ship is struck by another, and who must be rescued by his bewildered crew. To Marlow the incompetent old man is still admirable (" 'Just imagine that old fellow saving heroically in his arms that old woman—the woman of his life' ", the motto "Do or Die" is still profound, and although he can regard youth intellectually as " 'silly,' " a lure " 'to joys' " as well as " 'to perils' " and " 'to death,' " he is emotionally a slave to the past and enjoys wallowing in regret a good bit more than dealing with an uncongenial present.

In "Heart of Darkness," however, the anonymous narrator no longer assents to Marlow's tale-telling, indeed, he would rather have Marlow keep silent than suffer through "one of Marlow's inconclusive experiences." And although the narrator does get interested in Marlow's story, confessing that "[he] listened on the watch for the sentence, for the word, that would give [him] the clew to the faint uneasiness inspired by this narrative . . . ," one cannot be sure that the "clew" ever comes (we do know, of course, that the tale has impressed him, for he retells it to the reader). The narrator's final remark is inconclusive. It could involve simply the narrator's transposition of the diction he has heard for hours from Marlow onto his relating of the fact that during Marlow's tale the sun has set and it has grown dark: "The offing was barred by a black bank of clouds, and the tranquil waterway . . . seemed to lead into the heart of an immense darkness." The remark does not necessarily betray a completed "moral progress" (as Seymour Gross asserts), although it may. In "Heart of Darkness" Marlow speaks with a self-conscious aura of elite profundity that may annoy the reader even more than the maudlin triteness he displayed in "Youth." His contempt for the remainder of humanity after his return from the Congo betrays an unjustified egoism on Marlow's part which is significantly akin, I feel, to Gulliver's downright insanity upon his arrival in England in book IV of *Gulliver's Travels.* As he shows in works like *The Secret Agent,* Conrad is aware that the "darkness" can be encountered anywhere, within civilization or outside of it, an awareness that Marlow in his pride does not share: " 'I found myself back in the sepulchral city resenting the sight of people hurrying through the streets . . . because I felt so sure they could not possibly know the things I knew.' " Indeed, one wonders whether the Director of Companies's comment at the end of Marlow's tale, " 'We have lost the first of the ebb' " is really "banal," and not an ironic qualification of the supposedly overwhelming profundity of Marlow's story.

In any case, as the character of Marlow and his relationship with the anonymous narrator (and other listeners) alter, the narrative perspective of the volume of stories progresses significantly from a protagonist who idealizes the state of imperceptive innocence while in harmony with his companions and in a tearful, alcoholic haze himself, to a protagonist who values, to an equally exaggerated degree, a blighting recognition of what he sees as a moral darkness at the heart of Man, while his shipmates and he can relate only in a remote and discordant manner. Only the incisive third-person narrative voice of "The End of the Tether" can clear the air of the disturbing (but thematically relevant) subjectivity that has dominated the first two stories, and give the reader some sort of objective, factual information and philosophical construct, even though this validity is derived only from the artistic convention of an omniscient narrative voice, and functions only within the framework of the work of art in which it appears.

—WILLIAM W. BONNEY, "Joseph Conrad's Discontinuous Point of View,"
Journal of Narrative Technique 2, No. 2 (May 1972): 103–6

STEPHEN ZELNICK

Lord Jim has a critical form, a philosophically adventurous form. It follows no obvious spatial or temporal pattern and disassociates itself from the authority of omniscience. It has a form allowing discoveries by its openness, rather than resolving tensions by the arc of its plot. It is a subversive form because it dislocates us from our rationalized categories and prepares us to know the world dialectically. The tension between appearance and reality, between "is" and "ought", is probed in the light of the contingency of the given world and subjected to a search for truth at a higher level of reason and feeling. It is a form well suited for catching a glimpse of what conventional rationality would censure or make unthinkable or unexpressible; it invites us to participate in a search requiring our sharpest attention and our readiness for revelations of what lies under the neatly administered surfaces of our convenient understanding.

Near the opening of *Lord Jim* Conrad alerts us to the issue of false ideals and the purpose they serve in masking the social order. We are informed that Jim's father, a clergyman, "possessed such certain knowledge of the Unknowable as made for the righteousness of people in cottages without disturbing the ease of mind of those whom an unerring Providence enables to live in mansions." This settled home world, centuries deep in idealistic complacency, is founded on fixed beliefs never challenged by the rough edge of reality. Jim emerges from this static world, a model of Britain's thrust outward, carrying a stiff set of heroic fantasies into a world of action and change.

Conrad demands that we see the period of his story historically. As Marlow looks about, he recognizes a world order dominated by the narrow rationality of imperialism. Where once there was adventure and wonder, Marlow witnesses the triumph of trade and administration. At points far East he finds telegraph offices, clusters of European shop-keepers, administrative courts, and trade and mail routes mapped over the seas. Gentleman Brown, a modern buccaneer, is "being financed on the quiet by a most respectable firm of copra merchants," and even the South Seas are being closed off to the pirate's trade "what with High Commissioners, consuls, men-of-war, and international control..." In his meditations Marlow remembers an open world and his response to Jim reveals his desire for open potentialities.

Not only is the world Marlow sees about him increasingly bound in a commercial net, it is tired and complacent. Though trade still preserves an afterglow of adventure (Chester and Robinson indicate how debased this ideal has become), Marlow realizes a qualitative shift has come about. Once romantic individualism held sway, now commercial traders dominate. The influential men to whom Marlow tells his tale are without wonder, desire, or imagination. They "wallow" in their "good chairs" and take life to be "an after-dinner hour with a cigar; easy, pleasant, empty." Their common table companion is "the usual respectable thief of commerce." They are said to have "starved their imaginations to feed their bodies." For them, "it is respectable to have no illusions—and safe—and profitable—

and dull"; Marlow wonders whether they can at all remember "the intensity of life."

This aura of complacency and decay is also associated with the two groups of European seamen. One group gets by on "the distinction of being white" and waits for "turns of luck" and a "soft thing". They have "the soft spot, the place of decay, the determination to lounge softly through existence." A second group displays restless avidity, the dialectical opposite of the first: "They appeared to live in a crazy maze of plans, hopes, dangers, enterprises, ahead of civilisation, in the dark places of the sea; and their death was the only event of their fantastic existence that seemed to have a reasonable certitude of achievement." Both groups are united in having no purpose and no community of values to shape their lives. They live over against the rationality of imperialism, but not outside it.

These general versions of devitalization are corroborated by the particular characters Marlow encounters. Captain Brierly might at first seem to be a figure of great energy and purpose. He is neither a lounger nor a restless adventurer; his career in the merchant navy has been exemplary. Brierly is motivated by no narrow commercialism but instead by an ideal of perfect order. However, his ideal is a rigid abstraction and relates to no comprehensible social value. Regarding Jim's disgrace, Brierly explains that "the only thing that holds us together is just the name for that sort of decency." As for the lives jeopardized by Jim's desertion, "I don't care a snap for all the pilgrims that ever came out of Asia." Brierly serves a "name" and regulates his life by his chronometer. His suicide, introduced in a terse ironic explosion, reveals an unseen depth. Brierly's rigidity—the perfect expression of a fixed standard of conduct—is one of those apparently solid surfaces, rational and efficient, that give way to incalculable human forces.

The French lieutenant also seems to have mastered the complexities of life, his untroubled surfaces persuading Marlow of his power. But Marlow learns that the veteran's mastery is a victory won by deadening routine, avoidance, and repression. He turns out to be one of those who "go through life with eyes half shut, with dull ears, with dormant thoughts." When Marlow presses him on what he has buried in his thoughts, he responds "as a startled ox might scramble up from the grass" and rushes from the room. Power is rigidity; mastery is torpor; control is repression.

Marlow finds ghosts everywhere in the imperialist era. Like the derelict ship that cripples the *Patna*, each of the orderly, placid, rational surfaces is threatened by a vagrant dream, a buried memory, and unacceptable yet unavoidable recognitions that haunt complacency out of all assurance. When Marlow contemplates too long and too freely Jim's vitality in Patusan—his life-serving purpose, the swift congruence of ideal and act, the love and respect he evokes without compulsion— Marlow catches a glimpse of the emptiness of his world and is forced to discard his ironic distance that keeps him from knowing his own buried longings: "For a moment I had a view of a world that seemed to wear a vast and dismal aspect of disorder, while, in truth, thanks to our unwearied efforts, it is as sunny an arrangement of small conveniences as the mind of man can conceive. But still—it was only a moment: I went back to my shell directly. One *must*—don't you know?—though

I seemed to have lost all my words in the chaos of dark thoughts I had contemplated for a second or two beyond the pale."

The subtle yet deep alienation Marlow's meditations reveal is historical and specifically bound up with imperialism. Marlow recalls the heroic world-view of the seventeenth-century traders for whom ideal and act were a confident unity. Though they were rude materialists, their "passion for pepper seemed to burn like a flame of love" and "the bizarre obstinacy of the desire made them defy death. . . . It made them great. . . . they appear magnificent, not as agents of trade but as instruments of a recorded destiny, pushing out into the unknown in obedience to an inward voice, to an impulse beating in the blood, to a dream of the future." Yet Conrad is no romantic reactionary suggesting that such a crude romantic individualism has a place in his world. The new unknown, represented in Jim's quest, is in the social realm; the new historical boundary is between a commercial ideal that serves a narrow interest and a social ideal belonging to a whole community. This is the "dream of the future" toward which Jim is impelled and that strikes Marlow's complacent ironies like a submerged phantom, overturning his rational assurance.

—STEPHEN ZELNICK, "Conrad's *Lord Jim:* Meditations on the Other
Hemisphere," *Minnesota Review* NS No. 11 (Fall 1978): 80–83

GARY GEDDES

Marlow's task ⟨in *Chance*⟩ is first one of historical reconstruction. In order to make sense of Flora's situation, he has to engage in some elementary research; he ferrets out the facts of her life from the Fynes, from Powell, and from his own encounters with her. As the narrator observes, Marlow is the 'expert in the psychological wilderness. This is like one of those Redskin stories where the noble savages carry off a girl and the honest backwoodsman with his incomparable knowledge follows the track and reads the signs of her fate in a footprint here, a broken twig there, a trinket dropped by the way. Marlow cannot adequately penetrate to the essential 'truth' of Flora's situation by means of abstract theorizing, but must render it in terms of the elements of art: 'The purely human reality is capable of lyrism but not of abstraction. Nothing will serve for its understanding but the evidence of rational linking up of characters and facts'. 'Fiction', as Conrad explains in his essay on Henry James, 'is history, human history, or it is nothing . . . and a novelist is a historian, the preserver, the keeper, the expounder, of human experience'. The importance of this imaginative reconstruction, Marlow explains to the narrator, arises from our general

> inability to interpret aright the signs which experience (a thing mysterious in
> itself) makes to our understanding and emotions. For it is never more than
> that. It always remains outside of us. That's why we look with wonder at the
> past. And this persists when from practice and through growing callousness of
> fibre we come to the point when nothing that we meet in that rapid blinking

stumble across a flick of sunshine—which is our life—nothing, I say, which we run against surprises us anymore. Not at the time, I mean. If, later on, we recover the faculty with some such exclamation: 'Well! Well! I'll be hanged if I ever, ...' it is probably because this very thing that there should be a past to look back upon, other people's, is very astounding in itself when one has the time, a fleeting and immense instant to think of it.

Through this by-play between Marlow and the narrator, a kind of dialectic or ironic counterpoint is established, which allows for the clarification of important issues in the novel. When the narrator asks Marlow whether their 'inestimable advantage of understanding what is happening to others' has any value other than that of amusement, Marlow states emphatically: 'But from that same provision of understanding, there springs in us compassion, charity, indignation, the sense of solidarity; and in minds of any largeness an inclination to that indulgence which is next to affection'.

Marlow's function in *Chance* parallels that of the novelist, which Conrad describes as 'rescue work, this snatching of vanishing phases of turbulence, disguised in fair words, out of the native obscurity into a light where the struggling forms may be seen, seized upon, endowed with the only possible form of permanence in this world of relative values—the permanence of memory'. By holding up this rescued fragment, the novelist is able to 'show its vibration, its colour, its form; and through its movement, its form, its colour, reveal the substance of its truth—disclose its inspiring secret'. The analogy is by no means far-fetched, since the same phrase appears on the lips of Fyne in *Chance*, as he thinks of Flora and Anthony taking on the responsibility for her ex-convict father: 'They mean to drag him along with them on board the ship straight away. Rescue work'.

In *Chance*, Marlow engages in imaginative rescue work; in fact, one might argue that the subject of *Chance* is not so much the story of Flora de Barral as the *rescue* of the story of Flora de Barral from the dust and ashes of obscurity. In terms of the romance pattern Anthony is the knight who rescues Flora, but it is really Marlow who rescues the facts about Flora, who analyses them and gives them imaginative shape. He is, of course, undertaking the central Conradian task of making us 'see'—that is, of making us understand.

Thus the significance of his speculations, his conjecture, his sallies back and forth in time, the fragmentation of his narrative. Misunderstanding Conrad's aims in *Chance*, Frederick Karl says of the narrative technique: 'One is tempted to suggest that Conrad was coming close to a satire on the Conradian method.' One is tempted to suggest that Karl's observation comes unwittingly close to the truth; for Conrad is aiming in *Chance* not a satire but at an *elaboration* of his essential method. And this method of coming to terms with the truth of experience is, as he suggests in the Author's Notes to his novel, 'indissolubly allied' to the vision of imaginative sympathy that we have seen emerging from his pages.

In comparison to the other characters in *Chance* who have dealings with Flora, Marlow stands out as an inquisitive man. He makes no claim to the 'pure compassion' of the Fynes, the religiosity of de Barral's cousin, or the magnanimous idealism of Anthony; yet, he is the only one who fully understands Flora, the only one with sufficient imagination to bring to fruition the prolonged 'courtship' between Powell and the widowed Flora. Marlow's success in dealing with Flora's story implies a peculiar attitude to experience. For Marlow, things do bear looking into. Where Anthony's ideal of generosity proves to be 'but a flaming vision of reality', Powell's curiosity is instinctive; it is more 'neutral'. Marlow possesses this curiosity in abundance. His encounter in the East End with the pressman who had covered de Barral's trial is important in this connection. The shallow pressman, who was 'glad' that de Barral 'got seven years', disapproved of the convicted man's last gesture in court, the raising of a hard-clenched fist above his head. Marlow takes a significantly different view of de Barral's final gesture:

> The pressman disapproved of that manifestation. It was not his business to understand it. Is it ever the business of any pressman to understand anything? I guess not. It would lead him too far away from the actualities which are the daily bread of the public mind. He probably thought the display worth very little from a picturesque point of view; the weak voice, the colourless personality as incapable of an attitude as a bedpost, the very fatuity of the clenched hand so ineffectual at that time and place—no, it wasn't worth much. And then, for him, an accomplished craftsman in his trade, thinking was distinctly 'bad business.' His business was to write a readable account. But I, who had nothing to write, permitted myself to use my mind as we sat before our still untouched glasses. And the disclosure which so often rewards a moment of detachment from mere visual impressions gave me a thrill very much approaching a shudder. I seemed to understand that, with the shock of the agonies and perplexities of his trial, the imagination of that man, whose moods, notions, and motives wore frequently an air of grotesque mystery—that his imagination had been at last roused into activity. And this was awful. Just try to enter into the feelings of a man whose imagination wakes up at the very moment he is about to enter the tomb.

Marlow describes himself as 'an investigator—a man of deductions', who is concerned with 'the facts of the case'. The narrator contrasts Marlow's complicated hypotheses and imaginative leaps with the 'artless talk' of Powell; and with the single-mindedness of Anthony whose knowledge of Flora does not go beyond 'the bare outline of her story'. Constantly we find Marlow 'piecing here bits of disconnected statements'. Marlow makes mistakes as a result of faulty assumptions. He is scrupulously faithful to facts, as far as they go; but, ultimately, the facts must be supplemented by his own active imagination.

Unlike Powell and the pressman, Marlow theorizes about facts; and in that 'moment of detachment from mere visual impressions' he perceives the essence of an object, a person, a gesture. His attitude to experience parallels that which so often finds expression in Conrad's letters. The artist, Conrad wrote, 'is a much more subtle and complicated machine than a camera, and with a much wider range, if in the visual effects less precise'. In rejecting photographic realism, Conrad laboured to leave his work indefinite and suggestive, in order not to 'call attention away from things that matter in the region of art'. Conrad found his inspiration in the forms and sensations of the real world, but he was a realist only insofar as he was concerned with the truth underlying every aspect of experience. 'All my concern', he explained, 'has been with the "ideal" value of things, events and people. That and nothing else. The humorous, the pathetic, the passionate, the sentimental *aspects* came in of themselves—*mais en verité c'est les valeurs idéales des faits et des gestes humains qui se sont imposés à mon activité artistique'*.

In his art Conrad is striving for that deeper psychology that we have learned to associate with the works of Hawthorne. What matters in *Chance* is not Flora's story but rather the vision of things embodied in the novel's structure. Marlow is always speaking of his search for the psychology of events, the inwardness, the motivations. 'Don't you think that I have hit on the psychology of the situation?' he asks the narrator about his assessment of Anthony. His existence is not merely passive, or aesthetic; he represents the ideal of imaginative sympathy which informs the whole novel. His relation to the world of *Chance* resembles Conrad's own relation to the world, as expressed in *A Personal Record:*

> The ethical view of the universe involves us at last in so many cruel and absurd contradictions, where the last vestiges of faith, hope, charity, and even of reason itself, seem ready to perish, that I have come to suspect that the aim of creation cannot be ethical at all. I would fondly believe that its object is purely spectacular: a spectacle for awe, love, adoration, or hate, if you like, but in this view—and in this view alone—never for despair! Those visions, delicious or poignant, are a moral end in themselves. The rest is our affair—the laughter, the tears, the tenderness, the indignation, the high tranquillity of a steeled heart, the detached curiosity of a subtle mind—that's our affair! And the unwearied self-forgetful attention to every phase of the living universe reflected in our consciousness may be our appointed task on this earth. A task in which fate has perhaps engaged nothing of us except our conscience, gifted with a voice in order to bear true testimony to the visible wonder, the haunting terror, the infinite passion and the illimitable serenity; to the supreme law and the abiding mystery of the sublime spectacle.

It is Marlow's detached curiosity that enables him to listen to Flora's moving confession without becoming sentimentally involved. The steeled heart is not a cold heart or a heart of darkness; as the narrator observes, Marlow's eyes wear a 'slightly mocking expression, with which he habitually covers up his sympathetic impulses of mirth and pity before the unreasonable complications the idealism of mankind puts into the simple but poignant problem of conduct on this earth'.

—GARY GEDDES, "*Chance:* The Sympathetic Structure," *Conrad's Later Novels* (Montreal: McGill-Queen's University Press, 1980), pp. 21–26

WILLIAM M. HAGEN

Toward the end of *Apocalypse Now* we reach that supremely Conradian moment when Willard, the Marlow figure, confronts the object of his journey, Colonel

Kurtz. Does he come to rescue Kurtz and, in so doing, test himself? If Francis Ford Coppola had chosen to follow Joseph Conrad here, he might have gotten some desperately needed U.S. military assistance. But that was not the kind of script conclusion the director of *The Godfather* and *Godfather II* had planned for his war epic.

Still, Coppola underscores the significance of the meeting by altering his style. When Willard is taken into the temple for the first time, the whole pace of the film slows down, as if in imitation of the ponderous immensity of Brando. Brando-Kurtz slowly emerges into the light and pats water on his gleaming bald head, in a kind of ritual cleansing. The camera holds the shots for a much longer period than usual, allowing movement to be dictated by the actors rather than by focusing in or editing. Dialogue too proceeds at a much slower pace, with pauses occurring within sentences as well as between them. Questions are left hanging for a few extra beats, even when there is nothing particularly threatening about them. Of course, the pace has been slackening ever since the Do Lung Bridge sequence, but this scene is so slow it borders on worship. Brando is meant to be mythic, the still center of darkness, worshipped and self-worshipping, capable of every atrocity including self-annihilation through his double. Willard is so affected by the atmosphere of disorder and stasis, that he has to force himself to kill Kurtz. Through lighting, camera angles, and cross-cutting, the murder itself is transformed into a kind of dance in and out of darkness, creating a visual-aesthetic experience quite as isolated as the slow-motion destruction of a Sam Peckinpah film. The acquiescence of Kurtz and the preliminary appearance of Willard out of black water make the whole affair a kind of rite of rebirth-initiation into the world of Kurtz through slaying of the king.

With the exception of the rather abrupt thematic cross-cuts between the murder and the ritual killing of a caribou, the encounters are quite stunning and organic . . . visually. We could perhaps accept the deliberate departure from Conrad's novel if the director did not also seek to build in the psychological-moral dimensions of *Heart of Darkness*. His characters may be caught in a ritual death and rebirth, but he wants them to have depth all the same. He wants viewers to confront the immensity of this war one more time. Above all, he wants to explain everything through Kurtz. So Coppola picks up Kurtz' last words and tries to build a structural theme for the last portion of the film. By the time we hear "The horror!" for the last time, in a memory replay, we are likely to have worked up that fine wrath normally reserved for all those who quote outrageously out of context.

Conrad's Kurtz mouths his last words as a message to himself and, through Marlow, to the world. He has not really explained himself to Marlow before this final exclamation. Through Marlow's summary and moral reactions, we come to a sense of the possibilities of meaning rather than definite meaning. The message is more Marlow's and the reader's than it is Kurtz'. By contrast, Coppola's Kurtz precisely defines "horror"; the only way we can make his definition our message is to see his horror and enact his definition with Willard. The way to judgment lies through vicarious violence. Judgment is self-judgment.

The problem with even this transaction is that Willard seems almost unmoved by his experience. He certainly expresses no moral judgment. The worst he says is that he sees "no method" in Kurtz' operations. This statement may strike the reader of Conrad as uncomfortably similar to the Station Manager's amoral judgment of Kurtz' atrocities as merely "unsound" or bad for company business. The separation of reason from civilized morality, the fragmentation of the self so typical of the technocrat, causes Marlow to prefer the nightmare of Kurtz. Better to commit atrocities passionately than to account them wrong on grounds of efficiency. Like Dante—whose traditional moral hierarchy he reflects—Marlow can summon up a measure of sympathy for those who succumb to their emotions or appetites and reserve unmeasured scorn for those who pervert reason. Within the film, only the general at the briefing and Chef show the rational or emotional repugnance toward Kurtz; Willard, the professional soldier, is more than halfway friendly with this horror. After Chef joins the heads and Willard becomes part of the horror, we may realize that the whole point of the scenes at the Kurtz compound is to make the audience confront Kurtz' horror without moral mediation. From the very beginning, the shots of the compound were carefully filled with more separate images and actions, especially around the edges of the frame, than the eye could integrate. The eye was always kept moving and focusing on different parts of the screen. We did not have Marlow's field glasses or his sensibility to distance us or focus in sympathetically; we were entrapped and overwhelmed in an amoral medium range. Thus, instead of judgment or self-judgment, we are likely to come away from this perceptual overdose with the feeling that it has been a bad trip, and nothing more.

—WILLIAM M. HAGEN, "*Heart of Darkness* and the Process of *Apocalypse Now*," *Conradiana* 13, No. 1 (1981): 45–46

DANIEL R. SCHWARZ

In *Chance*, Marlow becomes an unintentional caricature of his former self. If we have any doubts that Marlow's richness as a character in prior works depends upon his embodying Conrad's psyche, we have only to look at what happens when he becomes hardly more than a narrative instrument, a mere garrulous device to tell a tale. He is a surrogate for Conrad's middle-age prejudices rather than for his quest for values and for emotional stability. Conrad returned to Marlow during a time of personal trial; based on the prior Marlow tales, we expect Conrad to use him as a means of defining himself. During this period his letters reveal the most serious neurosis since the 1890s if not his life: 'I've lost all self-respect and have abandoned myself to a debauch of illness and laziness. . . . I am all of a shake yet. I feel like a man returned from hell and look upon the very world of the living with dread' (28 June 1910). But he seems to have deliberately avoided transferring his own doubts and anxiety to his character. Much of the effectiveness of the prior Marlow tales depends upon the reader's intuitive understanding that Conrad's own psyche is a dramatised presence within his text. Conrad tries to establish continuity with the early Marlow tales by giving him his identity as a thoughtful seaman and by reviving his meditative syntax. But his meditations are only tangential to the issues dramatised by the narrative episodes. Unlike the earlier Marlow tales, the past and present do not interact as he narrates; more importantly, Marlow is fundamentally unaffected by his tale, as if it were peripheral to his values and even, alas, to his imagination.

Recalling no doubt the grounds of Marlow's appeal to Jim and of Marlow's own relationship to his audience in both *Lord Jim* and 'Heart of Darkness', Conrad has Marlow remark to the narrator about his London interview with Flora, 'A confession of whatever sort is always untimely. . . . You seek sympathy, and all you get is the most evanescent sense of relief—if you get that much. For a confession, whatever it may be, stirs the secret depths of the hearer's character. Often depths that he himself is but dimly aware of.' But in *Chance,* although the narrator tries to build up Marlow's stature (note his 'sympathetic impulses of mirth and pity'), he is an opinionated, cranky, indifferent and rather dense speaker. At times, Conrad does not know what to do with Marlow, even though he requires him to continue his narrative. What Palmer calls 'Marlow's analytic improvement of other characters' understanding' is often irrelevant to the characters' experience (such as the French Lieutenant or Bob Stanton) to create contexts in which to evaluate Jim, in *Chance* he often uses abstractions which, because undefined by the dramatic action, fail to stir the reader's imagination. The following analyses of the conduct of Fyne's *dog* reveals, behind an unsuccessful effort at irony, a self-indulgent pleasure at using multisyllabic words for trivial events: 'The dog, a vivacious and amiable animal which for some inscrutable reason had bestowed his friendship on my unworthy self, rushed up the bank demonstratively and insinuated himself under my arm.'

Not only Marlow's cynicism but also his verbosity undermines the fulfilment of the romance possibilities implied by the terms 'Knight' and 'Damsel'. When the narrator remarks that 'one never could be sure' whether Marlow meant what he said or not, he proposes the possibility that Marlow is playing with his audience. Conrad undoubtedly proposes this Catch-22 formulation to excuse whatever foolishness his narrator speaks; surely, there is no factual explanation or psychological reason for Marlow's speaking *other than what he meant.* But then, again, there are no dramatised reasons for much of Marlow's intermittent philosophising and occasional polemics; for example, the following epigrammatic passage *sounds* important, but does it derive from experience within the novel, or, indeed, does it really make much sense? 'I think that to understand everything is not good for the intellect. A well-stocked intelligence weakens the impulse to action; an overstocked one leads gently to idiocy.' If, as Guérard claims, Captain Anthony 'initiates the line of immature, passive, irritable and unintelligent heroies', Marlow initiates that line of tellers. What kind of psychological or moral analyses is the following remark to the nameless narrator? 'The idea of the son of the poet, the rescuer of the most forlorn damsel of modern times, the man of violence, gentleness and generosity, plunged up to his neck in ship's accounts amused me.' Such a sentence conveys Marlow's complacency, self-indulgence, and generalising propensity. One can neither identify nor empathise with a speaker prone to such generalisations as the following: 'the incapacity to achieve anything distinctly good or evil is inherent in our earthly condition. Mediocrity is our mark'.

Conrad replaces Marlow with Powell to report the psychodrama on board ship. Powell is supposed to be a sympathetic but conventional character with whose perspective the reader will feel comfortable. While he transmits to the narrator what he learns from Powell, Marlow lacks a substantial relationship with both of them. Either Marlow or the first-person narrator should be an active seeking mind in the process of coming to terms with experience or, alternatively, an imperceptive, myopic narrator whose telling is self-indicting. Marlow is really an *explanation of omnisience;* because he has had the opportunity—the 'chance', in an intended irony—to speak to and observe the major characters at crucial moments, he can tell the tale. The tale is undermined—'deadened' might be a better word—by the elaborate narrative technique whereby the anonymous narrator tells us what Marlow learned from Flora, Powell and Fyne; and, at times, what Fyne learned came from Mrs Fyne via Flora. The unintended effect of this process is to make the action remote and to reduce it to Lilliputian stature. As in *Clarissa,* the inefficiency of narrative technique becomes itself the focus of interest; the characters self-indulgently immerse themselves in a word world as an outlet for repressed libidinous energies. While the constant retelling of private dramas *seems* to transform them into semi-public events, the reader's interest is in the intricacies and idiosyncracies of the characters' psyches.

At times Conrad tries to duplicate the dramatised crises that make Marlow function so effectively in 'Heart of Darkness' and *Lord Jim.* Such a moment occurs when Mrs Fyne's remark that Flora 'has chosen to disappear' overwhelms Marlow, and he experiences such disorientation that he thinks of himself as a trained dog: 'In an instant I found myself out of the dance and down on all-fours so to speak, with liberty to bark and bite.' If one has any doubts that this bathetic image of dislocation transparently reveals Marlow's lack of seriousness and moral energy, one only has to compare it with Marlow's psychological agony when he loses his temper in the face of Jewel's challenge to Jim, or when he explains why he could not lie to the Intended in 'Heart of Darkness'. Indeed, Marlow now lives in a word world which is often an echo chamber of his past narrations; Conrad's frequent use of 'inscrutable' is a facile mnemonic device to recall the Marlow of 'Heart of Darkness'.

Rather than a dynamic, evolving personality, Marlow is a disguised version of the anonymous omniscient narrator that Conrad had previously avoided in his major works, even when he nominally used that convention. When Marlow's comments reinforce the dramatised action, they serve a functional choral role but they do not distinguish him as an individual moral identity in whom the reader is interested. Although hardly profound, his references to man's powerlessness and loneliness within the 'cruel', 'horrible', 'Infinite' universe—a universe that is indifferent to man's aspirations—are confirmed by the action. Like the omniscient narrator in *The Secret Agent,* he alludes to enduring traditions and thus proposes alternatives to the standards of the mediocre characters whose actions he describes; implicitly he emphasises the ironic discrepancy between his subject and the world evoked by such allusions. For example, Marlow describes de Barral in terms that suggest a religious visionary: 'His appearance was ecstatic, his motionless pale eyes seemed to be gazing down the vista of future ages . . .'; at his trial, he cries out 'in accents of passionate belief'.

Since Conrad interrupted *Chance* to write *Under Western Eyes* and 'The Secret Sharer', it is not surprising that *Chance* also contains the double motif. *Chance* lacks the kind of doubling in which a character confronts another who is not himself, but because of crucial resemblances seems *of himself.* In *Chance,* 'doubling' is really no more than Conrad's insistence upon superficial resemblances. For example, at first Powell confuses the captain with de Barral: 'he received an absurd impression that his captain . . . was sitting on both sides of the aftermost skylight at once. He was too occupied to reflect on this curious delusion, this phenomenon of seeing double . . .' To be sure, each is a prisoner on board the ship; each is the jailer of the other. They are contesting for the love of the same woman; feeling that her father is a martyr, no doubt because she identifies with his suffering, which she had shared because of society's verdict, Flora acknowledges his claims. But, these similarities are either at the verbal level or they define parallels that an attentive reader already understands. Such putative character doubles in *Chance* provide a refuge for Conrad from intense psychological and epistemological analysis.

Chance has historical interest as an unintentional parody of the self-conscious narrator that was perfected by James, Ford and Conrad. Like most parodies, *Chance* teaches us something about the limitations and possibilities of the form that is caricatured. Henry James has made the most acute comment about the form of *Chance:*

> It literally strikes us that [Conrad's] volume sets in motion more than anything else a drama in which his own system and his combined eccentricities of recital represent the protagonist in face of powers leagued against it, and of which the denouement gives us the system fighting in triumph, though with its back desperately to the wall, and laying the powers piled up at its feet.

The almost geometric form threatens to snuff out content. The form, like a series of Chinese boxes, imprisons the characters and mirrors their repression; it is a form that dilutes and undermines passion by setting it at a distance. The reader becomes anaesthetised to the characters' passions and to dramatic situations because they are remote from his experience. The seemingly baroque form of *Chance* lacks a radial centre, a unifying core that informs the various episodes. Hence, beneath the sophisticated scaffolding is really an inchoate form reflecting Conrad's inability to master his narrative materials. The reader finds himself discarding multiple explanations that eschew the psychosexual complexities and, as a result, making little headway into what is going on. Because of Marlow's evasion and verbiage, the reader often must provide his own analyses of character and moral implication. This is quite contrary to the reader's experience in *Lord Jim* and *Nostromo,* where the

novels' rhetoric shapes the reader's responses. Unwittingly in *Chance,* at times
Conrad puts the reader in the position of the crewmen in *The Nigger of the
'Narcissus'* struggling to rescue Jimmy Wait from beneath the wreckage and clutter.

—DANIEL R. SCHWARZ, *"Chance:* Manners as Psychosexual Drama," *Conrad:
The Later Fiction* (London: Macmillan Press, 1982), pp. 42–46

JEROME MECKIER

One must remember that Marlow does not tell *Heart of Darkness.* An unidentified
speaker, who heard the story of Kurtz from Marlow, actually spins the tale. He
could be Conrad but probably is not, since Marlow sounds like the only experienced sailor in the five-man group. The opening voice most likely belongs to a
landlubber by profession, as are the Lawyer, the Accountant, and the Director of
Companies. Only such a person would talk of "the bond of the sea" uniting a
gathering of week-end navigators on the deck of a cruising yawl or have to remind
himself that the Director, who is dressed like a pilot for this little party, works in the
City instead of "out there in the luminous estuary."

   Heart of Darkness is about the night the unnamed speaker heard of Kurtz
from Marlow during a marathon storytelling session on the deck of the *Nellie.* This
session has serious consequences not only for Marlow and the unidentified narrator
but also for Kurtz. The story resurrects the man of genius whom the jungle spoiled
and preserves his tragedy for posterity. At the same time, it supplies Marlow with
an opportunity to make amends for the lie he told Kurtz's fiancée. The impact of
the tale on the outlook of the unnamed first speaker, who is disillusioned by it,
makes an honest man of Marlow once again. An important part of the action is the
reinstatement of Marlow as an utterly reliable, veracious mariner. The disconcer-
tion he causes the first speaker, who seems to be a literary man, insures that Kurtz's
story will be retold again and again, which is already happening as one reads.

   Marlow does not speak until the seventh paragraph. His startling observation
that London "also . . . has been one of the dark places on the earth" cuts sharply
across the opening speaker's romantic mood. This speaker characterizes England's
capital as "the biggest, and the greatest, town on earth." Comfortable aboard the
yawl, he sees the day ending in "a benign immensity of unstained light." His political
philosophy can be deduced from this cloying mixture of picturesque travelogue and
patriotic rhetoric. He is satisfied with England, past and present. For him, the
Thames is "the venerable stream," which has done "ages of good service" and must
be viewed "in the august light of abiding memories." He calls the Thames "a
waterway" of "tranquil dignity" that leads to "the uttermost ends of the earth," one
that is "crowded with memories of men and ships it had borne to the rest of home
or to the battles of the sea." In prose that practically scans, the first speaker
glamorizes the "great knights-errant of the sea," whose ships "are like jewels flashing
in the night of time." He exalts the "Hunters for gold or pursuers of fame" who
sailed off to explore "the mystery of an unknown earth!" In a final burst of elo-

quence, his exclamations reach a crescendo of clichés: "The dreams of men, the seed of commonwealths, the germs of empires." Then Marlow speaks the truth about the ivory trade in the Belgian Congo and the roof falls in on such nonsense.

Prompted by the unidentified speaker, Marlow redeems himself for the compassionate but cowardly lie he used to pacify Kurtz's fiancée. He tells a new tale of piracy that puts the exploits of adventurers from the past into better persepctive. The clash of moods generated by Marlow's seemingly unpremeditated interruption is comic in effect but serious in intent. Kurtz's downfall is primarily important as a satiric commentary on the tensile strength of the humanitarian ideals supposedly underlying Western civilization. But it also changes the unnamed speaker's view of human nature. To the extent that the opening narrator sits in for everyone, the reader's conception of civilization becomes Conrad's ultimate target. Marlow wants to revise the opening speaker's perception of English history and Conrad to rewrite the story of empire for what it is: a dance of death in which the strong kill their better selves while exploiting the weak. Politics and metaphysics in the twentieth century are inseparable for Conrad. He regards the accumulation of empire as the life process in capitals. Colonialism, the form of cannibalism practiced by so-called advanced civilizations, reveals the nature of things. It becomes a satiric metaphor for the permanently active darker side of human nature.

Conrad's novella is so funereal that each new locale—the somber offices of the Trading Society, the dark Congo, even the Intended's drawing room—resembles a mortuary. The wages of spoliation, Conrad strenuously implies, are clearly death. But the final demise Conrad's death-riddled story contains is the collapse of the first speaker's unfounded romanticism; this is a victory for truth, a triumph for sanity. Many such collapses will be required to break the cycle whereby victims turn into criminals and places like the Congo become colonies of European countries once colonized by Rome. The historical outlook that the first speaker cherishes—the view that barbarity inevitably ceases with the advent of more developed societies, that darkness is gradually replaced by light—is a reprehensible lie, like the illusions a dedicated Marlow carried with him into the jungle.

Heart of Darkness raises doubling to a fine art. Besides Kurtz, doubles for Marlow include an anonymous Swedish captain and the murdered Fresleven, whom Conrad's favorite storyteller has been hired to replace. These "dead or dying *doppelgängers*," a recent critic (Garrett Stewart) argues, die for Marlow by proxy so that he can both witness and survive his own demise. Admittedly, the Marlow who returns to Europe is a man come back from the dead, but the emphasis is more readily Victorian than Freudian, closer to Dickens than to modern psychology. Marlow's proxies are a series of warning signs advertising the evil of the colonial enterprise in which he has been caught up. After sharing vicariously in Kurtz's terrible epiphany, Marlow fights his nearly fatal bout with fever and is invalided home. He dies not only by proxy but figuratively as well. Like the malaria that assails Martin Chuzzlewit in Eden or the equally figurative death Oliver Twist must suffer to pass from Fagin's world into the heavenly household of the Maylies, Marlow's illness is chiefly a dying to his old self. It is also a secularized rebirth and resurrection. Seen in this way, Marlow's doubles combine with his serious illness to make him modern: he will be a missionary to, not from, civilization; for, as an enlightened emissary of darkness, he brings the cautionary truth about man with him out of the jungle.

The opening speaker becomes Marlow's final *doppelgänger*. Next to Kurtz, he is the most important of the doubles. But in this instance, the procedure is noticeably reversed to indicate Marlow's maturation. He functions as the agent-half of this final partnership, the enlightener; whereas formerly he was almost always the recipient, the one needing enlightenment. Marlow does for the initial speaker the same epiphanic favor an expiring Kurtz once performed for him, a favor which the disillusioned narrator is now doing for the general reader. Conrad's narrative technique pits this cycle of truth-telling against the ongoing historical process of doubling and duplicity that encourages former colonies to become colonial powers.

Unless one appreciates the truth-telling cycle that informs *Heart of Darkness,* Marlow's interview with Kurtz's fiancée will continue to be misinterpreted. The scene with the Intended cannot be read as a subversive codicil in which Marlow, by lying, suddenly overturns the reader's confidence in everything that has already been related. Critics confuse Conrad's time scheme by arguing that the Marlow who states his detestation for lies ruins his reliability by lying to the Intended: Marlow "pontificates early on" about the evils of falsehoods and "later submits himself to his spiritual death" by "squandering . . . Kurtz's delegated revelation on a squeamish deceit." But it is Marlow's old self, the self that shared Kurtz's illusions, that dies in the Congo, not his spiritual self, which, on the contrary, is born there. Marlow's final act in *Heart of Darkness* is confessional, not deceitful; far from telling a lie, he tells about having once told one. If one ignores the narrative situation in *Heart of Darkness,* the lie to the Intended, swelling beyond its importance in the text, replaces the yarn aboard the *Nellie* and becomes Marlow's last act as self-ordained executor for Kurtz. The result is a cheapening of Kurtz's deathbed integrity and an undermining of Marlow's avowed dedication to truth. Much of the hitherto unacknowledged comedy in Conrad's dark novella gets thrown overboard.

The temptation to transform Marlow into an undependable narrator, to make Conrad more modern than he is, has always been latent in the criticism of *Heart of Darkness.* But the Marlow who recalls the story of Kurtz for his companions on the *Nellie* speaks only the truth. He tells his tale about Kurtz now. He told his falsehood to the Intended long ago. The lie happened first; the repudiation of lying takes place later on, a repudiation Marlow underlines as he spins his yarn. The interview with the Intended can be identified as the episode that may have convinced Marlow to equate prevarication with death. Condemnation of lying comes from the wiser man who recalls not only the agony of Kurtz but the defeat he himself suffered in shielding the fiancee from the truth.

Marlow's lie to the Intended has become an integral part of his involvement with Kurtz and must be scrupulously recorded. The interview forms an important link in the long chain of absurd vignettes that is *Heart of Darkness.* By retelling his conversation with Kurtz's fiancée, Marlow certifies himself as Conrad's exemplary modern man: he has learned to recognize and excoriate absurdity even in himself. Were Marlow truly the mendacious mariner, he would conceal this defeat at the hands of a pathetically inexperienced and misguided woman, instead of recounting the incident in detail as a joke against himself. Coming clean about this fiasco, Marlow enhances his credibility. The listeners aboard the *Nellie* and readers in general believe Conrad's highly moral tale because it includes an incident in which a lie, told with good intentions and clearly less serious than the untruths used to justify Western imperialism, nevertheless could have denied Kurtz justice had it remained Marlow's last word. Marlow proves his honesty by confessing his lie. His depiction of an infernal Congo is therefore accurate beyond doubt.

Thus one cannot refer to Marlow's "appended lie," which allegedly trans-mogrifies *Heart of Darkness* into "main plot and coda" and "leaves its acrid taste throughout the last scene," as if the lie, instead of being recalled and corrected, were actually being told. Rather, *Heart of Darkness* contains clever variations on the theme of the inadvisability of lying, whether it is done culturally as a collective enterprise or privately as a means of extricating an individual from difficulties. First, the Marlow-Kurtz encounter explores the tragic consequences of cultural lies, including the absurd belief that civilized man is morally superior to the primitives he exploits under pretence of raising them to his own level. Then the interview with the Intended illustrates the rapidity with which personal discomfort proliferates whenever truth is suppressed. Marlow tells his shipboard audience both episodes and does so truthfully.

The interview scene is bursting with ironies. Marlow fares worse by not detailing the evils of rapacity for the Intended than he did in his pre-Congo inter-view with his aunt, in which he suggested profit as the motive behind exploration. Before lying, Marlow does precisely what Kurtz could not: he gets a grip on himself. "I pulled myself together," he reports. Ironically, he prevents the darkness from pouring into the fiancée's drawing room, whereas Kurtz could not keep it from seeping into his heart. Marlow is on the verge of "crying" Kurtz's last words, of actually shouting "The horror! The horror!" Instead of crushing the Intended, how-ever, he practices the restraint that, under different circumstances, might have saved Kurtz. Between Marlow and Kurtz there is a bond of failure: Kurtz was unable to sustain his belief in colonialists as apostles of civilization, and Marlow was initially incapable of delivering the message he believed was entrusted to him by Kurtz.

To the fiancée's questions an increasingly panicky Marlow utters a sequence of trite responses that entitle the interview scene to recognition as a comic master-piece: "Intimacy grows quickly out there," "We shall always remember him," and "His works will remain." When the Intended cites Kurtz's "goodness," which "shone in every act," and proceeds to "His example—," Marlow replies: "Yes, his example. I forgot that." He has to go through all the cliches. The interview illustrates the way untruths multiply. Similarly, false claims made for the benevolence of Western imperialism constantly require fresh lies to support them. Only when Kurtz's fian-cée ventures the tritest observation of all—"He died as he lived"—does Marlow, angry at traps he has set for himself, add to the irony by exaggerating the ambiguity: "His end . . . was in every way worthy of his life."

The actual lie need never have been spoken had Marlow not blurted out that he heard Kurtz's "last words." Having done so, he recalls that he "stopped in a fright." From his vantage point on the yawl, Marlow can see what an idiot he was. "The last word he pronounced," Marlow finally forced himself to say, "was—your name." Even now he nearly chokes on the last two words, and the pause acquires comic effect. The Marlow of the present quotes the Intended ironically: " 'I knew it—I was sure!' " . . . "She knew. She was sure." He repeats her words sarcastically to underline the dark comedy in such total misunderstanding and the disgrace it brought him to have caused it.

The scene with the Intended depends for its success on the interaction between the Marlow who actually lied, vanquished by an inability to tell a woman harsh truths, and the regretful Marlow who looks back at his failure. On the yawl he is still apologizing: "But I couldn't. I could not tell her," even though he was drawn to her apartments by a need to unburden himself. To repair the damage as best he can, he relates the whole story to the group the Director has assembled to see if, indeed, the heavens come crashing down. For the unidentified speaker who began *Heart of Darkness,* they apparently do. This speaker returns after the story of Kurtz's deterioration is over so that he can record its paralyzing impact: "Nobody moved for a time." The sailing party, the Director notes, has been so engrossed that it has missed "the first of the ebb." The "serenity of still and exquisite brilliance," with which day was ending when Marlow began, also seems irretrievable. "I raised my head," the unnamed speaker concludes, and "The offing was barred by a black bank of clouds, and the tranquil waterway leading to the uttermost end of the earth . . . seemed to lead into the heart of an immense darkness."

Such dramatic change in the opening speaker's view of the Thames seems to portend a complete overhaul for his political philosophy. The unnamed speaker doubles not only for the Marlow who partook of Kurtz's horrific vision but for the delusions of the fiancee, who did not. Subversion of the initial speaker's lightheaded romance supplies an additional frame, thanks to which Marlow's lie loses its "flavour of mortality." It no longer compromises irreparably Kurtz's bleak but saving vision. The instant of death-victory that turned the failed idealist from debased savage to oracle and martyr was once concealed from his fiancée but it is now transmitted to Marlow's shipboard audience and then passed on by one of them to all who have read Conrad's novella during the past three-quarters of a century. Although retained merely as an experienced sailor to supervise weekend cruises, Marlow deserves to be called "a meditating Buddha" in European clothes because he tries to broaden the awareness of his involuntary pupils. His satire takes away conceptions of man's greatness based on self-aggrandizement but gives back, as compensation, renewed confidence in the worth of being human, in the power of man, even in extremity, to pass moral judgement upon himself and his fellows. Marlow supplies his listeners with something more reliable to live with.

Lying and dying become identical when a lie is allowed to grow and fester, when illusions, once set up, are preserved at all costs. Using the network that stretches from Kurtz through Marlow to the unidentified speaker and the general reader, Conrad performs a life-giving act to offset the deaths in his novella. If lies are deadly, truth-telling is salvationary. Aboard the *Nellie*, Marlow again lives through his ordeal with Kurtz, but this time he remains loyal to the dying man's vision until the end. Kurtz's revulsion from the horrors of colonialism, which he recognizes as an emanation from the blackness within himself, is a victory over savagery for mankind's inextinguishable humanity only if, indeed because, Marlow finally reports it accurately. He includes his blunders with the Intended to emphasize the folly of doing Kurtz's final wisdom less than justice.

Since Marlow tells his shipboard audience events he withheld from Kurtz's fiancée, Conrad's attitude toward women remains unregenerate. Yet this works well as a pedagogical ploy. It allows for an appeal to male vanity. The listeners on the *Nellie*, Marlow implies, will digest hard truths because it is their duty as men to do so. More important, however, is the realization that Marlow recites his tale truthfully. He brings Kurtz back to life, thereby completing the rescue mission he was sent into the Congo to perform.

—JEROME MECKIER, "The Truth about Marlow," *Studies in Short Fiction*
19, No. 4 (Fall 1982): 373–79

AARON FOGEL

The Conradian novel ⟨. . .⟩ as defined here—along with a small group of novels since Scott to which it belongs—has a very strong will to objectify and contemplate dialogue as constrained form, and the plurality of such dialogue forms in their social distribution. In this light, consider "Heart of Darkness" as a story about the progressive objectification of its own disproportionate and forced dialogue forms. It is, of course, easy to take Conrad's most famous story as an instance of free-spoken "oral literature," in which Marlow is the skaz, yarn spinner, or ancient mariner. But the story itself has to be seen as having for one of its main actions the increasing objectification of the speaking narrator himself, so that as it proceeds, the reader has an increasingly uncanny—partly comic, partly disappointed—feeling that Marlow's long-winded yarn is proportionally and therefore somehow morally linked to the more obviously imperial and abject forms of excessive talk like Kurtz's. That is, Marlow and Kurtz, as speakers, are progressively identified with each other through a covert appeal to the reader's sense of "normal" prose masses, and of the ordinary length of a talk. We increasingly see that each does "almost all" the talking in his own dialogical context: Marlow to his audience, Kurtz to the natives and to his clownish Russian disciple.

Here is a typical short passage from "Heart of Darkness" which in its onrush might go unnoticed but which is meant to make us contemplate and "equate" three or four dialogue scenes formally. Marlow has come ashore and is listening to the young Russian, exploding with a need to talk, tell about Kurtz:

"In the next breath he advised me to keep enough steam on the boiler to blow the whistle in case of any trouble. 'One good screech will do more for you than all your rifles. They are simple people,' he repeated. He rattled away at such a rate he quite overwhelmed me. He seemed to be trying to make up for lots of silence, and actually hinted, laughing, that such was the case. 'Don't you listen to him,' he exclaimed with severe exaltation."

These sentences set up a hierarchy of dialogue scenes—which the reader is invited to tear down. Lowest, apparently, are the simple natives, overwhelmed by a boat's whistle. On the next level, the Russian's talk itself, a kind of social chatter, here ironically overwhelms Marlow. At the presumed highest level is philosophical discourse like Kurtz's, aweing disciples into pious silence. Implicitly, on the fourth level, framing all this, and making its own claim to truth, is Marlow's narration to his audience, who object and grunt a few times. We might, that is, easily organize these scenes of forceful speech and disproportionate dialogue, combined so rapidly and formally that they seem to make a "dialogue fugue," into a self-congratulatory hierarchy similar to the Russian's, but with the last—ours—fiction or art, at the top, as transcendent consciousness: Marlow's ironic contemplative art, the truest frame. But just as clearly, Conrad stands behind the analogous disproportionate dialogues to suggest that all the scenes, including Marlow's art, and his writing to us, are alike: imperial assertions of "overwhelming" force. In each scene, the speaker impresses the listener by the force of sound. If the jungle's "darkness" and civilization's "light" will nearly be "welded together without a joint" by the story, the same fusion applies to our preconceived images of some dialogues as civilized and some as uncivilized. The natives overwhelmed by the ship's whistle resemble the Russian himself (their narrator and explainer) being overwhelmed by the force of Kurtz's altruistic oratory. Less clear, but most important, Marlow's silent audience (representing ourselves) falls—at least potentially—into this field. But whether we accept or refuse this last irony, this passage shows *how* Conrad asks the reader to think about dialogue as formal and proportional rather than simply expressive: by seeing and hearing the parallel ratios so as to find startling affinities among apparently discrete dialogue scenes.

Note, in terms of the history of readings of "Heart of Darkness," that Marlow's portentous, forceful repetition of adjectives can be understood somewhat differently. Leavis' conversational idealism rejects some of Marlow's incessant rhetoric as hot air—which of course it is. But in this reading, Marlow's relentless insistences, his own excess of verbal steam (even the mist that pervades the landscape is an image of rhetoric), is part of the conscious imagery of the story, and of the dialogical words. The scene of "overwhelming" noise is the common denominator of the story's main theme—imperialism—and what Conrad called its "secondary" theme, Marlow's obsession with the image of Kurtz speaking. The "dialogic" here welds together the two themes "without a joint." The proportional resemblance of all dialogue scenes is both tragic and comic, even oddly hilarious, and appears as an irrationally temporal, rather than simply atemporal, simultaneity: Marlow the young man, we could say—if we break with rational time sequence—became obsessed with his image of Kurtz talking "because" Kurtz talks to his disciples in the same disproportion which Marlow the older man and narrator *how* has vis-á-vis his audience. Young Marlow was obsessed by the image of Kurtz speaking, which was itself the metaphoric and predictive image of older Marlow narrating. The "cause" of Marlow's inexplicable obsession with Kurtz's talk is his own "later" identity with its proportions during the time of the story's actual telling. From a perspective of speech production, of course, this is all rational, because the older Marlow's production of the story for his audience *is* the "origin" of the story. There is, then, a simple repetition of dialogue form in time (Kurtz's overwhelming verbosity generates Marlow's overwhelming verbosity about him), but also a simultaneity or "knot" of dialogue scenes, which has to do with the production of the story itself. Marlow's original obsession with Kurtz—which Conrad has to impose on the reader partly by fiat or pure force of insistence—has its strongest but most irrational explanation in his predestined identity with Kurtz as the current talkative narrator before us (almost in the way that Oedipus' rational power to conduct judicial inquiries and force speech from his witnesses is inherited from the Sphinx's earlier grosser power—which he dissolved and inherited—to demand the answer to the riddle, to force replies).

The fusion of categories such as "psychological" and "political" in and by dialogue form can be seen clearly here. While Marlow's resemblance to Kurtz can be read psychologically, so that each is the other's son and father in speech disproportion, and the two are "insanely" identified as willful speakers (Marlow of course trying but failing to eradicate this will to power in himself), there should be no question that this resemblance presents itself to us first as a historical and political idea. Disproportion and coercion in the speech scene become the constants because, as Conrad writes in one essay, "man is a conquering animal," and history is imperialist. The famous "horror" at the end of the story is partly a joke, said twice, narcissistically, by self-echoing Kurtz, and partly a non-answer, punch line, or "detonation" coming at the close of what we could call a "shaggy dog story" (the entire action of "Heart of Darkness" is more defiantly funny than most critics have argued); but it is lastly the identification of art and politics as imperial speech. The first sentence of the story describes how the ship "swings to" (describes a forced circle about) its anchor until it rests. The secondary action of the story is the "swing to" that Marlow's own freer telling makes toward Kurtz's compulsive talk, becoming slowly and inevitably linked to it in moral and political status. In this gradual parallelism, a universal "dialogic" is being contemplated and objectified: by the end of the story the "swing to" has implicitly united philosophical dialogue (Kurtz as mock Socrates), fictive narration (or the dialogue between writer and audience), and imperialist cant into a single scene of dialogue, and Conrad has assigned himself and the reader to the same unavoidable intention of conquest and the same imperial scene. Artistic force, the desire to make the reader see, hear, or feel, is a sublimation at most of the other desires to conquer. It "must" participate in the general dialogue form.

In *Don Quixote* the repeated dialogue, in addition to its comedy, mimicked a typical debate of the age, between biblical authority and sense experience; it was then also used in the second part for baroque paradoxes, in which the *Quixote* became a new profane Bible, a book determining reality. Conrad constructs "Heart of Darkness" on similar lines, to make a baroque "knot," a "mirror" of dialogues reflecting each other out onto the audience, so as to define the typical dialogue scene of his time. As *Quixote* mimics a typical dialogue of the age, Conrad brings contemporary imperialism home in his forced dialogues. The point is that the proportions of imperialism are everywhere in an imperial age—even in stories told on yawls on the Thames, or in our reading of the novella. What bothered Leavis— Marlow's incessant, insistent, domineering, adjectival style—was meant to bother. The story could not exist without an excess of fiat. The disproportions in Kurtz's speech, in Marlow's telling, and in Conrad's representation of Marlow's telling, resemble each other; from different angles each could be said to come first and "cause" the others. Conrad "repeats" the scene of dialogue abstractly, not merely in the story of the characters but from level to level of the story's production, until we finally see Conrad, or the author, in a dialogical relation to us that resembles, in its desire for conquest, all the others. What Conrad called the "secondary" plot of "Heart of Darkness," in this reading, is this gradual identification of all dialogue relations as disproportionate and imperial.

—AARON FOGEL, "Ideas of Dialogue and Conrad's Forced Dialogue,"
Coercion to Speak: Conrad's Poetics of Dialogue (Cambridge, MA:
Harvard University Press, 1985), pp. 17–21

DONALD M. KARTIGANER

At the heart of *Heart of Darkness* is the interdependency of Marlow's two jour- neys, as captain and interpreter, and of the two characters, Marlow and Kurtz. In minimizing his action as captain, Marlow is preparing to appropriate Kurtz as the vehicle for his vicarious insight into the deepest meaning of European exploitation, the African wilderness, and his own desires—an image of the darkness Marlow has endured yet not fully experienced. At the climax of the narrative, the moment of Kurtz's death and final utterance, Marlow continues to insist on the negligibility of his own actions: " 'And it's not my own extremity I remember best. . . . No! It is his extremity that I seem to have lived through.' " But even as he yields the priority of action to Kurtz, Marlow assumes for himself the privilege of reading it, ultimately providing for Kurtz an interpretation more articulate and profound than any he can provide for himself. In short, Marlow and Kurtz exploit and serve each other, achieving meaning only as the process of their reciprocal engagement.

Marlow's reliance on Kurtz, as he now recalls the episode years later, began early in the journey, as Kurtz became not only the obvious focus for the trip upriver but a source of relief from the inefficiency, aimless intrigue, and moral vacuity of the European imperialism Marlow was witnessing for the first time. Mistakenly identified with Kurtz by the brick maker and the manager (" 'You are of the new gang—the gang of virtue. The same people who sent him specially also recommended you' "), Marlow came to recognize Kurtz as the guiding spirit of his quest, according to Ian Watt "a magic helper or at least a secret sharer": " 'For me . . . [the boat] crawled towards Marlow—exclusively." And when it appeared at one point that Kurtz might be dead, before Marlow had had a chance to meet him, Marlow's sorrow " 'had a startling extravagance of emotion. . . . I couldn't have felt more of lonely desolation somehow, had I been robbed of a belief or had missed my destiny in life."

If Kurtz became a "destiny" for Marlow, a ground and guide for his river journey, so now, in the present, Marlow projects himself as a figure for Kurtz, through whom the largely invisible and enigmatic actor can achieve a meaning. Marlow's intrusion of himself into the interpretive act is dramatically signaled precisely at the moment of his greatest despair as interpreter: " '[Kurtz] was just a word for me. I did not see the man in the name any more than you do. Do you see him? Do you see the story? Do you see anything? It seems to me I am trying to tell you a dream—making a vain attempt." He appears to be on the verge of giving up: " 'No, it is impossible; it is impossible to convey the life-sensation of any given epoch of one's existence—that which makes its truth, its meaning—its subtle and penetrating essence. It is impossible."

With this abrupt outburst, Marlow seems to turn completely away from Kurtz, as if abandoning him to unmeaning, only to turn back to him with a new intensity. Instead of merely sympathizing with Kurtz, appreciating an isolation he himself has been made to taste (and is experiencing again now), Marlow offers his own person as the only possible image of what can be no more than a sound for his audience: " 'Of course in this you fellows see more than I could then. You see me, whom you know . . .' "

The identification between Marlow and Kurtz suddenly shifts, begins moving in two directions at once. Just as the rumors surrounding Kurtz, his mysterious presence in the jungle, provide Marlow with a goal to stabilize and direct his uneasy position as captain and interpreter, so Marlow provides a similar stability to the identity of Kurtz by putting himself forward as a surrogate for the man who he knows will otherwise never come completely clear, for his audience or for himself. Implicit to this substitution is the idea that Marlow can plunge to the heart of Kurtz only by duplicating him. It is at once a submission of self to a shadowy forerunner, barely discernible in his Inner Station, and usurpation: Marlow exploits his relative prominence for his audience in order to illuminate Kurtz by supplanting him. The form of substitution is Marlow's identification of his own struggle to reach Kurtz with the shape and meaning of Kurtz's struggle for the mastery of darkness—or, to be more exact, with what Marlow is in the process of discovering to be the meaning of that struggle.

As it turns out, Marlow's repetition of Kurtz is both more plausible and more problematic for his audience than he realizes. The outside narrator of the tale remarks at this point that Marlow, emphasizing his own visibility, *cannot be seen:*

"For a long time already he, sitting apart, had been no more to us than a voice. . . . I listened, I listened on the watch for the sentence, for the word, that would give me the clue." And yet by virtue of this invisibility, Marlow is already reenacting the object of his quest. No more than a "voice" for the outside narrator, Marlow is repeating the form of Kurtz's existence for himself: " 'of all his gifts the one that stood out pre-eminently . . . was his ability to talk, his words—the gift of expression.' "

Marlow's move here to the role of substitute-Kurtz indicates his recognition of the extent to which the mode of his interpretation and presence must necessarily be integral to any meaning at which he can arrive. Whatever the truth of Kurtz's experience of darkness, it will emerge only as the echo of Marlow's own. Marlow becomes the deliberate performer whose interpretation of a role speaks no word that is not already inscribed within it—and yet the role comes alive as a dramatic characterization, is truly seen, only in the tone, gesture, pause, pitch of the performer's personal enactment.

Despite his promise of personal insignificance, Marlow becomes the most conspicuous image in the story: as the nautical quester, repairing his steamboat, negotiating the natural and human hazards of river and shore, and as the interpretive quester, forcing from bits of hearsay and ambiguous personal experience his uneven, vacillating reading. Nonetheless, for all his visibility, Marlow never claims an unequivocal priority. Every detail of his life and art is woven of the stuff of Kurtz, every meaning complicated by the dual protagonists of whom, and by whom, it is being made. The result is a reality we see only as reflection, Marlow and Kurtz each casting back and creating the other.

Only in this contrived coexistence, in being situated as parallel, repeating figures, can Marlow and Kurtz have meaning at all. Each protagonist mediates and reenacts the other, each is tenor and vehicle for the other. Marlow appropriates Kurtz's adventure in the jungle as image for his own encounter with the darkness of meaning; at the same time Marlow submits himself as image through which Kurtz's action can become intelligible—and in turn useful as image: " 'You fellows see more than I could then. You see me.' "

Marlow thus necessarily transforms the conditions of his reading into a version of what he is trying to read. These conditions involve, more or less simultaneously, an appreciation of and a desire to share vicariously Kurtz's descent into darkness, and a need to screen that descent through a European cultural and moral tradition. Both of these needs in Marlow at once facilitate and block his approach to Kurtz. The vicarious interest in darkness provides a useful empathy with Kurtz, yet it also results in Marlow's romanticizing him, imagining Kurtz, for example, as an authentic alternative to a "papier-mâché Mephistopheles"—as if an outright thief were preferable to the coward who merely covets what he has no intention of taking. Such sentimentalizing can only separate Marlow from what is actually going on at the Inner Station.

Similarly, Marlow's European heritage provides him (as captain as well as interpreter) with the resources and skills to get his battered boat up the river and with a cultural context for understanding Kurtz. Even as Johannes de Silentio in his reading of Abraham resorts frequently to literary and religious traditions which he recognizes as ultimately inadequate, so Marlow makes continual use of the conventions available to him: conventions of sailing an unfit craft, of navigating an unfamiliar river, and conventions—both moral and aesthetic—for providing his audience aboard the *Nellie* with a coherent reading of a complex history.

The upshot of Marlow's cultural heritage, however, is that whereas it brings him nearer and nearer to Kurtz it protects him against just those physical and psychological dangers that Kurtz apparently has faced directly, and which are the core of his meaning. While attending to the "surface-truth" activity necessary to " 'get the tin-pot along by hook or by crook,' " Marlow has no time, he claims, to submit to the temptation to " 'go ashore for a howl and a dance." Nor is he at all sure, having established a communal bond with his doomed helmsman, that Kurtz is " 'exactly worth the life we lost in getting to him.' " As interpreter of Kurtz, Marlow's practice is more wayward. He shuns the "direct simplicity" of the typical sea yarn, engages in digressions, dislocations of chronology, even assaults on his audience. And yet his narrative, anchored by the figure of Kurtz, toward whom everything moves, is less prone than usual to what the outside narrator refers to as a characteristic inconclusiveness. In this tale, Marlow pursues closure and the emergence of a clear if complex moral judgment.

These traditions are surely a credit to Marlow, and a palpable and effective structure for his quests, the armature of his desire to reach Kurtz and understand him. They sustain the quests—and yet they also contain them. Ultimately they are no more than Marlow's own "monkey tricks" that guard the tale from its "inner truth". They guarantee that he will never fully encounter Kurtz, never bring him back physically or interpretively.

What is required of Marlow, to use the language of the novel, is that he "go ashore." He must break away from the method of his sailing and interpreting and explore a deeper darkness, the " 'remote kinship with this wild and passionate uproar.' " In performing this act, Marlow succeeds in bringing Kurtz back to the boat and in pushing past his personal desires and cultural standards to a new reading.

Marlow's literal confrontation with Kurtz on shore is the encounter that laid " 'the foundations of our intimacy,' " although it is an intimacy rooted in Marlow's new awareness of just how remote, how much the Other Kurtz is: " 'He had kicked himself loose of the earth. Confound the man! he had kicked the very earth to pieces.' " The intimacy, established at Marlow's furthest remove from his boat and all the enabling methods that have guided him this far, is extended and confirmed in Marlow's second leap ashore—the interpretive leap in the present when he finally takes hold of the darkness as something of his own.

The climax of interpretation is Marlow's reading of Kurtz's death-bed utterance, " ' "The horror! The horror!" ' "—a reading which threatens to violate the received facts of the story, but which ultimately casts back on those facts the only coherence that seems commensurate with their central focus: the actor " 'to whom I could not appeal in the name of anything high or low.' " In this interpretation

Marlow gives up whatever identity he has apart from Kurtz and builds a new one on the ground of their dependency. He underplays his own near-death—" 'a vision of greyness without form filled with physical pain, and a careless contempt for the evanescence of all things' "—for the illusion of having "lived through" Kurtz's "extremity." But the act of deferring his own experience to another's is the direct source of Marlow's claim to an *understanding* of what the experience means. Kurtz's final cry, according to Marlow, has been a perfect summing up: " 'It was an affirmation, a moral victory paid for by innumerable defeats by abominable terrors, by abominable satisfactions. But it was a victory!' "

Marlow's interpretation is an act of rhetorical defiance that defines Kurtz's acts by repeating them, abandoning the very traditions which Kurtz abandoned in his descent into darkness. Strewn with the bones of his humanitarianism, with the literal bones of the dead whose skulls adorn his fence posts, Kurtz's life is nevertheless wrenched by Marlow into a strange victory of the human spirit: a burst of clarity in the midst of gray confusion, a " 'supreme moment of complete knowledge.' " Marlow's judgment here breaks loose both from his moral tradition, which should find in Kurtz either moral corruption or psychic derangement, and his tradition of interpretive logic as well, which assumes a plausible, provable link between event and commentary, between evidence and meaning.

Kurtz's last words, " 'no more than a breath,' " are less an "affirmation" than naked sound bending in different directions, as if seeking rather than stating its meaning: a proper Christian repentance on the edge of hell, a brilliantly nihilstic defiance, a baffled vision of ultimate chaos. Coming from a man whose eloquence has been, for Marlow, his noblest talent, Kurtz's summation is scarcely utterance at all. Yet from it Marlow wrests an interpretation both affirmative and unequivocal: it was a victory. At a single moment Marlow has made his life subservient to Kurtz's and put forth his own vibrant creative identity. He has found in madness motive, has found in the maniacal self a profound moral layer. The "victory" in these pages is victory *for Marlow* as much as for Kurtz, and it is of the same violent quality. In fact, it is victory for Kurtz only *because* it is victory for Marlow; for the actor only as it is for the interpreter.

Within this climactic reading of Kurtz's history, Marlow is not only putting aside a large part of the heritage that has helped him toward that reading; he is also discovering the unexpected, appalling dimensions of his identification with Kurtz— just as Johannes de Silentio, to his shock, discovers his Knight of Faith in the man who "belongs entirely to the world." Once again, the reading discovers more than it intends. Formerly a romantic outlaw to whom Marlow turns as alternative to the men of sounder methods, a supportive sharer for the journey and the interpreting, Kurtz now bursts forth as a monster whose "soul was mad"—and yet to whom Marlow awards something called a victory. A useful and even self-serving empathy becomes a fearful responsibility, and a shocking knowledge of oneself. The link Marlow has forged between himself and Kurtz, and the affirmation he has bestowed as interpretation, arise from and signify a complicity between observer and actor that is both the validation of the interpretation and its consequence.

The complicity and its meaning do not wholly survive *Heart of Darkness*. At the end of his experience in the "sepulchral city" and of his telling on board the *Nellie*, Marlow is in a sort of limbo, belonging neither to the radical meanings he has read into his actor-double nor to the conventions of sailing and interpreting that have brought him to the edge, although not to the center, of his deepest insight. His lie to the Intended—his attempt to hold back " 'the wilderness . . . for the salvation of another soul' "—suggests the return of his questioned heritage. But Marlow's largest and most vibrant life—and Kurtz's—abides in the duration of his identity with the actor, that collaborative creation in which they both exist and mean.

—DONALD M. KARTIGANER, "The Divided Protagonist: Reading as Repitition and Discovery," *Texas Studies in Literature and Language* 30, No. 2 (Summer 1988): 161–67

CRITICAL ESSAYS

Alan Warren Friedman

CONRAD'S PICARESQUE NARRATOR

One of the notable phenomena of twentieth-century fiction is the extent to which it has become extended. Forster gave the term "novel" one meaning when he defined it as a prose work in fiction of a certain extent. But many novels have moved beyond "certain" to become "indefinite." For since the novel has become psychological and open, the novelist who would terminate the stream of his fiction finds that it has no necessary ending, that it goes on multiplying perspectives and possibilities—often into several or many volumes.

This is not to say that twentieth-century novels are simply longer than their predecssors—for certainly Samuel Richardson, Fielding, and Trollope, for instance, had few qualms about excessive verbiage. The later novelists, in fact, tend to write shorter novels, but once having written them they frequently find the job less than complete—and so write them again from a somewhat different angle or vision, and sometimes again and again. The result is a genre that might be called the modern multivalent novel.

In a sense, the very extension of a novel into several volumes is an ineffaceable act of self-consciousness, and therefore an assertion of multiple perspectives. The multivolume novel—almost invariably self-conscious and pluralistic because simultaneously both a series of discrete parts and a unity—necessarily creates and defines a context, a pattern, for itself. The separate volumes must stand on their own, and yet their interrelated existences require of us a comparatist's eye and judgment. The whole becomes the sum not only of the parts but also of something more: the interconnectedness between and through the parts that sweeps us back as well as forward as we move through the several volumes. For the temporally linear act of reading, like Proust's madeleine cake, creates responses that ripple outward both with and against the conventional current of time—and never more so than in the multivolume novel with its self-contained dramas that are yet acts

From *Joseph Conrad: Theory and World Fiction*, edited by Wolodymyr T. Zyla and Wendell M. Aycock (Lubbock, TX: Interdepartmental Committee on Comparative Literature, Texas Tech University, 1974), pp. 17–39.

within a larger play. On the grandest scale one might, with Balzac, call that play the human comedy and write a hundred of its countless acts.

Read as a unit, Conrad's Marlovian fictions—"Youth," *Heart of Darkness, Lord Jim,* and *Chance*[1]—differ markedly from what they are in isolation. In the four works taken together, Marlow himself becomes the moving center of an episodic, larger fiction in which characters and incidents spin off and revolve about him, as in one of the inner circles Lord Jim seems to emit characters like Brierly and the German captain, Brown and the French lieutenant—all aspects of the whirling, prismatic protagonist of one experiential focus. Conrad's seemingly depersonalized narrator emerges over the course of several works first as character and then as protagonist. In the beginning of *Heart of Darkness,* Marlow says, " 'I don't want to bother you much with what happened to me personally,' " which provokes the narrator to comment that Marlow showed "in this remark the weakness of many tellers of tales who seem so often unaware of what their audience would best like to hear" (*HD,* p. 179). Yet Marlow immediately indicates that his purpose in recounting his Congo experience is to have his listeners " 'understand the effect of it on me' "—Marlow's tales are self-revelatory above all.

Conrad constructs the Marlovian tales on two main series of relationships and two dynamic sequences. First, Marlow interacts both with the sympathetic yet dubious protagonists of his narratives, and with the narrators who frame him; second, temporal revelations portray not only the young Marlow, Kurtz, Jim, and Flora, but also Marlow's own picaresque journeying from one narrative stage to the next. The stories within the stories express an independent reality and validity like that which Chaucer creates within *The Canterbury Tales*—and as great a symbiotic interdependence with the framing context. The narrated tales are beguiling in their own terms, for each dramatizes an extraordinary sequence of adventures and misadventures in which an energetic questor reaches, with varying degrees of success, towards identity and control. The four narrated sequences lose in chronological ordering but gain in significance by being filtered through what James calls the "interpreting consciousness," Marlow's plus at least one other. Yet the four also exist—and perhaps most fundamentally, certainly most organically—as temporal stages in the development of Marlow himself. For through Marlow, Conrad achieves at once the intimacy and distance he sought in the shifting perspectives of *The Nigger of the "Narcissus."* It is our task, then, to consider how this oddly constructed tetralogy—growing much longer and more cumbersome each step of the way—negotiates the personal, moral, and esthetic evolution of its central spokesman.

"Youth" and *Heart of Darkness* are both narrated by an anonymous ex-seaman, one of five characters (along with the director of companies, the lawyer, the accountant, and Marlow) who recall and verbalize a similar past. "Between us there was, as I have already said somewhere [in "Youth"], the bond of the sea. Besides holding our hearts together through long periods of separation, it had the effect of making us tolerant of each other's yarns—and even convictions" (*HD,* p. 175). But "Youth" is straightforward, for in it Marlow has no moral lesson to learn or teach. The tonal difference between "Youth" and *Heart of Darkness* parallels the deepening passage from *Tom Sawyer* to *Huckleberry Finn,* but the three later Marlovian works erect structural and narrative complexities far more fundamental than tonal shifts. Kurtz in *Heart of Darkness,* Jim in *Lord Jim,* and Flora and Powell in *Chance* take us away from Marlow to a large extent; they appear to us with the force and validity of protagonists in their own right. We may even be annoyed at times by the incessant verbalizing of that infuriating word spinner who seems congenitally incapable of telling his tale, and who keeps intruding himself between us and it. Wayne Booth, however, suggests that teller and tale, like Yeats's dancer and dance, are indistinguishable: "Is 'Heart of Darkness' the story of Kurtz or the story of Marlow's experience of Kurtz? Was Marlow invented as a rhetorical device for heightening the meaning of Kurtz's moral collapse, or was Kurtz invented in order to provide Marlow with the core of his experience of the Congo? Again a seamless web, and we tell ourselves that the old-fashioned question, 'Who is the protagonist?' is a meaningless one. The convincing texture of the whole, the impression of life as experienced by an observer, is in itself surely what the true artist seeks."[2] And yet the question has meaning if we take the four Marlow narratives as a whole, as Conrad, by his interwining of them, encourages us to do.

Lord Jim, the greatest of the four Marlovian tales, is unique in including an *extra* narrative layer, a multifarious,[3] seemingly objective, commentator. He portrays the titular character: "He was an inch, *perhaps* two, under six feet, powerfully built" (*LJ,* p. 1; italics mine). Then he parlays that "perhaps" into a full-scale attack on the very validity of this type of narration: "They wanted facts. Facts! They demanded facts from him, as if facts would explain anything!" (*LJ,* p. 23). And then he merges into an auditor-narrator analogous to the one in "Youth," *Heart of Darkness,* and *Chance:*

> And later on, many times, in distant parts of the world, Marlow showed himself willing to remember Jim. . . .
> Perhaps it would be after dinner, on a verandah draped in motionless foliage. . . .   (*LJ,* p. 27)

The main difference between the multifarious and personal voices lies in the breadth of "many times" and the vagueness of that last "Perhaps"; but from this point until the return to multifarious narration at the end of Chapter XXXV, the narrative perspective of *Lord Jim* is identical to that of the other three tales: a companion of Marlow's narrates Marlow's narrative.

Why does Conrad employ a multifarious frame narrator for *Lord Jim?* The question admits of no easy and direct answer, but may best be approached by considering why Conrad abandons the strategy for the bulk of the novel. In a manner perhaps derived from the depiction of Henry Fleming in *The Red Badge of Courage* (a novel Conrad knew, admired, and consciously sought to surpass[4]), Conrad's multifarious narrator takes us inside Jim's youthfully foolish ego: "At such times his thoughts would be full of valorous deeds: he loved these dreams and the success of his imaginary achievements. . . . They had a gorgeous virility, the charm of vagueness, they passed before him with a heroic tread. . . . There was nothing he could not face. He was so pleased with the idea that he smiled, keeping perfunctorily his eyes ahead . . ." (*LJ*, p. 16). The narrator's mocking attitude speaks through the hollow rhetoric of "valorous deeds," "the success of his imaginary achievements," "gorgeous virility, the charm of vagueness," and "heroic tread"; this attitude is also apparent in the climactic self-deception of "there was nothing he could not face," and in the devastating betrayal of trust implicit (and retrospectively *explicit*) in "keeping *perfunctorily* his eyes ahead." As elsewhere, the narrator here verges on turning into the sarcastic presiding genius of *The Secret Agent.* The intense derision directed at Jim—increasingly obvious with each rereading—requires counterbalancing if Jim is to be afforded any sort of sympathetic response: thus, Conrad conceals from his reader what everyone else knows (that the *Patna* failed to sink), abandons the frame narrator, and offers Marlow as intercessor between Jim and the reader.

A further distinction between the narrators of *The Secret Agent* and *Lord Jim* is that the latter never really plays what John Fowles in *The Magus* calls "the god game"—dry, ironically detached, and near-solipsistic narration and manipulation. Rather, when Marlow passionately declares to Jewel that Jim is not good enough (because no one is good enough), it seems clear that he speaks also for the novel's uncertain multifarious narrator who, in the novel's first line, announces Jim's height as *perhaps* five feet ten inches and then rails out against facts just before the anonymous listener and Marlow take over the narration. Such a narrator is far removed from that of *The Secret Agent*, who accepts as valid the irony of facts and the triviality of all human endeavor.

Lord Jim's frame narrator, however, after denouncing facts in a manner wholly sympathetic with Jim's perspective, then depicts Jim's attitude toward the Inquiry as follows: ". . . he had come round to the view that only a meticulous precision of statement would bring out the true horror behind the appalling face of things. . . . He wanted to go on talking for truth's sake, perhaps for his own sake also; and while his utterance was deliberate, his mind positively flew round and round the serried circle of facts that had surged up all about him to cut him off from the rest of his kind. . . . He was made to answer another question so much to the point and so useless, then waited again" (*LJ*, pp. 24–26). Such an approach to facts precisely parallels the attitude and technique of the book as a whole and Marlow in particular, and has as a central purpose our continuing deception.

Here is the technique at its most blatant, though we do not realize it on first reading. Marlow is speaking about the Inquiry: "There was no incertitude as to facts—as to the one material fact, I mean. . . . Its object was not the fundamental why, but the superficial how, of this affair. . . . 'the questions put to him necessarily led him away from what to me . . . would have been the only truth worth knowing. You can't expect the constituted authorities to inquire into the state of a man's soul—or is it only of his liver?' " (*LJ*, pp. 47–48). The problem here is that we who are ignorant of factual reality are also made to believe that "there was no incertitude as to facts," and so we are unprejudiced by their actuality—or, rather, we are prejudiced by what we are deceived into assuming they are. We share Marlow's outrage at official insensitivity because we think we share his superior moral insight. Only later do we discover that we have done so because we have been duped. Yet such is the nature of moral commitment that it becomes virtually impossible for us to deny our initial identification, to distance ourselves from the moral trap that Marlow (perhaps unintentionally) and certainly Conrad have laid for us. Perhaps the only way out is to recognize, as R. W. B. Lewis has said of Faulkner, that the difficulty of such narratives "lies in the order of their telling. . . . What *happens* in a Faulkner story is the most important thing in it, except perhaps the moral excitement that produces the happening. But we are let in on the event secretively, gradually, almost grudgingly, from different viewpoints and at different times."[5]

But *Lord Jim*'s frame narrator, with his uncertainty and his attack on facts from a perspective we first accept as "omniscient," creates an aura of excessive reliability around Marlow's tale. It is the frame narrator preceding the introduction of Marlow who empathizes with Jim's platonic equation of esthetics and morality in responding to the German captain on board the *Patna:* "The odious and fleshy figure . . . fixed itself in his [Jim's] memory forever as the incarnation of everything vile and base that lurks in the world we love . . ." (*LJ*, p. 17). Without this context, this subtle and seductive use of the plural personal pronoun by the multifarious narrator, Marlow's similar perspective would be immediately suspect—the defensiveness of a partisan—and would thereby fail to elicit our sympathetic involvement with Jim, an involvement basic to the vertiginous ambivalence at which the novel aims. The multifarious narrator both gives license to Marlow's unreliability and lulls our suspicions concerning what Conrad is having him foist off on us. In this sense, *Lord Jim* is simply an elaboration of *Heart of Darkness,* for Marlow's concealing from us the real reason for Jim's flight (thus causing us to assume a less damning one) reworks in daringly expanded form the trick of keeping Kurtz from us until we, like Marlow, make the mistake of choosing him.

As character and narrator Marlow typically experiences and expresses what seem at first commonplace approach/avoidance attitudes—towards lies (smacking of mortality though sometimes necessary), towards work (he dislikes it, but likes "what is in the work, the chance to find yourself. Your own reality," *HD*, p. 203), towards exoticism ("the fascination of the abomination," *HD*, p. 177), towards youth and the sea (the time and place of fleeting glory), towards women (human beings "very much like myself," yet devoid of "masculine decency," *C*, pp. 53, 63). The accreted effect of such dualism, however, is ambivalence carried to the point of confusion, and Marlow, his masks of sarcasm and human sympathy simultaneously in place, becomes a curious Janus-faced guide whom we trust at our peril.

Thus, much of the tension in *Heart of Darkness* and *Lord Jim* arises from Marlow's failure to resolve major contradictions. The "one of us" theme in *Lord Jim,* for example, is as central to *Heart of Darkness,* though in the earlier work it goes by the name of "idea." Marlow complacently begins his Congo tale by dubiously asserting the moral superiority of English colonists to Roman conquerors. He adds: " 'The conquest of the earth, which mostly means the taking it away from those who have a different complexion or slightly flatter noses than ourselves, is not a pretty thing. . . . What redeems it is the idea only. An idea at the back of it; not a sentimental pretence but an idea; and an unselfish belief in the idea—something you can set up, and bow down before, and offer a sacrifice to . . .'" (*HD*, p. 179; Conrad's ellipsis). Marlow reiterates this notion halfway through *Lord Jim* when he speaks of being deeply impressed by earlier adventurers and traders: "'It seems impossible to believe that mere greed could hold men to such a steadfastness of purpose. . . . To us, their less tried successors, they appear magnified, not as agents of trade but as instruments of a recorded destiny, pushing out into the unknown in obedience to an inward voice. . . . They were wonderful . . .'" (*LJ*, pp. 195–96). Certainly this is historically a popular view (witness "manifest destiny"), yet Marlow also *repudiates* this position in *Lord Jim*, as he had in the earlier tale. Despite Marlow's pronouncements, *Heart of Darkness* depicts not only "the utter savagery" of the uncivilized, but the far more frightening darkness at the heart of men of ideas. Thus Marlow, heading for the crisis, begins to think of the howling natives as other than human—and then worse, *as* human: "one of us."

In *Lord Jim*, Gentleman Brown is also treated as "one of us" (e.g., pp. 337, 344). Marlow maintains that his accomplices "'were merely vulgar and greedy brutes, but *he* seemed moved by some complex intention'" (*LJ*, p. 306). In Brown's murder of Dain Waris, Marlow adds, "'there is a superiority as of a man who carries right—the abstract thing—within the envelope of his common desires. It was not a vulgar and treacherous massacre; it was a lesson, a retribution—a demonstration of some obscure and awful attribute of our nature which, I am afraid, is not so very far under the surface as we like to think'" (*LJ*, p. 352). Similarly, Marlow insists that "while Jim was one of *us*," Dain Waris was "one of *them*" (*LJ*, p. 314). And when Marlow comes to choose a soul-mate to receive word of Jim's death, that "privileged man," like Gentleman Brown, embodies Marlow's racial biases carried to their extreme. "You said," Marlow writes, "that 'giving your life up to them' (*them* meaning all of mankind with skins brown, yellow, or black in colour) 'was like selling your soul to a brute.' You contended that 'that kind of thing' was only endurable and enduring when based on a firm conviction in the truth of ideas racially our own, in whose name are established the order, the morality of an ethical progress. . . . In other words, you maintained that we must fight in the ranks or our lives don't count" (*LJ*, p. 294). Marlow's comment is an ambiguous "Possibly!" because a clear-cut response would deny the validity of either his racial views or else of what he sees as Jim's magnificent triumph of fate. Marlow characteristically wants it both ways.

The same concern for us and them surfaces as early as "Youth," where Marlow identifies with humanity (rejecting Carlyle who was not a man but "either more—or less," *Y*, p. 146), with Caucasians (fearing the fascination of the abomination, "'the lands of brown nations, where a stealthy Nemesis lies in wait, pursues, overtakes so many of the conquring race, who are proud of their wisdom, of their knowledge, of their strength,'" *Y*, p. 170), with Englishmen (exalting the *Judea*'s ragged crew: "'it was something in them, something inborn and subtle and everlasting. I don't say positively that the crew of a French or German merchantman wouldn't have done it, but I doubt whether it would have been done in the same way. There was a completeness in it, something solid like a principle, and masterful like an instinct—a disclosure of something secret—of that hidden something, that gift of good or evil that makes racial difference, that shapes the fate of nations,' " *Y*, p. 161).

On first encountering the Congo, Marlow discovers an absurd world anti-thetical to the natural or grotesquely mocking it: a boat "shelling the bush" causing nothing to happen; a "dead" railway truck "lying there on its back . . . [like] the carcass of some animal"; "objectless blasting"; emaciated slaves wearing masks of "deathlike indifference," unhappy savages who "were called criminals" (*HD*, pp. 186–88). With typical sarcasm, Marlow speaks of being greeted by the despicable manager as "a part of the great cause of these high and just proceedings" (*HD*, p. 189). In a somewhat similar tone he later alludes to the human heads on Kurtz's posts: " 'I am not disclosing any trade secrets. In fact, the manager said afterwards that Mr. Kurtz's methods had ruined the district. I have no opinion on that point, but I want you clearly to understand that there was nothing exactly profitable in these heads being there. They only showed that Mr. Kurtz lacked restraint in the gratification of his various lusts, that there was something wanting in him—some small matter which, when the pressing need arose, could not be found under his magnificent eloquence' " (*HD*, p. 234). Curiously and characteristically, Marlow suggests that Kurtz's actions are somehow less reprehensible because they are motivated not by greed but by undefinable desires.

Immediately there follows Marlow's climactic summary of Kurtz—"he was hollow at the core"—a chilling conclusion to his quest: " 'I was curious to see whether this man who had come out equipped with moral ideas of some sort, would climb to the top after all and how he would set about his work when there' " (*HD*, p. 205). Thus Marlow's thesis concerning the redemptive nature of ideas (above all, "the white man's burden") and his implication that the Congo represents unfortunately uncongenial soil for their implantation, are wholly misleading: Kurtz's "moral ideas" are hollow and he brings with him the evil he encounters. Like *Lord Jim*, *Heart of Darkness* becomes a very different work on second and subsequent readings because we become sensitive to the hollowness of Marlow's own position. There is a subtle horror in his thesis, perspective, choice, action, and justification, all of which he offers in his narrative with little or no examination. Similarly, he takes no note of his own telling imagery, like Kurtz's "ivory face" (*HD*, p. 247) and the Intended's "forehead, smooth and white" (*HD*, p. 254), a wonderfully sardonic pairing of form following function that he tosses out but fails to confront. Thus, Marlow's pose of Buddha-like inscrutability seems in the end to deceive no one so much as himself.

Marlow first uses the term "one of us" early in *Lord Jim*. He is fascinated by the dichotomy in Jim of his "sham and reality." Jim's appearance is compelling ("clean-limbed, clean-faced, firm on his feet, as promising a boy as the sun ever shone on . . ."), and Marlow is furious: " 'I was as angry as though I had detected him

trying to get something out of me by false pretences. He had no business to look
so sound.' " Not for the last time, Marlow finds Jim's casualness odious: " 'I waited
to see him overwhelmed, confounded, pierced through and through, squirming like
an impaled beetle—and I was half afraid to see it too. . . .' " And then comes
Marlow's identification and generalization, the basis for fear greater than that encountered in the heart of savage darkness.

> "From weakness that may lie hidden, watched or unwatched, prayed
> against or manfully scorned, repressed or maybe ignored more than half a
> lifetime, not one of us is safe. . . . he was one of us. He stood there for all the
> parentage of his kind, for men and women by no means clever or amusing, but
> whose very ixistence is based upon honest faith, and upon the instinct of
> courage . . . backed by a faith invulnerable to the strength of facts, to the
> contagion of example, to the solicitation of ideas. Hang ideas! They are tramps,
> vagabonds, knocking at the backdoor of your mind, each taking a little of your
> substance, each carrying away some crumb of that belief in a few single
> notions you must cling to if you want to live decently and would like to die
> easy!"   (LJ, pp. 33–36)

Having experienced the indecency of Kurtz's life and the difficulty of his death,
Marlow now condemns the moral supremacy of ideas, the thesis of Heart of
Darkness. Now older and more weary, he rejects them here as he had exalted
them there. In Lord Jim he espouses something more substantial, the reality and
validity of appearance and imagination—and they fail and betray him as well.[6]

The theme of "one of us," of "idea," intertwines as well with that of imagination
and duty. Conrad's simple "good" men—Singleton in Nigger of the "Narcissus,"
Captain MacWhirr in Typhoon, Lord Jim's French lieutenant—function well because their intellectual and moral makeup precludes their seriously entertaining
alternative courses of action; in Chance, Captain Anthony is essentially and ultimately of this same order. The successes of such characters are wholly admirable
(and precisely what Jim is circuitously seeking), yet they themselves are inadequate
because they are seemingly mechanical, lacking in divergent impulses, not "one of
us"—the very characteristics that insure their successes. The extreme of this type
are the presumably non-introspective helmsmen in Heart of Darkness and Lord
Jim. Marlow says of Kurtz, " 'I can't forget him, though I am not prepared to affirm
the fellow was exactly worth the life we lost in getting to him. I missed my late
helmsman awfully. . . . Perhaps you will think it passing strange this regret for a
savage who was no more account than a grain of sand in a black Sahara. Well, don't
you see, he had done something, he had steered; for months I had him at my
back—a help—an instrument' " (HD, pp. 226–27). Marlow opts for the nightmare
Kurtz represents over that of the rapaciously bourgeois manager—" 'Ah! but it was
something to have at least a choice of nightmares' " (HD, p. 239)—without ever
noting the possible unnightmarish choice that the helmsman's example offers. He
compares Kurtz unfavorably to his helmsman (as he later does Jim to those of the
Patna), but his racial scorn is strongly evidenced. The helmsman's surprising devo-

tion to duty and his failure to act like a bestial savage—like the cannibal crew's extraordinary restraint, their failure to "have a good tuck in for once" (*HD*, p. 216) as white men would presumably have done in their position—merits the respect due a faithful pet or a useful tool. Kurtz, a true savage in word and deed ("hollow at the core"), receives from Marlow, like Jim and Gentleman Brown, the homage due to "one of us."

Throughout his narratives but expecially in *Lord Jim*, Marlow's deceptive unreliability undercuts the values on which he and we presume to stand, while seeming at first to reinforce them. Intentionally or not, Marlow works to arouse our sympathy for Jim while denouncing him. He speaks of being pitiless, but immediately adds, " 'You must remember he believed, *as any other man would have done in his place,* that the ship would go down at any moment ...' " (*LJ*, p. 73; italics mine). Marlow exploits the advantage he has of us. At this point, near the start of his narrative, *we* still believe that the *Patna* did sink, and that Marlow is therefore holding Jim up to extraordinary moral criteria. Yet he then reverses himself and damns with faint praise where he had praised with faint damnation: " 'He was not afraid of death perhaps, but ... he was afraid of the emergency.... His confounded imagination had evoked for him all the horrors ... of a disaster at sea he had ever heard of. He might have been resigned to die but I suspect he wanted to die without added terrors, quietly, in a sort of peaceful trance' " (*LJ*, p. 75). As usual, Marlow's prophetic impulse is correct in a sense, in a way we would not have anticipated: Jim *does* "die ... quietly, in a sort of peaceful trance," but orchestrating it fully himself, on centerstage, with all eyes fixed upon him.

Halfway through *Lord Jim*, Marlow gives us what he calls "the last word" on Jim's Patusan success while characteristically denying the possibility of anyone's doing so: " '... the last word is not said,—probably shall never be said.... I have given up expecting those last words, whose ring, if they could only be pronounced, would shake both heaven and earth.... My last words about Jim shall be few. I affirm he had achieved greatness; but the thing would be dwarfed in the tellling, or rather in the hearing. Frankly, it is no my words that I mistrust but your minds. I could be eloquent were I not afraid you fellows had starved your imaginations to feed your bodies' " (*LJ*, p. 194). As elsewhere, Marlow gives himself away in every line: in forgetting the lesson of *Heart of Darkness* (that "those last words" may indeed be pronounced, and that they change nothing), in forgetting the lesson of "Youth" (that for him too "the romance of illusions" has long since yielded to "Pass the bottle!"), and especially in his typical thrusting of conclusions at us before the evidence. We are surely meant to question the ultimate authority of such a grand pronouncement occurring, as it does, halfway through the novel and before his narrative proper concerning Patusan. Had we come to experience Patusan uncontaminated by Marlow's prejudicial contextualizing, we would be in a position to distance ourselves from his conclusion and would likely do so. In addition, Marlow's attack on his listeners' lack of imagination has the force and validity of a *non sequitur* since only two pages before he had asserted that, unlike Jim, "I have no imagination."

Marlow's own *final* conclusion about Jim's achievement is very different from this early one. He first speaks with bemused wonderment of Jim's being " 'satisfied ... nearly. This is going further than most of us dare. I—who have the right to think myself good enough—dare not. Neither does any of you here, I suppose? ... But he is one of us, and he could say he was satisfied ... nearly. Just fancy this! Nearly satisfied' " (*LJ*, p. 281). But then after detailing Jim's death in richly lyrical terms, he says, " 'Is he satisfied—quite, now, I wonder? We ought to know. He is one of us—and have I not stood up once, like an evoked ghost, to answer for his eternal constancy? Was I so very wrong after all? ... Who knows?' " (*LJ*, pp. 362–63). Further, as Marlow reminds us, our experience of Jim is very different from his: " 'He existed for me, and after all it is only through me that he exists for you. I've led him out by the hand; I have paraded him before you' " (*LJ*, p. 194).[7] For us, Jim is a work of art and Marlow the artist with words; and, as the narrator of *Under Western Eyes* tells us, "Words ... are the great foes of reality."[8] No wonder, then, that we perceive Jim initially as Marlow would have us, and yet that Jim defies the static definition the artist would impose upon him. It thereby becomes incumbent upon us not only to perceive the product as process, but also to call into profoundest questioning the voice of the artist—not *qua* artist, but as purveyor of reductive pronouncements concerning what his art has wrought.

As he almost invariably does, Marlow again anticipates us, for he strikes exactly this note when, on taking leave of Jim for the last time, he speaks of re-entering the world of moral complexity and uncertainty: " 'I had turned away from the picture and was going back to the world where events move, men change, light flickers, life flows in a clear stream, no matter whether over mud or over stones. ... But as to what I was leaving behind, I cannot imagine any alteration. ... They exist as if under an enchanter's wand. But the figure round which all these are grouped—that one lives, and I am not certain of him. No magician's wand can immobilize him under my eyes. He is one of us' " (*LJ*, pp. 286–87). This may be the clearest indication yet of what "one of us" means: those born to inhabit the world of moral challenge and inadequacy, those doomed to imagination, freedom, and flux—as if this were not, as Marlow himself indicates elsewhere, the common fate of all mankind.

Marlow's response to Jim alternates from extreme to extreme throughout his narrative. He maintains that Jim had no business looking so sound (*LJ*, pp. 33–34) since there was a "subtle unsoundness" about him (*LJ*, p. 77), that there could be no "convincing shadow of an excuse" for his action(*LJ*, p. 43), for its "real significance [lay] in its being a breach of faith with the community of mankind" (*LJ*, p. 135). Jim had, Marlow tells us, "jumped into an everlasting deep hole. He had tumbled from a height he could never scale again" (*LJ*, p. 96). No wonder that Marlow's attitude is pitiless (*LJ*, p. 68), that he directs a "deep-rooted irony" at Jim. At a climactic moment, he declares himself "unexpectedly to be thoroughly sick of him" (*LJ*, p. 204). And yet, to counterbalance, he immediately adds "Youth *is* insolent; it is its right—its necessity; it has got to assert itself, and all asssertion in this world of doubts is a defiance, is an insolence" (*LJ*, p. 204). Further, Marlow simultaneously asserts a wholly opposed analysis, one that defines Jim as the victim of "a fiendish and appalling joke" (*LJ*, pp. 104–105), and who, on the *Patna*, "believed, as any other man would have done in his place, that the ship would go down at any moment..." (*LJ*, p. 73). He had helplessly faced and "had survived the assault of the dark powers" (*LJ*, p. 213), and then at the end "was overwhelmed by the inexplicable; he was overwhelmed by his own personality—the gift of that destiny which he had done his best to master"(*LJ*, p. 296). Marlow agrees with Jim that "You've been tried" (*LJ*, p. 107), that he is a gentleman (*LJ*, p. 112); he is pleased that the French lieutenant takes "the lenient view" (*LJ*, p. 127); he asserts Jim's greatness and devotion in the face of Jewel's bitter love and sense of betrayal.[9]

Ultimately and typically, Marlow seeks to resolve polar contradictions, to synthesize antitheses. Jim, he says, "appealed to all sides" (*LJ*, p. 80); at times Jim seems not univocal but unclear to Marlow and perhaps "not clear to himself either" (*LJ*, p. 152); it was hard to know "whether his line of conduct amounted to shirking his ghost or to facing him out" (*LJ*, p. 169); and finally Marlow sees Jim as great and pitiful "in the loneliness of his soul" (*LJ*, p. 343)—as, that is, a tragic hero who necessarily synthesizes and embodies *all* the contrarieties with which Marlow attempts, without success, to fix Jim in place like one of Stein's butterflies.

Perhaps the most glaring inconsistency in Marlow's entire narrative concerns Brierly's offer of money if Jim will flee. Marlow first tells us: "Of course I declined to meddle.... I became positive in my mind that the inquiry was a severe punishment to that Jim, and that his facint it ... was a redeeming feature in his abominable case.... Brierly went off in a huff" (*LJ*, p. 58). Later, Marlow recasts the events in a wholly different light. " 'He was guilty—as I had told myself repeatedly, guilty and done for; nevertheless, I wished to spare him the mere detail of a formal execution.... I don't defend my morality. There was no morality in the impulse which induced me to lay before him Brierly's plan of evasion...'" (*LJ*, p. 131). And Marlow's bitter anger at Jim's failure to run—" 'Better men than you have found it expedient to run, at times' " (*LJ*, p. 133)—comes to sound very much like Brierly. As elsewhere, Marlow successfully manipulates us both ways: his "Of course I declined to meddle" arouses our "braving it out" instinct; his laying before Jim "Brierly's plan of evasion" appeals to our sense of arrogant defiance—and only the most alert reader catches the blatant contradiction. Marlow plays upon the sensibilities of his listeners and readers with the sure touch of a skilled surgeon and the gall of a buccaneer.

Marlow's own untrustworthiness may be seen as finally focusing on Stein, whom he calls "one of the most trustworthy men I had ever known" (*LJ*, p. 174). Stein begins his self-revelation by suggesting that man is the product of an "artist [who] was a little mad" (*LJ*, p. 179), and then unconsciously offers himself as exemplum. He tells of calmly killing three men and finding "the clean earth smiling at me,"[10] and then of rapturously capturing a unique butterfly. "When I got up I shook like a leaf with excitement, and when I opened these beautiful wings and made sure what a rare and so extraordinary perfect specimen I had, my head went round and my legs became so weak with emotion that I had to sit on the ground.... 'On that day I had nothing to desire; I had greatly annoyed my principal enemy; I was young, strong; I had friendship; I had the love . . . of woman, a child I had to make my heart very full—and even what I once dreamed in my sleep had come into my hand, too!'" (*LJ*, pp. 181–82). The clue to Stein, and to the Marlow who finds him trustworthy, lies in the disproportion not only of emotion but also of language: "annoyed" as a euphemism for three killings. In the tradition of life-denying artists of nature, Stein now lacks all that his values implicitly negated: youth, friend, wife, child, and soon strength. Stein himself is what he tags his butterfly, "a remarkable specimen," but hardly what Marlow proclaims him: a reliable, Virgil-like guide through *Lord Jim*'s moral inferno. His deflation at the end, the revelation of hollowness we have previously associated with Kurtz, is in fact implicit in this moment of our first encounter with him.

Before depicting that deflation, Marlow offers us a description of Jim's death that is as lyrically ambiguous as anything Conrad ever wrote. He speaks of Jim's "'last flicker of superb egoism,'" of his final "'proud and unflinching glance,'" of

> "the alluring shape of such an extraordinary success! For it may very well be that in the short moment of his last proud and unflinching glance, he had beheld the face of that opportunity which, like an Eastern bride, had come veiled to his side.
>
> "But we can see him, an obscure conqueror of fame, tearing himself out of the arms of a jealous love at the sign, at the call of his exalted egoism. He goes away from a living woman to celebrate his pitiless wedding with a shadowy ideal of conduct."   (*LJ*, p. 362)

Marlow's romanticizing of Jim's death offers rich, metaphoric counterpointing to his early assertion of Jim's greatness. What seems to happen is that Jim's ritual suicide, unlike his youthful dreams and Patusan success, offers no moral guidance for Westerners ("us"), no exemplum for Marlow to puff and pass on. So he finds both Jim and the significance of his actions obscured by impenetrable shadows at the last.

Marlow then concludes *Lord Jim* with a series of unsettling questions concerning Jim and his death, and an even more unsettling picture of those who remain behind. "Is he satisfied—quite, now, I wonder? We ought to know. He is one of us—and have I not stood up once, like an evoked ghost, to answer for his eternal constancy? Was I so very wrong after all? . . . Who knows? He is gone, inscrutable at heart, and the poor girl is leading a sort of soundless, inert life in Stein's house. Stein has aged greatly of late. He feels it himself, and says often that he is 'preparing to leave all this; preparing to leave . . .' while he waves his hand sadly at his butterflies" (*LJ*, p. 363). Marlow seeks a final note of mystery, poetry, and sadness; yet what really is inscrutable here is not Jim—who is clearly defined by his own sense of worth and a repeatedly amazed awareness of his failure to realize it, a common enough form of schizophrenia—but Marlow and his pervasive despair over Jim's lack of single-facetedness. Marlow's refrain, "one of us," *should* suffice to define Jim as white and English, duty-bound, a successful embodiment of Western notions of fidelity and progress. Marlow revealingly says: "'He was like a figure set up on a pedestal, to represent in his persistent youth the power, and perhaps the virtues, of races that never grow old, that have emerged from the gloom. I don't know why he should always have appeared to me symbolic. Perhaps this is the real cause of my interest in his fate' " (*LJ*, p. 229). But despite appearances Jim fails to play the part he and Marlow assign him: " 'I would have trusted the deck to that youngster on the strength of a single glance, and gone to sleep with both eyes—and, by Jove! it wouldn't have been safe. There are depths of horror in that thought' " (*LJ*, pp. 36–38). Such a truth (and Marlow's need to learn it) invalidates his central assumption concerning racial superiority and the equation of appearance and reality, just as both *Heart of Darkness* and *Lord Jim* repudiate his faith in the nobility of evil done in the service of professed ideals.

Marlow's depictions, therefore, are *necessarily* of "inconclusive experiences" (*HD*, p. 179), for they neither support his initial theses nor cause him to confront and revise them after refutation by events. Marlow's virtues as man and narrator are also his vices: charming self-deprecation, humane and open questioning, refusal to make definitive pronouncements were warranted (or else an asserting of contradictory ones), sensitive if fruitless intruding of himself into the lives of others. And they represent a compelling self-depiction of one who is surely "one of us." Yet Marlow's hesitations and irreconcilabilities reflect an unreliability seriously at odds with the surface dependability of his narrative stance.

The one work of Conrad's that Wayne Booth cites in his "Gallery of Unreliable Narrators" at the end of *The Rhetoric of Fiction* is *Heart of Darkness* (presumably for Marlow's narration rather than that of the anonymous frame commentator); yet *Lord Jim* warrants inclusion at least equally as much, for in both of these, Marlow becomes profoundly, dynamically, and grotesquely unreliable— "grotesque" in the sense that Sherwood Anderson's writer uses that term at the beginning of *Winesburg, Ohio:* "It was his notion that the moment one of the people took one of the truths to himself, called it his truth, and tried to live his life by it, he became a grotesque and the truth he embraced became a falsehood."[11] As we have seen, Marlow seizes grotesquely on the morality of ideas (any ideas) in *Heart of Darkness*, and on the congruence of appearance and substance in *Lord Jim;* and yet his dartingly vital imagination causes them to remain problematical, a matter demanding continual struggle, always in motion.

Chance, however, is radically different, for such dynamics offer sharp contrast to the bland superiority of tone Marlow assumes toward Flora, Anthony, Powell, and the others in his last narrative. T. S. Eliot has noted that we are alive to the extent that we do good or evil; Marlow's intellectual and moral detachment in *Chance* has about it a stench of death and decay, what he calls mediocrity. He says, in *Chance*, " 'It's certainly unwise to admit any sort of responsibility for our actions, whose consequences we are never able to foresee.... the incapacity to achieve anything distinctly good or evil is inherent in our earthly condition. Mediocrity is our mark,' " (*C*, p. 23). There was a time, he notes, when he saw the world with different eyes: " 'When one's young human nature shocks one' " (*C*, p. 15). Nothing shocks, or even interests, Marlow very much in *Chance*—certainly not human nature, which he ceases to encounter on any but a mocking or trifling level. Conrad's mistake, like Shakespeare's in *Merry Wives of Windsor*, consists of reducing to domestication the natural scope and conflict of a profoundly mistaken moral spokesman; a mellow Marlow speaks to our deepest needs and joys no more than does a Falstaff playing at love.

Marlow seeks not only depth but scope as he journeys from "Youth" to *Chance*, yet Marlow has come full circle by *Chance*. *Chance* is far longer than "Youth" but attains no greater depth, for, as Conrad's defensive Preface implies, its amplitude depends largely on verbiage. The problem may be seen as focusing on the fact that *Chance* begins at the end not of *Lord Jim* but of "Youth." Marlow concludes "Youth" by asking rhetorically, " 'wasn't that the best time, that time when we were young at sea; young and had nothing, on the sea that gives nothing, except hard knocks—and sometimes a chance to feel your strength—that only—that you all regret?' " (*Y*, p. 170); and he begins *Chance* by agreeing with Powell "that the happiest time in their lives was as youngsters in good ships, with no care in the world..." (*C*, p. 4).

Marlow's attitude towards the sea represents a singular failure to evolve. Upon failing his first test, the youthful Jim scorns "the spurious menace of wind and seas. He knew what to think of it.... he exulted with fresh certitude in his avidity for adventure, and in a sense of many-sided courage" (*LJ*, pp. 6–7). We expect *Chance*'s Marlow to sound a good deal different, but halfway through his final narrative Marlow himself echoes Jim's naive assertion that the sea is "unchangeable, safe...sheltering man from all passions, except its own anger" (*C*, p. 292). Surely one of Jim's functions is to complete the process that Kurtz began: Marlow's initiation into disillusionment, his alienation from earlier visions of youth and sea. He speaks of Jim's being " 'the sort whose appearance claims the fellowship of those illusions you had thought gone out, extinct, cold...,' " and then of the destruction of that fellowship.

> "Surely in no other craft as in that of the sea do the hearts of those already launched to sink or swim go out so much to the youth on the brink.... In no other kind of life is the illusion more wide of reality—in no other is the beginning *all* illusion—the disenchantment more swift—the subjugation more complete.... He was there before me, believing that age and wisdom can find a remedy against the pain of truth.... I was aggrieved against him, as though he had cheated me—me!—of a splendid opportunity to keep up the illusion of my beginnings, as though he had robbed our common life of the last spark of its glamour."   (*LJ*, pp. 111–13)

After such an anguished outcry, it is no wonder that the opening note of *Chance*, sounding as it does like the end of "Youth," rings false.

In both "Youth" and *Chance* Marlow wryly but enviously shakes his head over the bravura successes of youth, but such nostalgia, while valid once, becomes brittle and aritificial after the confrontations with youth's flagrant excesses of ideas and imagination, and its consequent heart-rending doom, in *Heart of Darkness* and

Lord Jim. Like "Youth" and unlike *Heart of Darkness* and *Lord Jim, Chance* lacks a moral core and Marlow a moral stance. The problems of its plot are situational; they bear no relationship to the crisis of nightmare and conscience that Marlow, along with Kurtz and Jim, experience in *Heart of Darkness* and *Lord Jim.* Though used in various ways, "chance" primarily means coincidence rather than providence, happenstance rather than moral and symbolic aptness.[12] Thus Powell tells us that he got his first chance, a casual display of verbal irony indicative of the novel's level of profundity and wit. The story is the vehicle not for symbolic, philosophical, or moral exploration, but for what Marlow calls "the commonest sort of curioisty" (*C*, p. 40), for he finds what he narrates only mildly interesting, and his lack of temperamental involvement utterly denies any tension at the novel's core.

The tone of *Chance* is one of casual and bland superiority, and Marlow exhibits intense emotion rarely and incongruously, as when he rails out against confessions after presumably having sought to elicit Flora's. He says, " 'Never confess! Never, never!... a confession of whatever sort is always untimely. The one thing which makes it supportable for a while is curiosity.... And all of them [confessors] in their hearts brand you for either mad or impudent....' " The narrator says, "I had seldom seen Marlow so vehement, so pessimistic, so earnestly cynical before" (*C*, p. 212). Marlow may be correct about his motivation, but curiosity is an oddly feeble basis on which to construct the vast edifice of *Chance.*

In the analogous passage in *Lord Jim,* Marlow also contemplates himself as confidant, wondering what loosens men's " 'tongues at the sight of me for the infernal confidences; as though... I didn't have enough confidential information about myself to harrow my own soul till the end of my appointed time.... I am not particularly fit to be a receptable of conrressions' " (*LJ*, p. 28). Marlow's conclusion here is presumably wrong, and in fact he later qualifies it: " 'I would have been little fitted for the reception of his confidences had I not been able at times to understand the pauses between the words' " (*LJ*, p. 90). Marlow asserts that " 'My weakness consists in not having a discriminating eye for the incidental' " (*LJ*, p. 80), but he implies the opposite when he proclaims his admiration for the French lieutenant's discrimination. Yet with all their contrarieties, such pronouncements are not simply misleading—they are profoundly, supremely misleading, and they express something central and significant about Marlow in the same way as does the confession passage in *Hamlet* that this self-judgment seems to echo. Hamlet defines himself to Ophelia: "I am myself indifferent honest; but yet I could accuse me of such things that it were better my mother had not borne me: I am very proud, revengeful, ambitious, with more offences at my beck than I have thoughts to put them in, imagination to give them shape, or time to act them in. What should such fellows as I do crawling between earth and heaven: We are arrant knaves, all; believe none of us" (III, i, 123–32). The uses of literary sources are subtle and powerful in *Lord Jim;* in *Chance* they are cheap and superior, as when Marlow refers to Flora and de Barral as " 'Figures from Dickens—pregnant with pathos' " *C*, p. 162).

Marlow's attitudes toward *Chance's* central concerns—the sea and women—

are also disturbing, for his complacent categorization of each confronts endless contradictions while remaining unchanged. As with *Typhoon*'s Captain MacWhirr, the sea in *Chance* is defined as free from all moral challenge, "free from the earth's petty suggestions" (*C*, p. 310), offering professional satisfaction plus adventure with its simple, direct claims (*C*, pp. 31–32). Thus, life on the *Ferndale* must be seen as aberrant, its unrestfulness atypical of the sea but very like that associated with the land. This aberrance is compounded by the marriage of Flora and Anthony, for another of Marlow's *ex cathedra* pronouncements blithely generalizes about marriage and then marraige at sea:

> "With what we know of Roderick Anthony and Flora de Barral I could not deduct an ordinary marital quarrel beautifully matured in less than a year. . . . If you ask me what is an ordinary marital quarrel I will tell you, that it is a difference about nothing. . . . There are on earth no actors too humble and obscure not to have a gallery, that gallery which envenoms the play by stealthy jeers, counsels of anger, amused comments or words of perfidious compassion. However, the Anthonys were free from all demoralizing influences. At sea, you know, there is no gallery. You hear no tormenting echoes of your own littleness there. . . ."   (*C*, p. 326)

Once again, Marlow remains unperturbed by the failure of his definition and picture to square with each other.

Marlow maintains that he is out of his element on land (*HD*, p. 179; *C*, pp. 33–34), and he is certainly out of his depth with women, although early in *Chance* he asserts the opposite: " 'There is enough of the woman in my nature to free my judgment of women from glamorous reticency. . . . A woman is not necessarily either a doll or an angel to me. She is a human being, very much like myself' " (*C*, p. 53). Actually, this asserted affinity, this wilful misuse of his "one of us" thesis, serves merely as license for Marlow's endless pronouncements in the face of ignorance and gross inconsistency. Occasionally he sees women as superior to men, but his basic attitude toward them in *Chance*, in fact through all his narratives, is one of condescension.

Marlow then offers us a telling abstraction that gives the show away: " 'You say I don't know women. Maybe. . . . But I have a clear notion of *woman*' " (*C*, p. 353). Of course Marlow has nothing of the kind; he not only knows far less than he asserts, but he cannot keep his assertions straight. Thus, he defends his lie to Kurtz's Intended at the end of *Heart of Darkness* by insisting that he had a duty to keep from her a truth that, as a woman, she would have found "too dark—too dark altogether . . ." (*HD*, p. 256). But in *Chance* he reverses the formula while managing to remain equally patronizing: " 'I call a woman sincere when she volunteers a statement resembling remotely in form what she really would like to say, what she really thinks ought to be said if it were not for the necessity to spare the stupid sensitiveness of men. . . . We could not stand women speaking the truth. . . . It would cause infinite misery and bring about most awful disturbances in this rather mediocre, but still idealistic fool's paradise in which each of us lives his own little life. . . . And they know it. They are merciful' " (C, p. 144). Trying to determine his complexly ambivalent attitude toward Jim, Marlow reveals something of his own depths: " 'It is when we try to grapple with another man's intimate need that we perceive how incomplete, wavering, and misty are the beings that share with us the sight of the stars and the warmth of the sun. It is as if loneliness were a hard and absolute condition of existence . . .' " (LJ, p. 155), This sort of intensely personal confrontation with human relationships lies at the polar extreme from the "common curiosity" that motivates Marlow in Chance.

In his "Author's Note" to "Youth," which appears five years after Chance, Conrad identifies Marlow as his alter ego from first conception to last farewell. Conrad is credible when he denies having merely used Marlow, when he denies that Marlow is a charlatan, "a clever screen, a mere device, a 'personator,' a familiar spirit, a whispering 'daemon.' " Their relationship, he continues, grew "very intimate in the course of years. . . . The man Marlow and I came together in the casual manner of those health-resort acquaintances which sometimes ripen into friendships. This one has ripened. For all his assertiveness in matters of opinion he is not an intrusive person. He haunts my hours of solitude, when, in silence, we lay our heads together in great comfort and harmony; but as we part at the end of a tale I am never sure that it may not be for the last time. Yet I don't think either of us would care much to survive the other."[13] Conrad's statement has a poignant validity whose outline has become clear in retrospect, for though Conrad lives and writes until 1924, both Marlow and his important writings are behind him by Chance in 1913. And this fact seems more than coincidence, no more mere chance than Jim's arrival in Patusan or the marraige of Flora and Powell through Marlow's intercession. Jim's death seems to necessitate that of Marlow as artist; Marlow's demise signifies that of Conrad as artist. Art imitates life and life returns the compliment.

Conrad had reached a dead-end from which, apparently, there could be no returning. Marlow's rites of passage from "Youth" to Lord Jim expand parameters and deepen vision, but Chance depicts a narrowing, a domestication, as Marlow shifts from morally involved participant to fussily detached busybody making banal pronouncements: " 'Pairing off is the fate of mankind' " (C, p. 426). Marlow's curiosity in Chance lacks empathy, the deep solace and despair of his earlier narratives—Flora, after all, is much younger, alien in temprament as well as inferior in sex. Unlike Powell, Marlow doesn't take her seriously until the very end, and even then he manipulates her with condescending superiority and against his own initial condemnation of such interference (C, pp. 23–24). Marlow intrudes at the end to change the shape and direction of Powell's and Flora's lives, but apparently without the conviction that his is a significant action. And that the consequences may be presumed unequivocally fortuitous, like Marlow's banality throughout, suggests that Conrad himself respects and shares Marlow's cheery and dull complacency. No wonder Conrad abandons him here—no beyond is possible once he ceases to take him seriously.

One central question remains concerning the Marlovian narratives. Is Marlow himself aware of and controlling the attitude implicit in his perspective, and thus as cynical as *The Secret Agent's* narrator from first to last? Or is he as unconscious of many of his words' implications as is the professor of languages who narrates *Under Western Eyes?* By and large, *Chance* does not raise such questions because in it Marlow's sarcasm and sympathy are both distinct and superficial. But *Heart of Darkness* and *Lord Jim,* which are, in Booth's word, "seamless," remain two of Conrad's inscrutable fictions because they both raise such questions and seem to deny all the possible answers. Yet whether or not Marlow is fully a party to the plot, Conrad is surely at great pains to frustrate the part of us craving certitude. In one sense, Conrad (an ironist in all his major fiction) is simply having fun at our and Marlow's expense; yet he is also recognizing that our deepest experiences never sort themselves out neatly: they berate and confound us with their multiple moral claims: they perversely demand contradictory responses of us—and in the process truth and validity must sort themselves out neatly: they berate and confound us with their multiple moral claims: they perversely demand contradictory responses of us—and in the process truth and validity must sort themselves out as best they can. Our most difficult and important task may well be to dismiss the ambivalent "Possibly" Marlow offers *Lord Jim's* "privileged man" as wholly inadequate, and yet to perceive that it lies at the heart of truth—if, that is, one may even speak of truth as having a heart. Marlow's journey, though it finally loses the momentum that is its *raison d'être,* derives its validity by becoming what it seeks—the way into the self-confronting realm of modern art and life, where the artist, burdened by tradition like all of us, nonetheless asserts his claim to "making it new," to striking out for unknown territories of the human psyche like the bold, free, but criminal Leggatt of Conrad's "The Secret Sharer." Marlow agrees with Jim that his clean slate is a magnificent chance and then adds, "but chances are what men make them, and how was I to know?" (*LJ*, p. 209). The only answer to such a question must be the quest implicit in the question.

NOTES

[1] All quotations from these four works are from the following editions: "Youth" and *Heart of Darkness*, in *Great Short Works of Joseph Conrad* (New York: Harper & Row, 1966), pp. 143–71, 175–256; *Lord Jim* (New York: Holt, Rinehart, 1963); *Chance* (New York: Norton, 1968). References to these works will be made in the text as follows: Y, HD, LJ, C.

[2] Wayne C. Booth, *The Rhetoric of Fiction* (Chicago and London: University of Chicago Press, 1961), p. 346.

[3] The term "multifarious narrator" is taken from Robert Scholes and Robert Kellogg, *The Nature of Narrative* (New York: Oxford Univ. Press, 1966). It is intended to replace "omniscient" since even the most objective and removed commentator "is not everywhere at once but now here, now there, now looking into this mind or that, now moving on to other vantage points. He is time-bound and space-bound as God is not" (pp. 272–73).

[4] See Jocelyn Baines, *Joseph Conrad: A Critical Biography* (New York: McGraw-Hill, 1967), p. 205.

[5] R. W. B. Lewis, *The Picaresque Saint* (Philadelphia and New York: Lippincott, 1959), p. 197.

[6] Marlow never seems to learn the lesson of appearances. His initial reaction to the French lieutenant is that "he looked a reliable officer . . . he was seamanlike" (*LJ*, p. 120). Marlow happens to be right in this case, as Jim happened to be right about the *Patna's* captain; but such judgments reduce values to a dangerously myopic conflating of morality and esthetics.

[7] At the end, as Marlow writes to the "privileged man," Jim is even further removed from us, even more an artifice of others' constructing. Marlow says, " 'It is impossible to see him clearly—especially as it is through the eyes of others that we take our last look at him' " (*LJ*, p. 294). Oddly, as Marlow would have it, the more Jim becomes shaped and final for some, the more he becomes inconclusive process for others.

[8] Joseph Conrad, *Under Western Eyes* (New York: Anchor Books, 1963), p. 1.

[9] This encounter, like Marlow's earlier one with Kurtz's Intended, also emphasizes that "one of us" is a sexual as well as a racial distinction.

[10] It is no mere coincidence that Jim, become a killer, replays with uncanny exactitude the Stein role, as Marlow describes it. " 'He held his shot, he says, deliberately. He held it for the tenth part of a second, for three strides of the man—an unconscionable time. He held it for the pleasure of saying to himself, That's a dead man! . . . He found himself calm, appeased, without rancour, without uneasiness, as if the death of that man had atoned for everything' " (*LJ*, p. 261).

[11] Sherwood Anderson, "The Book of the Grotesque," *Winesburg, Ohio* (New York: The Viking Press, 1967), p. 25.

[12] See, for example, *Chance*, pp. 16, 126, 272, 311, 328, and 446.

[13] "Author's Note" to *Youth*, quoted in *Heart of Darkness: An Authoritative Text, Backgrounds and Sources, Criticism*, ed. Robert Kimbrough (New York: Norton Critical Editions, 1963), p. 155.

Jacques Berthoud

"HEART OF DARKNESS"

I confounded the beat of the drum with the beating of my heart ...'
—Marlow in 'Heart of Darkness', p. 142

I

It is appropriate that 'Heart of Darkness' should begin in the Thames estuary—the very place where *The Nigger of the 'Narcissus'* ended—for it is, in a special sense, a continuation of that novel. 'Heart of Darkness' takes up the affirmations of its predecessor, and exposes them to a process of systematic questioning. The test of the sea generates values which are submitted to the test of the wilderness.[1]

In respect of the positives it discovers, the world of *The Nigger of the 'Narcissus'* is a self-sufficient one. This does not mean that its inhabitants are unrepresentative, particularly in the weaker side of their nature; or that the redemption they achieve together cannot be sought in other forms of service. On the contrary, the voyage of the *Narcissus*—particularly in its final phase—is susceptible of wider application. As the ship approaches England, a sudden glimpse of the coast leads the narrator to imagine the island as some mighty vessel in its own right, which its subjects can serve much as its crew serves the *Narcissus*. And later, after the ship has berthed, and a swarm of strangers has taken possession of her 'in the name of the sordid earth', and the narrator sees the men, now paid off, drifting in front of London's historic Tower, he immediately associates them with their 'fighting prototypes'—the great line of English maritime heroes. Yet for all this wider relevance, *The Nigger of the 'Narcissus'* achieves its affirmation at the cost of a certain abstraction. By deliberately contrasting the ethnic of service at sea with the principle of self-seeking on land, Conrad suggests that service is intrinsically meaningful, an end in itself—irrespective of the further purposes it may advance. He does not, of course, disregard the commercial interests that send sailing-ships out on their

From *Joseph Conrad: The Major Phase* (Cambridge: Cambridge University Press, 1978), pp. 41–63.

voyages. As early as the second chapter, he remarks: 'The august loneliness of her path lent dignity to *the sordid inspiraction* of her pilgraimage'.[2] [My italics.] The inspiration of the ship's journey may be sordid; but once she has shaken herself free of the land she acquires a solitary beauty that neither her origin nor her destination seems to be able to affect. And there can be no mistaking the meaning of our last sight of the 'dark knot of seamen' drifting away in a pale shaft of English sunlight. 'The sunshine of heaven fell like a gift of grace on the mud of the earth ... And to the right of the dark group the stained front of the Mint, cleansed by the flood of light, stood out for a moment, dazzling and white.'[3] The work of men who take no thought beyond their immediate task—and who by virtue of that, and that alone, achieve a purifying disinterestedness—cannot altogether abolish the taint of minted currency; but, like a sudden gleam from heaven, it can momentarily transfigure it.

If no such shaft of light interrupts the gloom brooding over Marlow's London, it is essentially because his tale forgoes all pretence of a distinction between land and sea. The men on the deck of the yawl *Nellie*, like their predecessors of the *Narcissus*, share the bond of the sea. But three of them are also landsmen—and businessmen to boot: a director, an accountant, and a lawyer, each serving commercial interests in his own way. As for the fourth, Marlow (if we ignore the anonymous narrator who opens and closes the narrative), he is a tested seaman who has stepped out of the circle that insulates the sailor's life. For ordinary sailors, 'there is nothing mysterious ... unless it be the sea itself'; hence, 'a casual spree on shore suffices to unfold ... the secret of a whole continent'. In this respect, Marlow does not represent his class. Although he has learnt the lesson of the sea and is wholly committed to integrity in word and deed, he is also a 'wanderer', urged on by a most unseamanlike curiosity about life on land, which takes him (as he is about to disclose) into a region where the values he upholds are deprived of most of their moral effectiveness.

The four men who constitute Marlow's audience are uncritical products of a powerful maritime civilization. It is not surprising, therefore, that, as they talk among themselves, waiting for the tide to turn, they should offer a view of English history which unconsciously elaborates the idea of the 'ship of state' evoked in the closing pages of *The Nigger of the 'Narcissus'*. We have seen that life at sea depends on a number of factors: the sea itself, of which the rigours have to be faced; the ship, of which the demands have to be met; and the tradition of service, of which the requirements have to be observed. As Marlow's companions contemplate the waterway 'leading to the uttermost ends of the earth', they discover analogous qualities in England's imperial past. The selfless mariners are now 'the great knights-errant of the sea', the challenge they face is 'the mystery of the unknown earth', and the cause they serve is the 'torch' or 'sacred fire' of their inherited civilization.

Marlow's initial response to this grandiose prospect ('Heart of Darkness', pp. 48–51) is a profoundly disturbing one. 'Light came out of this river since—you say knights? ... But darkness was here yesterday.' For the vision of a heroic England bearing the torch into unknown lands he substitutes another and earlier picture: England herself an unknown territory, receiving the attentions of a Roman invader. In this perspective English civilization begins to look much less permanent—the 'flicker', as he calls it, of 'a running blaze on a plain, like a flash of lightning'; and imperialism, which is the expansion of this civilization, begins to seem much less glamorous. The imagined invader, dismayed and demoralized by the surrounding wilderness, loses his chivalric zest; his struggle with exhaustion, disease and death tarnishes whatever ideal of service he may have brought in with him. In this predicament, says Marlow, 'what saves us is efficiency'. The significance of this wry comment should not be missed: what in the context of the sea had become redemptive labour is now reduced to a merely mechanical means of survival. Taken all in all, 'the conquest of the earth, which mostly means the taking it away from those who have a different complexion or slightly flatter noses than ourselves, is not a pretty thing when you look into it much.' The imperialist is obviously even more in need of justification than the merchant seaman. But what justiciation *can* there be? 'What redeems it is the idea only . . . An idea at the back of it; not a sentimental pretence, but an idea—something you can set up, and bow down before, and offer a sacrifice to.' This seems to be a return to the solution of *The Nigger of the 'Narcissus'*. But even here resemblances are deceptive. The sailor who serves his ship is governed by a practical tradition; the imperialist, at best, has to rely on the justification of an abstract idea—an idea which, moreover, acquires in Marlow's presentation of it the connotations of a dubious idolatry.

The elaborate preamble to Marlow's narrative with which 'Heart of Darkness' opens does more than provide an appropriate physical setting for the telling of the tale. It also raises the questions which the tale will explore. Considered as a test, Marlow's venture into the African jungle can be compared to the ocean voyages he has accomplished. In its scale, power, aloofness, and inscrutability, the virgin forest bears a certain resemblance to the sea. Marlow, for example, can describe it in terms that recall the storm scenes of *The Nigger of the 'Narcissus'*.

> 'The great wall of vegetation, an exuberant and entangled mass of trunks, branches, leaves, boughs, festoons, motionless in the moonlight, was like a rioting invasion of soundless life, *a rolling wave of plants, piled up, crested, ready to topple over the creek, to sweep every little man of us out of his little existence.'* [My italics.]   ('Heart of Darkness', p. 86)

But there is one essential difference. Whereas the sea is an absolutely alien element, the land-locked jungle is part of man's abode. It contains human beings who are not unrelated to the ancestors of the modern Englishmen listening to Marlow's story. This means that as we move from one work to the next, we have to change our bearings. Whereas a voyage on the 'immortal sea' can be seen as taking place under the gaze of eternity, a journey into the jungle is also a descent into man's history, a return to his primordial origins. The darkness into which Marlow ventures has a heart which can be found within his own breast.

II

We have seen that *The Nigger of the 'Narcissus'* dramatizes a conflict between fidelity to a defined tradition of service and the temptation of self-regarding individualism. What is in question in 'Heart of Darkness' is man's fidelity to the general tradition of civilization. But whereas the crew of the Narcissus could rely on objective structures and imperatives—that is, on a tradition embodied, independently of themselves, in such tried veterans as Alistoun and Singleton—the imperialist invaders of Africa, sundered as they are from the regulating context of their society, are left wholly to their own devices. There is, to be sure, an essential difference between Marlow, who has passed the test of the sea, and so can distinguish between words and deeds, professions and performances, and the agents of the exploitative company he encounters in the Congo. But the Marlow who takes up his appointment as captain of the river-steamer has not yet undergone the ordeal of the jungle—and in having to do so, he is as cut off as everybody else.

'Heart of Darkness', then, can be considered as an inquiry into how strong the hold of civilization is on its members. It is therefore necessary to note the degree to which this tale, particularly in its initial phase, exhibits the consequences of abstracting men from their native contexts. One of the salient features of Marlow's narrative is his insistence on the 'unreality' of his experience. This is more than a matter of what he says; it is also implied in the presentation of his story. That 'Heart of Darkness' makes extended, and sometimes obtrusive, use of non-naturalistic devices has been widely recognized. Mythical correspondences (the journey as a quest), literary allusions (the Dantesque grove of death), symbolic oppositions (light/darkness, white/black), anthropomorphism (the forest as 'an implacable force brooding over an inscrutable intention'), and the like, are not solely or even mainly (as some critics have complained) means of inflating significance; they also express—and on the whole with remarkable success—the sense of dream, of phantasmagoria and nightmare, which Marlow claims is of the essence of his experience. But if such devices help to convey Marlow's feeling of unreality, it is because they work within the context of a much more directly mimetic use of language.

Let us consider a justly famous example of this. Marlow is sailing down the coast of West Africa.

> 'Once, I remember, we came upon a man-of-war anchored off the coast. There wasn't even a shed there, and she was shelling the bush. It appears the French had one of their wars going on thereabouts. Her ensign drooped limp like a rag; the muzzles of her long six-inch guns stuck out all over the low hull; the greasy, slimy swell swung her up lazily and let her down, swaying her thin masts. In the empty immensity of earth, sky, and water, there she was, incomprehensible, firing into a continent. Pop, would go one of the six-inch guns; a small flame would dart and vanish, a little white smoke would disappear, a tiny projectile would give a feeble screech—and nothing happened. Nothing could happen. There was a touch of insanity in the proceeding, a sense of lugubrious drollery in the sight; and it was not dissipated by somebody on board assuring me earnestly there was a camp of natives—he called them enemies!—hidden out of sight somewhere.'

('Heart of Darkness', pp. 61–2)

Why Marlow feels there is a touch of insanity about these proceedings is because what should be a recognizable human action presents itself as an arbitrary event. In this alien environment, where the tepid, echoless air, the sluggish, greasy swell, and above all the sheer scale and emptiness of land and sea defeat the purposes of European precision, the phrase 'to fire a cannon' loses all connotation. The shattering report becomes a 'pop', the death-dealing shell a 'tiny projectile', the target to be destroyed a 'continent'. In other words, we are made to witness an action that claims to be intentional, but can no longer be regarded as such. What this incident brilliantly demonstrates is that the intelligibility of what men do depends upon the context in which they do it. The first important thing that Marlow's journey reveals to him is that what made sense in Europe no longer makes sense in Africa. As he disembarks, for instance, he notices that a railway is apparently being built; but he can make little sense of it. The activity of the engineers reduces itself to 'objectless blasting'; familiar artifacts are transformed into strange beasts: a boiler is 'wallowing in the grass', a truck lies 'on its back with its wheels in the air'. And if displaced action and objects behave peculiarly, displaced concepts go hopelessly adrift. The term 'enemy' is applied to bewildered and helpless victims, the word 'criminals' to moribund shadows, the concept of 'law' to those to whom it comes 'like bursting shells,... an incomprehensible mystery out of the sea'. Such words as 'worker', 'rebel', 'custom-house', 'seat of government', presuppose the entire social apparatus of European life; sundered from their natural contexts, they can find little purchase in the 'darkness' of the African continent. Most disturbing of all, death itself—the one absolute experience of a man's life—becomes a commonplace triviality. The first information about Africa that Marlow imparts concerns the fate of his predecessor—a man who loses his life over a misunderstanding about two black hens. The insignificance of the cause is matched only by the casualness of the event itself: 'some man ... made a tentative jab with a spear at the white man—and of course it went quite easily between the shoulder blades'. This nightmare disorientation becomes a familiar aspect of his African experience. It is indeed important, for it demonstrates that the sense of reality is not absolutely founded, but the product of a long process of cultural assimilation.

Really to possess a concept is to know when it does not apply. One of the essential differences between Marlow and his fellow-Europeans in Africa is that he can recognize the unreality of the notions that have been arbitrarily imported into the country, whereas they cannot or will not. This of course implies that he is capable of acknowledging the reality of the alien context. How far he does so is indicated by his encounter with some African canoes immediately after sighting the French warship.

'Now and then a boat from the shore gave one a momentary contact with reality. It was paddled by black fellows. You could see from afar the white of their eyeballs glistening. They shouted, sang; their bodies streamed with perspiration; they had faces like grotesque masks—these chaps; but they had bone, muscle, a wild vitality, an intense energy of movement, that was as

natural and true as the surf along their coast. They wanted no excuse for being
there.'   ('Heart of Darkness', p. 61)

Paradoxically, it is because of his firm grasp of the norms and conventions of his
own society that Marlow is able to recognize the humanity of the members of a
'primitive' culture. Knowing what he is, he can accurately measure the gap that
separates the Europeans in their steamer from the black men in their boat. He does
not pretend that the latter are anything but unfamiliar to him: their faces, for
example, seem to him to be 'grotesque masks'. Yet this very recognition of difference is an acknowledgement of otherness; the grotesque masks belong to 'these
chaps': because he accepts dissimilarity, he is able to affirm a common humanity.
Conscious of the fact of cultural relativity, he can contrast the vitality of the 'black
fellows' with the flabbiness of the invaders. The blacks are real because they want
'no excuse for being there'. They belong to their environment, and their environment belongs to them.

Marlow's possession of his own reality is complete enough for him not to have
to erect it into some kind of absolute. Hence he does not feel compelled to reject
what is alien to him as abnormal or absurd. A striking example is his response, as
he navigates up the river, to the throb of jungle drums. 'Perhaps on some quiet
night', he recalls, 'the tremor of far-off drums, sinking, swelling, a tremor vast, faint;
a sound weird, appealing, suggestive, and wild—and perhaps with as profound a
meaning as the sound of bells in a Christian country' (p. 71). An even more
searching illustration is his discovery of the cannibalism of his native stokers. What
would be unspeakable horror in London and Brussels becomes, on the Congo
river, an unremarkable topic of conversation. Halted by dense fog near their
destination, Marlow and his companions hear an outburst of shrieking from the
invisible bank (pp. 102–5). The stokers' headman turns to Marlow:

' "Catch 'im . . . Give 'im to us."
    ' "To you, eh?" I asked; " what would you do with them?"
        ' "Eat 'im!' he said, curtly, and, leaning his elbow on the rail, looked out
into the fog . . .'

Marlow's response is typical: 'I would no doubt have been properly horrified, had
it not occurred to me that he and his chaps must be very hungry: that they must
have been growing increasingly hungry for at least this month past.' Remembering
who and where he is, he is not stampeded into indiscriminate revulsion. Indeed, far
from casting the cannibals beyond the pale of humanity, he discovers in them a
quality which in one important respect sets them above the very moralists who
condemn them: their restraint in leaving untasted, despite the 'exasperating tor-
ment' of their 'lingering starvation', the defenseless cargo of so-called 'pilgrims'
virtually at their disposal. To Marlow, Africa and all it contains may seem strange,
mysterious, and even unintelligible: but it is not unreal. And for that very reason he
retains, displaced as he is, a sense of his own reality.

It is not the native inhabitants of Central Africa that Marlow regards as unreal, but their European invaders and colonizers. *Their* unreality, moreover, does not arise merely from the fact of geographical and cultural dislocation, but from their failure to recognize it. That is to say, their alienation is an internal one: their inability to understand the values which they are supposed to represent leads them to regard foreign ways as nothing more than illegitimate deviations from their own. And this has sinister reprecusioons. The fact that the society that sustains them is not merely different from, but also stronger than, the tribal communities they encounter abolishes every external check and makes it possible for them to treat the populations they deal with as if they were exploitable raw material, though of considerably less intrinsic value than the ivory they seek.

The trial of the jungle, therefore, can be considered as a test of the degree to which civilization, understood as the sublimation of primitive energies, is more than a mere word. Within advanced communities like Brussels or London one cannot tell whether the citizen is *really* civilized: whether the values he professes are really his—or his merely by virtue of 'the holy terror of scandal and gallows and lunatic asylums' (p. 116).[4] Transport him, however, into a region where every external control is abolished—not only the steadying presence of butcher and policeman, but also the regulating effects of good health and a temperate climate—and he may abandon every vestige of the restraint on which civilization is founded, and without which it becomes a mere fraud. It is just such a collapse, of course, that Marlow witnesses on his arrival in Africa. In 'the blinding sunshine of that land' he finds that the whites, far from retaining possession of civilized norms, have themselves become possessed by 'a flabby, pretending, weak-eyed devil of a rapacious and pitiless folly' (p. 65). Thus considered, the trial of the jungle is like the trial of the sea, distinguishing Marlow from his demoralized colleagues very much as service at sea is distinguished from self-seeking on land.

III

Up to this point, then, 'Heart of Darkness' might be said to develop the moral distinction established in *The Nigger of the 'Narcissus'*. However, as soon as we begin to scrutinize Marlow's relations with his fellow-whites, this distinction becomes problematic. Broadly speaking, the company officials with whom he comes into contact fall into two main categories: the established traders, whose task is to exchange worthless trinkets for as much ivory as they can lay their hands on; and a new kind of agent, sent out in deference to the pressure of philanthropic opinion, part of whose purpose is—in the words of Marlow's aunt—to wean 'those ignorant millions from their horrid ways'. After his arrival in the Congo, Marlow—who is assumed to belong to what the brickmaker of the Central Station cynically calls 'the gang of virtue'—quickly starts suspecting that the two groups are engaged in some sort of power struggle; and despite his attempts to remain uninvolved he is willy-nilly drawn into the contest. As this process of engagement forms the central part of his narrative, it is necessary to look more closely at his relationship first with the anonymous Manager of the Central Station, the leader of the 'exploiters', then with Kurtz, the chief agent of the Inner Station, the representative of the 'civilizers'.

The Manager, who is Marlow's immediate employer, reveals himself at once as the very type of the exploiter. His single virtue, invulnerable health, frees him from the sole remaining check operative in Africa—tropical fever; and as none of his rivals is able to withstand this disease, he has had an unprecedented stretch of nine years in which to consolidate his position. In all other respects, however, he is—like the 'pilgrims' who loiter about his run-down station—an unredeemable mediocrity, incapable of any guiding principle other than that of maximum profit for minimum effort. 'He had no genius for organizing, for initiative, or for order even . . . He had no learning and no intelligence . . . He originated nothing, he could keep the routine going—that's all.' Marlow's contemptuous summing-up of the qualities of his employer seems merely to reinforce the distinction between the two men; his tone makes it clear that at least *he* owes his self-respect to his capacity for efficient service. Yet at the same time it defines the essence of Marlow's dilemma. For serving an employer like the Manager is a very different proposition from serving one like Captain Alistoun. To work for a man for whom the ideal of service has no meaning whatsoever instantly revives the problem which *The Nigger of the 'Narcissus'* seemed to have resolved: can labour in the service of a vicious end retain its redemptive character? 'Heart of Darkness' as a whole makes the evasion of this problem quite impossible. During the whole of his sojourn in the Congo, Marlow meets only a single case of integrity in work—that of the Chief Accountant of the Lower Station whose meticulous bookkeeping, together with his stunning sartorial correctness, strikes him, in the context of the general demoralization, as evidence of real 'backbone'. Yet this exception only raises the problem in a more acute form. The Accountant's competence is achieved at the cost of an inhuman detachment. While he continues to make 'correct entries of perfectly correct transactions' in the Company's ledger, he remains oblivious of the appalling consequences of exploitation that are being enacted outside his door: the monotonous groans of a dying man; the 'rascally grin' of a 'redeemed' black in charge of a chain-gang; and, worst of all, the immobility of the broken slaves thrown out like refuse into the despairing hush of the 'grove of death' (pp. 67–70).

In such a situation, it is obviously impossible for Marlow to suggest that fidelity to the task in hand is any sort of justification. All he can claim is that it preserves him from the worst of the surrounding disintegration. The fact that he has to repair his steamer helps him to retain some sort of hold on his identity. 'No, I don't like work', he confesses '—no man does—but I like what is in the work,—the chance to find yourself. Your own reality—for yourself, not for others—what no other man can ever know' (p. 85). Yet even in this reduced form the ideal of service is not secure. The reason why he has to repair the steamer, Marlow understands, is that it has been accidentally wrecked by the Manager, as he set out to rescue an apparently ailing Kurtz. Yet there remains something disturbing about this incident, although Marlow does not spot it immediately: 'I did not see the real significance of that wreck at once . . . Certainly the affair was too stupid—when I think of it—to be altogether natural.' So although the Manager inspires a general sense of uneasiness, Marlow does not suspect him of anything specific. However, the more he learns about Kurtz—about his singular success as an ivory collector, but also about the multiplicity of his talents: as the painter of an allegorical figure of justice, as author of an eloquent tract against 'savage customs', as musician, orator, journalist—the more he becomes aware that Kurtz is universally loathed and envied by his colleagues. He receives his first inkling of an actual conspiracy against him only when he overhears the Manager assent to a proposition that 'anything—anything can be done in this country'. But it is only some months later, when Marlow notices the Manager displaying 'a beautiful resignation' at the fact that their rescue of Kurtz has been delayed yet again, that he becomes fully conscious that 'the essentials of this affair lay deep under the surface'. He is now certain that the Manager did not confine himself merely to *hoping* that delay would let the wilderness finish Kurtz off. The events of the recent past suddenly appear in an entirely new light. For example, when the Manager originally claimed that it would take three months to repair the steamer Marlow had taken him for 'a chattering idiot': how could anyone confidently predict that the work would take so long? But now he adds: 'Afterwards I took it back when it was borne in upon me startlingly with what extreme nicety he had estimated the time requisite for the "affair".' Whatever the meaning of the word 'affair'—whether it refers to the repair of the steamer (which the Manager would have been able to prolong at will since he controlled the supply of rivets), or to the destruction of Kurtz (which with his unprecedented experience of tropical climate he would have been able to calculate to a nicety)—Marlow can now see that the Manager has all along remained in complete control of events. What he has to face is something more disconcerting than the mere fact of perfidiousness: that the rescue operation, a task with which he had been professionally entrusted and from which he had derived a modicum of self-respect, has proved itself to be from beginning to end a cynical masquerade. It is not surprising that he feels himself caught in a situation in which, as he says, 'my speech or my silence, indeed any action of mine, would be mere futility' (p. 100, generally).

IV

If in his relationship with the inscrutable Manager of the Central Station Marlow is brought into contact with moral cynicism, in his relationship with Kurtz he is confronted with the phenomenon of idealistic self-deception. Kurtz seems to be a passionate and eloquent defender of the policy which holds, against the more pragmatic views of the Manager, that every station should be 'a centre of trade of course, but also for humanizing, improving, instructing. It is understandable that Marlow, surrounded as he is by an exploitation that has 'no more moral purpose at the back of it than there is in burglars breaking into a safe', should find himself drawn towards the idea of a man who, by all accounts, seems to be 'equipped with moral ideas of some sort'. In complete contrast to the Manager, Kurtz seems to be a person of exceptional talents and culture. Indeed he appears to be a very embodiment of that civilization which the African wilderness has so comprehensively annihilated. 'All Europe contributed to the making of Mr. Kurtz', says Marlow. His elaborate advocacy of European values, however, turns out to be even more disturbing than the Manager's uncomplicated denial of them.

As Marlow, navigating upstream towards Kurtz, penetrates more and more deeply into the wilderness, his feelings towards it undergo a substantial change. It is no longer a merely alien environment: it acquires the force of a positive presence. 'We are accustomed to look upon the shackled form of a conquered monster', he tells his listeners; '—there you could look at a thing monstrous and free.' He even admits to responding atavistically to the spectacle of unchained nature. The sight and sound of savage dancing, so much a part of its primeval setting, awakens in him the sense of his 'remote kinship with that wild and passionate uproar'. As Lionel Trilling has pointed out,[5] this marks one of Conrad's more striking originalities, for whereas most of Conrad's contemporaries would have been moved by the primitive only as an idyll in the tradition of Rousseau, Marlow responds to it precisely because of its sheer savagery. In it he finds what he calls 'truth stripped of its cloak of time'—that is, a truth which antedates the truth that civilization has brought about, and which is therefore timeless or permanent. But what he goes on to do is even more striking. Having acknowledged that the primitive is fundamental, he at once sets up a contradictory truth: a man 'must meet that truth with his own true stuff—with his own inborn strength ... I hear; I admit, but I have a voice too, and for good and evil mine is the speech that cannot be silenced.' In this view, civilization is thought of not merely as a given, but as something achieved—something deliberately constructed and upheld in defiance of an elemental nature. This *antithetical* conception of reality—in which the recognition of a basic truth prompts the affirmation of a counter-truth—is at the centre of 'Heart of Darkness'. Without it one cannot fully understand the spectacular degradation of the Kurtz whom Marlow finally comes upon when he reaches the Inner Station. We have seen that what distinguishes Marlow from the Manager is his refusal to countenance the exploitation of the primitive; we now see that what differentiates him from Kurtz is his refusal to condone a surrender to the primitive. A man cannot shed his inheritance of civilization with impunity, for primitivism, like innocence, once outgrown or lost cannot be recovered. Kurtz has stripped himself of all the cultural values he took so ostentatiously into Africa. But he has not thereby regained the reality possessed by his primitive ancestors. Instead, he has, in Marlow's words, 'taken a high seat amongst the devils of the land' (p. 116). What exactly does this imply?

Like his meeting with the Manager, Marlow's meeting with Kurtz is preceded by an encounter with a subordinate figure—the Russian sailor who makes an even more unexpected appearance in the remote Upper Station than the Accountant did in the Lower (pp. 122–5 and 126–33). He has, incredibly, managed to survive the jungle—not, like the Accountant, by insulating himself, but by remaining completely incapable of registering experience. He too is defined by his attire—a brilliant harlequin's patchwork which suggests a man without a fixed identity. His extraordinary eagerness, his buoyancy, his childlike spirit of adventure seem to Marlow 'to have consumed all thoughts of self'. But this is not moral strength: it is moral naïveté. Hence, while it may enable him to survive the trials of Africa, it leaves him completely exposed to the influence of Kurtz. Marlow quickly discovers that he has become a kind of neophyte, and he asks him what Kurtz's talk is really like. 'It was in general. It made me see things—things.' This reply (which recalls the inexpressible yearnings of the crew of the *Narcissus*) indicates that the young man's enthusiasm is completely uncritical. Reflecting back on it, Marlow ominously concludes: 'He had not meditated over it.' Thus the disciple has no inkling of what is quite plain to Marlow: that in his reverence for his master he has crawled 'like the veriest savage of them all'. What price fidelity now? The riddle posed by the young Russian's navigation manual—which, when Marlow had chanced upon it downstream, had imparted both a 'delicious sensation' of reality by its content, and a feeling of bewilderment by its marginal glosses in 'cipher'—is now solved. At once recognizable and baffling, it marks the ambiguous condition to which the certainties of maritime service have been reduced.

Some critics have complained that Conrad has been insufficiently specific about the inconceivable ceremonies and nameless lusts to which Kurtz is supposed to have abandoned himself. Yet Marlow's encounter with the young Russian enables us to see that what finally damns Kurtz is not the horror of the shrunken heads which decorate his house, nor even the ferocity of his raiding excursions, but what these things indicate: the appalling fact that he has taken upon himself the role of God. This is tantamount to saying that he has entered into a state of final self-deception. In this, as the interview with the young Russian again suggests, Kurtz is the victim of his own gifts—specifically of the gift of speech. Of itself, expression is a fatally ambivalent power—an instrument of truth or of deceit. When Marlow, before his arrival at the Inner Station, has a premonition that he may not see Kurtz after all, he suddenly realizes the reason for his disappointment.

> 'The point was in his being a gifted creature, and that of all his gifts the one that stood out preëminently, that carried with it a sense of real presence, was his ability to talk, his words—the gift of expression, the bewildering, the illuminating, the most exalted and the most contemptible, the pulsating stream of light, or the deceitful flow from the heart of an impentrable darkness.'

('Heart of Darkness', pp. 113–14)

Without what Conrad calls impersonality—the moral capacity for resistance or restraint—the gift of speech can prove catastrophic. It enables Kurtz to establish an ascendancy over the blacks which the Manager, with all his rifles, cannot even remotely approach. At the same time it allows him to continue to believe in himself as the apostle of disinterested altruism. Unquestionable virtue added to inviolable power instantly produces self-deification. But although he may be very dangerous, this new god, being hollow at the core, is a complete sham.

Albert Guérard has argued that there is a contradiction in Conrad's presentation of Kurtz: that he cannot be both an evil man and a hollow man.[6] But this seems based on a misunderstanding, Kurtz is only hollow with respect to what he *says* he is; there is nothing insubstantial about what he *does*. Or, to put the matter in another way, he becomes hollow by virtue of his lack of moral identity; but he does not remain hollow. The vacated space, in obedience to a well-known law, is immediately filled by primitive powers—whether mounting from below or invading from without. Marlow's own diagnosis of the case seems unanswerable: 'Everything belonged to him—but that was a trifle. The thing to know was what he belonged to, how many powers of darkness claimed him for their own.' He who wants to be a god becomes a devil.

It is only in the context of Kurtz's self-deception—of his turning the gift of speech from a 'stream of light' into a 'flow . . . of darkness'—that Marlow's special insistence on the virtue of honesty makes proper sense. 'You know I hate, detest, and can't bear a lie, not because I am straighter than the rest of us, but simply because it appals me', he declares. 'There is a taint of death, a flavour of mortality in lies—which is exactly what I hate and detest in the world—what I want to forget (p. 82).' Kurtz is a living incarnation of everything Marlow claims to hate. His condition of dishonesty substantiates the view that lying is related to death, not only because his self-deception is the immediate cause of his collapse (one cannot pretend to be God without running certain risks), but also, more subtly, because it dissolves the substance of his moral identity (one cannot yield to one's instincts without falling into their power). That Marlow, therefore, should find himself obliged to go over to his side is an even stronger shock to his convictions than having to work for the Manager. It does not make him into a self-deceiver—any more than the Manager's incompetence rendered him inefficient. But, without doubt, it calls into question the point or purpose of his commitment to veracity.

It is Marlow's meeting with Kurtz that precipitates the decisive crisis of the book. As in *The Nigger of the 'Narcissus'*, a choice has to be made between two alternatives. But these alternatives no longer consist of men who affirm and men who deny the ideal of service. They are the Manager and Kurtz. Marlow's predicament is not unlike that of a member of the crew of the *Narcissus* who, having been abandoned by Alistoun and Singleton, is obliged to decide between Donkin and Wait. (The parallel is less fanciful than it might seem: for example, one of Kurtz's last remarks, 'This noxious fool [i.e. the Manager] is capable of prying into my boxes when I am not looking', brings to mind the moribund Wait's dispossession by Donkin.) The confrontation takes place after Kurtz has at last been stowed away into his cabin (pp. 137–8). The Manager, who knows now that his opponent is finished, tries to secure Marlow's support.

> " 'We have done all we could for him, haven't we? But there is no disguising the fact, Mr. Kurtz has done more harm than good to the Company. He did not see the time was not ripe for vigorous action. . . . I don't deny there's a remarkable quantity of ivory—mostly fossil. We must save it, at all events—but look how precarious the position is—and why? Because the method is unsound.' "

It is this final declaration that brings Marlow off the fence. What he cannot take is the reference to Kurtz's murderous raids. Looking at the shore, he asks: 'Do you call it "unsound method"?' And when he receives a hotly affirmative answer, his sole rejoinder is 'No method at all.' The Manager's complacent nihilism so revolts him that his thoughts turn towards Kurtz 'positively for relief': better moral collapse than sub-moral success. After his attempts to remain free of Company politics, he now feels obliged to declare himself. So, facing the Manager, he deliberately says to him: 'Nevertheless I think Mr. Kurtz is a remarkable man.' These words are a sentence of instant banishment. From now on he finds himself ostracized as an advocate of the party of 'unsound' method. This, obviously, is no great loss; however, that the only alternative to the Manager's unfeeling meanness should be Kurtz's megalomaniac raving is a very different matter. Marlow is under no illusions: what has been forced upon him is 'a choice of nightmares'.

Marlow's association with Kurtz produces the final stage of what one could term his ordeal by darkness. What it implies is brought out by an incident that takes place during the evening that follows his conversation with the Manager (pp. 140–5). Unable to sleep, Marlow looks into Kurtz's cabin and finds it vacant. After the first thrill of terror (Kurtz, it seems, can make even Marlow momentarily superstitious), he realizes that the sick man has managed to escape, and that if the expedition is to survive, he must be prevented from rejoining his tribesmen. Without betraying this absence to the sleeping guards ('it was written I should be loyal to the nightmare of my choice'), Marlow slips ashore by himself. 'I was anxious to deal with this shadow by myself alone', he explains, '—and to this day I don't know why I was so jealous of sharing with anyone the peculiar blackness of that experience.' Marlow may not know why, but Conrad makes sure *we* do. Marlow had been thinking of Kurtz as a potential ally; he now instinctively regards him as a sort of anti-self or inverted double. The essential difference between Kurtz and himself is not that Kurtz has been exposed to a different kind of temptation, but that, for all his gifts, he has proved incapable of restraint, and thus of fidelity to the values he has professed. What has finally counted with him is the gratification of his desires. Even his advocacy of civilized values has had no impersonal or objective foundation, but remained a mere self-indulgence, an expression of vanity or conceit. So in going after Kurtz, Marlow sets off in pursuit of what presents itself to him as his own antithesis; and the ultimate test of the wilderness comes to him as a confrontation, not directly with savagery, but indirectly with a ghastly parody of civilization.

When Marlow finally overtakes Kurtz crawling in the long grass towards the flicker of the camp-fires, he discovers to his horror that there is nothing in him to which he can appeal. Kurtz's solipsism has become so perfect that he seems to have 'kicked himself loose of the earth'—that is, to have lost contact with everything outside himself. Marlow is left with one last possibility: to 'invoke him—himself' directly, as one would invoke a god. Incapable as Kurtz is of seeing any contradiction between his words and his deeds, between his professed values and his actual practices, he remains a creature in conflict, torn between his 'European' ambitions and his 'European' fantasies, he alternately adores and abominates his barbaric existence, first launching his tribesmen into an attack against the steamer coming to deprive him of it, then persuading them to allow the rescuing party to take him away from it unmolested, then again—as now—irresistibly possessed of a fiery thirst for its lawless gratifications. So in the absence of any reason or morality in Kurtz, Marlow is obliged to appeal directly to that aspect of his self-love which makes him recoil from the primitive. He encourages him to indulge dreams of his 'immense plans'; he flatters him with the prospect of his success in Europe which 'in any case is assured'. Marlow has no doubt of what is really at issue in this struggle: it is more than survival—it is salvation.

> 'If anybody had ever struggled with a soul, I am the man [he tells his auditors]. Believe me or not, his intelligence was perfectly clear—concentrated, it is true, upon himself with horrible intensity, yet clear ... But his soul was mad. Being alone in the wilderness, it had looked within itself, and, by heavens! I tell you, it had gone mad. I had—for my sins, I suppose—to go through the ordeal of looking into it myself. *No eloquence could have been so withering to one's belief in mankind as his final burst of sincerity.*' [My italics.]

Up to the moment of Marlow's encounter with Kurtz, it is Marlow's strength, that is, his capacity to serve a moral idea, that the wilderness has challenged; what it now calls into question is his faith, that is, his capacity to believe in the value or meaning of such an idea. The very sincerity of Kurtz's belief in his humanitarian mission—in other words, the very completeness of his self-deception—provides an insane parody of the values for which Marlow stands. Faith in humanity, as it were, must look into a deranged mirror—and overcome the mocking image. For Marlow, to prevent Kurtz from returning to the jungle is not only necessary for his physical survival; it is also a last-ditch affirmation of the reality of the civilized against that of the primitive. His success in bringing Kurtz back to his cabin, therefore, is some sort of spiritual victory.

V

In thus committing himself to Kurtz, of course, Marlow is unable to affirm civilized values unequivocally. He has wrested Kurtz out of the clutches of the wilderness, but only in the name of his insane egoism. The humanitarian he now holds is a mere fake, sealed up in his self-deception by his self-generated eloquence. 'He could get himself to believe anything', says an admiring journalist after Marlow's return to Europe. But to believe anything is to believe nothing. What Kurtz endlessly says, whether to Marlow or to himself, is flatly contradicted by what he is. What then does Marlow gain by this nightmare alliance? Is an essentially empty affirmation of value, like Kurtz's, really preferable to the Manager's open cynicism? Is Marlow's claim that Kurtz is 'a remarkable man' really defensible? Just as Marlow is to remain faithful to Kurtz in his fashion to the last, so Kurtz finally vindicates Marlow's faith in him—although he keeps him in suspense, as it were, until his ultimate moment. The scene of Kurtz's death, and particularly his last cry, has become perhaps the most notorious crux of interpretation in modern literature; it is, however, not as problematic as it is commonly supposed to be.

'Anything approaching the change that came over his features I have never seen before, and hope never to see again. Oh, I wasn't touched. I was fascinated. It was as though a veil had been rent. I saw on that ivory face the expression of sombre pride, of ruthless power, of craven terror—of an intense and hopeless despair. Did he live his life again in every detail of desire, temptation, and surrender during that supreme moment of complete knowledge? He cried in a whisper at some image, at some vision—he cried out twice, a cry that was no more than a breath—

' "The horror! The horror!"

'I blew the candle out and left the cabin.' ('Heart of Darkness','p. 149)

It has sometimes been forgotten that this is not the only, or indeed the first, death that Marlow witnesses in 'Heart of Darkness'. There is the earlier killing of the careless and excitable steersman during the skirmish in the approach to the Inner Station (pp. 111–13). The parallel is quite explicit: as an 'improved specimen'—culturally disorientated too, in his way—the steersman 'had no restraint, no restraint—just like Kurtz—a tree swayed by the wind'. And although as he dies he does not actually say anything, he casts on Marlow a 'lustrous and inquiring glance ... like a claim of distant kinship'. The moment of death, it would seem, has a meaning that is relevant to all mankind. So that what the dying Kurtz perceives may not only be true of himself as an individual; it may also be significant for humanity at large.

We have to take the moment of death, then, as Marlow presents it: not as a cuase of terror, but as a condition for insight. As far as Kurtz is concerned, it is the instant in which, for the first and last time, he sees his past for what it has truly been; it is the point at which, in a rending flash, his values at last connect with his life and reveal it to be a 'darkness'. Retrospectively, Marlow finds this ultimate summing-up, in contrast to his own indifference as fever brings him close to extinction himself, 'an affirmation, a moral victory'. And he is right to do so, for by recognizing that the values to which he had paid lip-service apply to himself, Kurtz has made them real at last. The words with which he passes judgement on 'the adventures of his soul on this earth' are no longer merely pronounced, but meant.

But there is more. Kurtz has achieved self-knowledge: but thereby he has also achieved knowledge of mankind. His verdict against himself is also a verdict against human life. Looking back on Kurtz's death, Marlow concludes that the reason he can now affirm—and not merely gamble or speculate—that Kurtz was indeed a re-markable man is that he had something to say: that his final appalled stare 'was wide enough to embrace the whole universe, piercing enough to penetrate all the hearts that beat in darkness'. And what was it that Kurtz had to say?—'He had summed up—he had judged. "The horror!" ' Problematic as the further meaning of Kurtz's cry has proved, there are two things that can be confidently said about it. The first is that it records some sort of 'ultimate truth' about man; the second is that it implies that this truth is morally abhorrent.

One of the major assumptions on which 'Heart of Darkness' rests is that if we want to find out the 'real' truth about man—what his 'essential' nature is—we must inquire into his origins. This basically evolutionary view holds that civilization is something merely imposed on man's essential nature—that culture does not eradicate, but merely keeps in check, his primitive instincts. In this sense, Marlow's journey to the Inner Station—to the heart of the African darkness—is a voyage into his ancestral past; and what Kurtz in the end discovers for himself is what Marlow has already grasped: that the ideals of European life form no part of man's essential self—that the heart of the European citizen, for all the endeavours of his education, remains an abode of darkness. But this is only part of Kurtz's meaning. The rest is that this truth is a terrible one—that is to say, that the values it denies survive the denial, in the sense that they remain supremely important. According to this view, teleological rather than evolutionary, the 'real' truth about man is not merely where he comes from, but where he is going to: his 'essential' nature is not found merely by uncovering his past but also by defining his future. Thus civilization cannot be dismissed, as it were, as a defective actuality: it should more properly be regarded as a potential to be sustained, or a destination to be pursued. The criterion for reality is no longer existence, but possibility. Man's goals do not have to be realized in order to be made 'real': it is enough that they be taken seriously. That Kurtz's last cry should not have been 'a word of careless contempt' is, as Marlow emphasizes, a fact of supreme importance to him, for it proves that Kurtz—and again in this like Marlow before him—has felt the need, in the face of what he has at last recognized as darkness, for an alternative reality.

In a brilliant paragraph in his essay 'The Teaching of Modern Literature', Lionel Trilling suggests that Kurtz, in contrast to Marlow whom he calls 'the ordinary man', must be considered 'a hero of the spirit', for he has dared to venture beyond the security of permitted experience and thereby earned the right to pronounce judgement.[7] This comparison is suggestive, but it does not seem to me to be precise enough. Both Marlow and Kurtz end by perceiving the same thing: that so-called 'civilized' man, unlike (as we have seen) savages in a state of nature or (as we shall see) women in a state of innocence, is trapped between two antithetical realities. But their mode of perception is quite different. It is only in his relation to Kurtz that Marlow might be taken for the ordinary man; in relation to everyone else in the story he represents, surely the moral man. For him, the dual reality revealed by the test of the jungle poses a problem of conduct: in its aspect of primitive truth, it demands his courage, for it has to be outfaced; in its form of civilized goal, it requires his fidelity, for it has to be upheld. For Kurtz, on the other hand, this duality is not so much something to be dealt with, as something to be embodied or enacted. He *is*, on his death-bed, the horror he perceives. His last cry, like that of Faustus, is the cry of a man who can only learn what his soul is worth as he discovers that it is irretrievably lost, or of one who can only affirm moral value as he perceives that it cannot exist. If Marlow is the moral hero, Kurtz becomes, for a visionary instant, the tragic hero.

It would be a mistake, however, to conclude that 'Heart of Darkness' is an essentially tragic narrative, for it is finally Marlow, not Kurtz, who retains the centre of the stage. Marlow's story is one of survival. He has successfully endured the immediate onslaught of the jungle. But how is he going to adapt to its consequences? And in particular, how will he cope with the duality that has been revealed to him? It seems at first as if he opts for a cynical discounting of one of its imperatives. For almost a year after his return to Europe, he can scarcely endure the complacent certainties of his fellow-citizens. Their very normality, based as it must be on wholly untested assumptions of security and superiority, strikes him as derisory in its blindness. He seems well on his way to spurning every claim on behalf of civilization, when he is abruptly halted by an unexpected event—his interview with Kurtz's 'Intended' (pp. 154–62).[8] What disturbs him most about her is not that she is deceived about what Kurtz really is, but that her faith in him should be so disinterested, and her fidelity so unswerving. 'I perceived', says Marlow, with scarcely concealed consternation, 'she was one of those creatures who are not the playthings of time.' He cannot dismiss her with her compatriots as an 'irritating pretence'. Indeed, she constitutes, in what she is, a living reproof of every kind of cynical evasiveness.

Whether or not Conrad has sacrificed reality to symbol in his portrayal of Kurtz's Intended—as many have felt—there is no uncertainty about the problem she poses for Marlow. Her trustfulness earns her the right to be told the truth; yet the only truth there is for him to tell must destroy the basis of that trust. This is a knot that cannot be untied, but only cut. And this Marlow does by telling her a lie: by making her believe that Kurtz's fidelity to her—and so to the ideals she embodies—has shone untarnished to the very last.

All attempts to explain this act merely in terms of Marlow's compassion for her must remain unsatisfactory, for they fail to take into account its central irony—that the lie which concludes 'Heart of Darkness' is uttered by a man whom the entire narrative has taught us to regard as the very apostle of veracity. Marlow himself tells us that if he deceives her, it is not simply out of concern for her, but also out of concern for himself. This, rather than vulgar male protectiveness, is the real point of his subsequent reflections on the event. 'I laid the ghost of his gifts at last with a lie ... Did I mention a girl? Oh, she is out of it—completely. They—the women I mean—are out of it—should be out of it. We must help them to stay in that beautiful world of their own, *lest ours gets worse.'* [My italics.] For all his tone of retrospective—and offensive—self-indulgence, Marlow here presents his lie as the guarantor of a certain truth: it preserves intact the innocence of Kurtz's Intended. For a moment, as he senses the depth of her grief for the man she has loved, he sees two antithetical truths overlap: 'I saw her and him in the same instant of time—his death and her sorrow—I saw her sorrow in the very moment of his death.' Kurtz's vision of horror is not replaced by her pity, but it is in some sense exorcised by it. Kurtz's Intended offers Marlow an image of that ideal reality which his despair had latterly threatened to deny. But she can only continue to do so as long as she remains innocent of the actuality. As the narrative draws to its conclusion, this paradox is given an almost schematic representation. Marlow notices that, in all the purity of her sorrow for the ideal Marlow, she unconsciously mimics the equally passionate grief of the savage mistress to whom the real Kurtz gave himself in the depths of the African wilderness. Should the Intended once suspect this truth, she would instantly be deprived of all redemptive virtue, and find herself on a level with Marlow under the shadow of Kurtz's legacy. Marlow's lie, arguably itself an act of darkness, is also a means of keeping back the darkness.

The concluding episode of Marlow's narrative measures the full extent of the gap that separates the man who set out for his African ordeal, and the man who returned from it. The difference isn't that the latter renounces the principle of service, but that he now knows that it cannot be simply affirmed. If the world we propose to serve is found to be comprehensively corrupted, there would seem to be only two alternatives left to us, each equally unsatisfactory: to give way to the corruption and cynically abandon all notion of service; or to ignore the corruption and continue to uphold a now vacuous ideal. Faced by this choice, however, Marlow is able to discover a third alternative, perhaps less desperate than the other two in that it can preserve what we are and what we should be in some sort of connection with each other. Characterizing his attitude to Kurtz's Intended, he describes himself as 'bowing my head before the faith that was in her, before that great and saving illusion that shone with an unearthly glow in the darkness'. If service is to be vindicated, it can only be in terms of the concept of what may be called *positive illusion*. The girl's belief in the essential virtue of mankind, as instanced by her faith in her betrothed, is an illusion, for it is contradicted by the facts; yet it is not unreal, for it is held with all the force of a truly unselfish conviction. It serves to keep alive, in the darkness of Marlow's experience of actuality, the light of visionary purpose.

What the concept of positive illusion allows Marlow to do is to survive tragic knowledge without incurring self-deception—that is to say, to affirm the values of the active life without blurring his sense of its underlying contradictions. But it is more than the culminating idea of an extraordinarily complex and concentrated work of fiction. It is also one of the central preoccupations of the major works of the first half of Conrad's career as a novelist, enabling him to do full justice to the paradoxes within his own nature—to his urge towards scepticism and to his need for faith.

NOTES

The *Collected Edition of the Works of Joseph Conrad* (22 vols., J. M. Dent, 1946–54) has been used throughout.

[1] This famous narrative has provoked a mass of critical material, a good deal of which is irrational and self-indulgent. Some of it has been collected by L. F. Dean, *Joseph Conrad's 'Heart of Darkness': Backgrounds and Criticisms* (Englewood Cliffs, 1960); and by B. Harkness, *Conrad's 'Heart of Darkness' and the Critics* (San Francisco, 1960).
[2] *The Nigger of the 'Narcissus'*, p. 30.
[3] Ibid., p. 172.
[4] Cf. p. 114.
[5] Lionel Trilling, 'On the Teaching of Modern Literature', in *Beyond Culture*, originally published 1965 (Penguin, 1967), p. 32. The incident referred to is in 'Heart of Darkness', pp. 95–7.
[6] Guérard, *Conrad the Novelist* (Cambridge, Mass., 1958), p. 131.
[7] Trilling, 'Modern Literature', p. 33.
[8] See p. 115.

Ian Watt

MARLOW AND HENRY JAMES

It was in connection with *Heart of Darkness* that Conrad made what appears to have been his most explicit attack on symbolism in fiction. In 1902, when the publication in book form had provoked critical discussion in the public press and in his private circle, Conrad responded to a friend's objections to what he called "my pet Heart of Darkness" by allowing only one criticism: "What I distinctly admit is the fault of having made Kurtz too symbolic or rather symbolic at all."[1] Conrad may have found it easier—not for the first time—to avoid discussing adverse criticism by presenting himself as a much simpler kind of writer than he was. He certainly continued in this vein: "The story being mainly a vehicle for conveying a batch of personal impressions I gave the rein to my mental laziness and took the line of least resistance. This is then the whole Apologia pro Vita Kurtzii—or rather for the tardiness of his vitality."

That Kurtz comes late upon the scene, and that he then proves rather one-dimensional and theatrical has been widely felt; but Conrad's pejorative use of "symbolic" here seems to imply the fixed and limiting conception of the word symbol, according to which Kurtz would merely "stand" for some set idea or ideas. This sense is quite contrary to the larger ambitions of Symbolist theory, and so Conrad's comments do not really bear on the question of whether his intentions in *Heart of Darkness* were or were not close to those of the Symbolists. The general view that Kurtz is not very fully characterised, however, could be taken as in some sense confirming the Symbolist presence in *Heart of Darkness,* since the novels of the French Symbolists tend to centre so much on the inner life of the protagonist that the other characters do not emerge very clearly. Kurtz is the victim of a similar subordination; both the form and the content of *Heart of Darkness* are centered on the consciousness of Marlow, and so Kurtz, in effect absorbed into Marlow's subjectivity, can have no independent existence. For *Heart of Darkness* is a "roman de la vie cérébrale,"[2] to use the phrase which Rémy de Gourmont applied to his Symbolist novel *Sixtine* (1890); it largely conforms to what de Gourmont thought "the only excuse for a man to write": "to unveil to others the

From *Conrad in the Nineteenth Century* (Berkeley: University of California Press, 1979), pp. 200–214.

kind of world which he beholds in his own personal mirror";[3] and Conrad's agent for this unveiling is Marlow.

In the Author's Note (1917) to the volume in which *Heart of Darkness* appeared in book form, *Youth—A Narrative: and Two Other Stories* (1902), Conrad devoted three of his eight paragraphs to Marlow, "with whom my relations have grown very intimate in the course of years." The terms in which this intimacy is expressed are both ironic and touching: "He haunts my hours of solitude, when, in silence, we lay our heads together in great comfort and harmony." About the origins of their relationship, however, Conrad says virtually nothing; he merely disclaims having had any "meditated plan for his capture," and adds: "The man Marlow and I came together in the casual manner of those health-resort acquaintances which sometimes ripen into friendships. This one has ripened." Conrad is equally noncommittal about Marlow's literary function. He limits himself to reporting without comment that others had "supposed" him to be "all sorts of things: a clever screen, a mere device, a 'personator,' a familiar spirit, a whispering 'daemon.' "

We must then, enquire into Marlow's origins and functions without any help from Conrad; and one way to begin is to consider how Conrad had handled the narrative point of view in his earlier writings, and especially in those closest in subject or time to *Heart of Darkness*.

Conrad's early works mainly employ impersonal third-person narration, and he continued to use it when, after finishing *An Outcast of the Islands* late in 1895, he attempted a change to a more subjective theme in his unfinished novel "The Sisters." Its subject, the intellectual and spiritual history of an isolated individual, was somewhat similar not only to that of *Heart of Darkness* but to that of J. K. Huysmans's *A Rebours;* and like Huysmans and other Symbolist novelists, Conrad had used the impersonal, distant, and omniscient point of view which tended to discourage the reader's active participation in the inner life of the protagonist. "The Sisters" was also a tale of individual quest, and even had something of the esoteric religious overtones of the Symbolists. It opened, for example, with: "For many years Stephen had wandered amongst the cities of Western Europe. If he came from the East—if he possessed the inborn wisdom of the East—yet it must be said he was only a lonely and inarticulate Mage, without a star and without companions. He set off on his search for a creed—and found only an infinity of formulas."

"The Sisters" remained a fragment, and its failure must have influenced Conrad's development in many ways. Ford suggests in his introduction that Edward Garnett's very adverse criticism decisively turned Conrad away from "the misty problems of the Slav soul" and its "introspections passing in Paris," and set him firmly on the path of being an Anglo-Saxon novelist (*T S*, 29; 16). But it may be that the experiment also planted the idea that a different narrative point of view would be needed to "make us see" the individual's subjective life.

Between 1896 and the writing, some two years later, of the first two Marlow stories, "Youth" and *Heart of Darkness*, it is likely that the main innovations in narrative technique which influenced Conrad were those of Henry James.

Many critics have seen James as one of Conrad's masters; F. W. Dupee, indeed, calls Conrad James's "greatest disciple."[4] We know that Conrad had been an admiring reader while he was still at sea, and when *An Outcast of the Islands* came out, he thought of sending James a copy; but it was very difficult to pluck up courage. In one letter (16 October 1896) Conrad wrote to Garnett: "I do hesitate about H. James. Still I think I will send the book. After all it would not be a crime or even an impudence." Then, after two further letters from Garnett, Conrad finally announced (27 October 1896): "I have sent *Outcast* to H. James with a pretty dedication; it fills the flyleaf" (*E G*, 50; 54).

Conrad's self-mockery about the "pretty dedication" only partly prepares us for the lacerating embarrassment of its terms. The letter begins:

> I address you across a vast space invoking the name of that one of your children you love the most. I have been intimate with many of them, but it would be an impertinence for me to disclose here the secret of my affection. I am not sure that there is one I love more than the others. Exquisite Shades with live hearts, and clothed in the wonderful garment of your prose, they have stood, consoling, by my side under many skies. They have lived with me, faithful and serene—with the bright serenity of Immortals. And to you thanks are due for such glorious companionship.[5]

The effusions continue until the letter closes with Conrad asking James to accept his book, and thus "augment the previous burden of my gratitude."

One senses the paralysing apprehension of an insecure worshipper approaching a redoubtable deity, or of a lover whose very fear of rebuff invites humiliation. However, after some four months, James reciprocated by sending Conrad his just-published *The Spoils of Poynton,* with the characteristic inscription: "To Joseph Conrad in dreadfully delayed but very grateful acknowledgment of an offering singularly generous and beautiful" (*L L*, I, 201, n. 2). Then, a week later, on 19 February 1897, Conrad announced jubilantly to Garnett: "I had a note from James. Wants me to lunch with him on Thursday next—so there is something to live for—at last!" (*E G*, 76).

The meeting probably took place in James's London apartment—it is there that Conrad later remembered that he had chanced upon the Pepys epigraph for *The Nigger of the "Narcissus".* But it was only in October 1898, and in the period immediately preceding the composition of *Heart of Darkness,* that James and Conrad became neighbours; a period of quite close literary frequentation ensued. There is no question of Conrad's profound reverence for James's achievement. Conrad habitually addressed James, and James alone, as "cher maître";[6] one imagines that for Conrad the veteran writer who had been the friend of Flaubert and Turgenev was a captain under whom he would willingly learn the last secrets of the novelist's craft.

The period was a momentous one in the careers of both men. James, genial as never before, was producing the works which precede *The Ambassadors,* and in which his method of narration through the registering consciousness of one of the characters is already perfected—*The Spoils of Poynton* (1896), *What Maisie*

Knew (1897), and *The Awkward Age* (1898). Conrad, for his part, was finally turning away from the French influence, as James had long before. The first story which Conrad began after his meeting with James early in 1897 was "The Return." It had a somewhat Jamesian subject—"the fabulous untruth" of a society husband's "idea of life." In a letter to Garnett, Conrad analyses the failure of the story in somewhat Jamesian terms: "if I did see it [the reason for his failure] I would also see the other way, the mature way—the way of art" (*E G*, 94; 98); but if "The Return" taught Conrad any permanent lesson, it was probably that he should avoid the Jamesian subject matter.

There remained, however, James's narrative technique, and especially that of his most recent novels. There is no doubt that Conrad deeply admired *The Spoils of Poynton*. Ford reports "the rapturous and shouting enthusiasm of Conrad over that story," and suggests that it "must have been the high-water mark of Conrad's enthusiasm for the work of any other writer."[7] The possible significance of this for the development of Marlow is that *The Spoils of Poynton* is, as J. W. Beach called it, "the first absolutely pure example of the James method."[8] It was there that James developed the indirect narrative approach through the sensitive central intelligence of one of the characters. Technically this was halfway towards avoiding both the intrusive authorial omniscience of earlier fiction and the obtrusive detachment of Flaubert. James went only halfway because he usually retained a discreet form of authorial narrative, and both his selection of a particular registering consciousness, and the terms in which he presented it, implied the author's full understanding of that consciousness. But the psychological and moral effects of James's way of registering the experience of the novel as a whole through the subjectivity of a protagonist were enormous: our sympathetic and authorially-endorsed closeness to the inward fineness of Fleda Vetch in *The Spoils of Poynton,* or of Maisie Farange's groping awareness of the horrors of the adult world in *What Maisie Knew,* did much to counter the refrigerating tendency of third-person narration as Flaubert had developed it.

Several critics have suggested that Conrad may have developed Marlow from James's use of a central observer. William York Tindall, for instance, though un-willing to go so far as to see Marlow as "a kind of bearded Maisie,"[9] concedes that Conrad may have got a "possible hint" from James. There is some circumstantial support for this view. For one thing, Conrad, though very evidently a conscious artist, had paid little attention to technical consistency as regards narrative point of view in his earlier fiction; and for another, we know that Conrad noticed and admired the formal perfection of James's narrative technique in *The Spoils of Poynton* as soon as he read it. In a letter of 13 February 1897 to Garnett, he commented on the novel's transparency: "The delicacy and tenuity of the thing are amazing. It is like a great sheet of plate glass—you don't know it's there till you run against it. Of course I do not mean to say it is anything as gross as plate glass. It's only as *pellucid* as clean plate-glass" (*E G*, 74). As we have seen, notably in the case of Maupassant, Conrad carefully studied the technique of new novels that he admired. There is no such direct evidence of his technical study of James, perhaps because Conrad was now past his apprenticeship; but the possibility remains that it was Conrad's reading of James's current novels which influenced him in adopting the very different narrative method of his next works—"Youth," completed in the summer of 1898, and *Heart of Darkness,* completed early in 1899.

Conrad's use of Marlow, of course, has no equivalent in James: it represents, above all, a much more extreme and overt break with the distance, impersonality, and omniscience of third-person narration; and it does so in the interests of a dual concreteness of visualization—dual because Marlow not only tells us what he saw and heard in the past, but as readers we see him telling his auditors about it in the narrative present. With Marlow, in fact, James's registering consciousness is wholly dramatized as regards both the tale and its telling; it is also internalised in the sense that it is as fully adapted to the direct relation of the individual's inner thoughts and feelings as to the description of the external world. One way of summarising these aspects of the function of Marlow in *Heart of Darkness* would be to say that Conrad takes the impressionist direction much further than anything in James, and in a number of ways.

James and Conrad are both impressionists in one broad sense: as E. K. Brown puts it, their novels focus the reader's attention not on "what will happen, but rather with what the happening will mean to the principal character or characters."[10] But whereas James as author selects and orders the "meaning" of what happens, in the Marlow stories and especially in *Heart of Darkness,* Conrad lets his protagonist muddle out the meaning of his own experiences as best he can. This total subordination to the subjective limitations of the vision of one particular character is very different from James, and Conrad emphasises the limitation by giving both Marlow's personal presence and the occasion of his narration a fully described impressionistic particularity in space and time.

The external aspect of the polarity between the inner and outer world is much more marked in *Heart of Darkness* than in the other three Marlow tales; it is the only story which is told on board ship, and in a setting whose time and place—the coming of night on the Thames estuary—are themselves to become important elements in the narrative. The occasion is unique in another respect: the teller and his audience have been physically immobilised by the tide, and are isolated from all else; both circumstances favour intimacy of disclosure. This intimacy is also given a psychological basis: Marlow's hearers apparently know him well, whereas in "Youth" the narrator was not even sure how Marlow "spelt his name" (*Y,* 3). All these elements—the particularity of time and place, the physical isolation, the closeness of the group—combine to dramatise the telling; and the reader's attention is focussed on the physical immediacy of Marlow's presence as he sits far aft, cross-legged and leaning against the mizzenmast, with "an aspect of concentrated attention" on a face that is "lean ... worn, hollow, with downward folds and dropped eyelids" (46; 114).

Henry James was no admirer of Marlow as a character, or of *Heart of Darkness.* James would refer to him in conversation as "that preposterous master mariner" (*F M F,* 161); and Marlow is indeed difficult to believe in as a fictional character. He belongs to a class of one, a class composed of British ship's officers whose minds and interests have been produced by the unique circumstances of Conrad's own national and personal history; he emerges before us weighed down by the knowledge and experience of a lifetime, and yet devoid of a biography—no birthplace, no home, no school, no fixed social or domestic ties. But James's deepest objection to Marlow, however, was probably on technical grounds. In a diary entry of 5 January 1903, Olive Garnett reports Elsie Hueffer as telling her that James "objected to the narrator mixing himself up with the narrative in 'The Heart of Darkness' & its want of proportion; said that we didn't really get hold of Kurtz after all the talk about him, but said the Russian was excellent.[11]

James's phrase about Marlow's "mixing himself up with the narrative" surely discloses a myopic resistance to the technique of *Heart of Darkness* that only James's invariable veneration for his own methods can explain. But there are probably much larger considerations behind James's objections, considerations affecting his own theory and practice as regards two of the crucial structural changes that were occurring in the tradition of the novel: Conrad goes much further than James both in the abandonment of authorial omniscience, and in the related transition from a closed to an open fictional form.

Both James and Conrad were very much aware that the way a novel ended reflected a general view of life, and they broke with the traditional closed form of ending which attempted a complete resolution of the main problems of the novel's plot and characters. This is one structural aspect of Henry James's fiction which Conrad specifically endorsed. In a 1905 essay, Conrad wrote of how James had rejected "the usual methods of solution by rewards and punishments, by crowned love, by fortune, by a broken leg or a sudden death." This rejection, Conrad argued, involved a breach with the tradition of the novelist's god-like control of the life he portrayed:

> Why the reading public which, as a body, has never laid upon a story-teller the command to be an artist, should demand from him this sham of Divine Omnipotence, is utterly incomprehensible. But so it is; and these solutions are legitimate inasmuch as they satisfy the desire for finality, for which our hearts yearn, with a longing greater than the longing for the loaves and fishes of this earth. Perhaps the only true desire of mankind, coming thus to light in its hours of leisure, is to be set at rest. One is never set at rest by Mr. Henry James's novels. His books end as an episode in life ends. You remain with the sense of the life still going on.[12]

Conrad was surely right in assuming that Henry James had denied his readers the satisfying illusion that the conflicts of life could ever be completely or finally resolved; on the other hand James had nevertheless regarded it as part of the task of art to produce out of life's continuing conflicts and endless bewilderments the appearance of resolution and finality. This appearance was generated by the perfection of the novel's own intrinsic formal organization. James summed up the matter in the famour words of the preface to *Roderick Hudson:* "Really, universally, relations stop nowhere, and the exquisite problem of the artist is eternally but to draw, by a geometry of his own, the circle within which they shall happily *appear to do so.*"[13]

Conrad's praise of James had not suggested that his narrative technique as such incorporated the incompleteness of life; Conrad was, rather, recognising how James had represented the complexity and incompleteness of life in the content of his plot. The representation of life's incompleteness had also been an important part of Conrad's own aim in *The Nigger of the "Narcissus".* As he wrote to Garnett, it expressed "the incomplete joy, the incomplete sorrow, the incomplete rascality or heroism" (*E G,* 61); and it was this aim, Conrad thought, which had made it so difficult to bring his novel to "the end, such as it is." But in *Heart of Darkness,* Conrad took the incompleteness of the fictional action and the indeterminacy of its moral implications much further.

Most obviously, the whole structure of the tale rejects linear chronological development. In this respect *Heart of Darkness* is very different from "Youth": Conrad was aiming, he wrote in his Author's Note, at "another art altogether" which would produce "a continued vibration that, I hoped, would hang in the air and dwell on the ear after the last note had been struck." In more general terms Conrad uses Marlow to give his tale neither the full close of the plot of earlier fiction, nor James's more limited completeness in the formal structure, but a radical and continuing exposure to the incompleteness of experience and the impossibility of fully understanding it.[14] This has been recognised by Alan Friedman, who argues, in *The Turn of the Novel,* that Conrad goes far beyond his contemporary novelists in making his structure and his narrative point of view reflect "the progressive emergence of a finally open experience as normative for fiction.[15]

What Conrad called the omnipotence of the author can obviously affect both the substance of *what* happens in the novel and *how* the fictional happenings are told. Henry James may have been sceptical about the possibility of seeing a character completely, but the form of his fiction did not fully embody this doubt. James disclaimed authorial omniscience, in the sense that the narrative usually presented the characters mainly from the point of view of the effect they made on others; as Ezra Pound noted of *The Awkward Age:* "Only real thing the impression of people, not observation or real knowledge."[16] But the liberty which James allowed to the impressionist approach to reality was limited; although the events and characters in *The Spoils of Poynton* were presented through the sensibility of the heroine, Fleda Vetch, these contents had first been selected and ordered by the author; and we feel as we do with the clarifying and unifying focus of Strether in *The Ambassadors,* that the central intelligence has fused its multiple impressions of others into a single, coherent, and reliable report. In any case James does not give us the impressions of his central intelligence directly, but as they have been translated into the lucidity of his own analytic style, and given the relatively impersonal and authoritative status which is implied by the use of the *style indirecte libre.* As a result the narrative, to a considerable degree, gives an impression of "happily appearing" to achieve completeness and reliability.

James, then, found a way by which the central intelligence could take over much of the direct responsibility of the author, and yet achieve a work which was as susceptible to complete understanding by the reader as if an omniscient author had been there to explain everything. James's objection to Marlow's "mixing himself up with the narrative" was probably based on how Conrad, by taking the sceptical aspect of impressionism much further, and making the observer an inseparable part of what he observed, interfered with the final effect of order and lucidity in narrative which James continued to require. Marlow is certainly very different from the Jamesian central intelligence; in effect he embodies what James thought the two essential faults of the first-person method—"the terrible *fluidity* of self-revelation," and the fact that the narrating "I" has "the double privilege of subject and object."[17]

It is because Marlow has this "double privilege of subject and object" that the reader cannot see him as a fictional object very clearly. Marlow is in effect his own author, and so there is no reliable and comprehensive perspective on him or his experience. Conrad's scepticism about understanding character had not really been embodied in his fiction until *Heart of Darkness;* but there Marlow prefigures how the modern novel was to reject much more fully than did James the assumption of full authorial understanding, and, in its formal posture at least, restrict itself to showing an individual consciousness in the process of trying to elicit some purely relative and personal meaning from its experience. What Marlow says is not lucidly pondered but random and often puzzled, leaving contradictions unresolved and allowing the less conscious elements of the mind, including those of reverie and dream, to find expression. Conrad's version of the Jamesian registering conscious-ness, in short, does not, as it does in James, induce the reader to zero in from every point within the story to view its centre more clearly; and this lack of any authorised objective clarity is one reason why we see Conrad as decisively closer to us than James.

One must concede part of James's general argument against first-person narration; there is indeed a "terrible fluidity" about the multiple roles which Marlow plays, even if the frame of *Heart of Darkness* prevents it from being a first-person narrative in a strict sense. Any final comparative evaluation of the two methods must largely depend on the price we are willing to pay for formal perfection in art, and the exclusions it dictates. By making us marvel at each move in his narrative strategy, James makes us forget or forgive the exclusions which that strategy involves. Conrad, on the other hand, so hypnotises us with the wide-ranging urgencies of Marlow's voice that we hardly notice our increasing bewilderment at the almost unmanageable inclusiveness of what we are being left to piece together.

Behind this contrast there is another: Conrad did not share James's belief that the secrets of the art of the novel had at last been uncovered.[18] Like James and many of his French contemporaries, Conrad thought Naturalism was a dead end; but, unlike James, he felt that there was no other model in sight which offered much hope. Thus he wrote to an admirer in 1902: "I doubt if greatness can be attained now in imaginative prose work. When it comes, it will be in a new form; in a form for which we are not ripe as yet. Till the hour strikes and the man appears, we must plod in the beaten track." (*L L*, I, 308). Allowance must no doubt be made for the strategy of polite self-deprecation which leads Conrad to place himself in the ranks of the dull plodders; still, it is a fact that he never claimed to be an innovator, and tended throughout his career to play down his characteristic fictional methods as mere devices of the craft. His consciousness of that craft certainly fell far short of any fully conceptualised fictional system; and while this may have encouraged a freedom in yielding to unformulated intuitions that played a part in making us, three generations later, see *Heart of Darkness* in the perspective of a profoundly original anticipation of many of the formal, as well as the ideological, aspects of the modern novel, it also explains why it stands rather alone in the Conrad canon, and for reasons about which Conrad is almost entirely silent.

Conrad's use of Marlow in *Heart of Darkness*, then differs not only from James's narrative point of view in many important respects, but also from the other Marlow tales. Some of these differences point forwards: Conrad's retreat from the omniscient author is applied much more radically to his characterisation and his mode of narration, and through them to the meaning of the story as a whole. As several critics have noted, Marlow's role turns *Heart of Darkness* into a story about—among other things—the difficulty of telling the "full story."[19] This difficulty is latent in both the Impressionist and Symbolist doctrines. Marlow is obsessively aware of it. "No, not very clear" (51), he ruminates aloud as he begins to recall his experience, and later he is driven to conclude that it is "impossible to convey the life-sensation of any given epoch of one's existence—that which makes its truth, its meaning—its subtle and penetrating essence" (82). Marlow's ironic consciousness of how far he is from being able to tell "the full story," and the overt enactment of this within the novel, are two of the ways in which *Heart of Darkness* anticipates the unauthoritative, self-reflexive, and problematic nature of such later fiction as Kafka's novels and Gide's *Les Faux-Monnayeurs.*

These comparisons, however, are themselves reminders of how far scepticism is from being the only or even the main burden of meaning in *Heart of Darkness;* Marlow is also the means whereby Conrad incorporates three of the oldest, and predominantly affirmative, elements in storytelling: the narrator as a remembering eyewitness; the narrator as the voice of his author's opinions; and the narrator as a friendly personal presence.

The most obvious of these traditional elements derives from the way that Marlow functions as a more direct expression of the preoccupation with writing as the voice of memory that informs most of Conrad's earlier fiction. In this respect *Heart of Darkness* formally harks back to that most ancient of the forms of storytelling which begins "I remember"; and Conrad may have been influenced by a traditional Polish form of such tales, the *gawęda,* which is told by a clearly defined narrator, and is usually of a retrospective nature (*N*, 16–17). Conrad at first thought of entitling his projected collection of short stories, which would include "Youth" and *Heart of Darkness,* "Tales from Memory," because he wished "to convey the notion of something lived through and remembered" (*B*, 55). The kinds of memory in the two stories, however, were essentially different: in "Youth" memory is there mainly to give a nostalgic appeal to a story which is mainly told in a very traditional kind of way; but in *Heart of Darkness* memory is the means for depicting an intense confrontation of Marlow's past with his present; and the mood of that confrontation, as Conrad commented in his Author's Note, is "anything" but that "of wistful regret, of reminiscent tenderness."

The fact that Marlow is not the primary narrator, however, has the effect of giving him an objective status that is in accord with more recent modes of story-telling. It can, indeed, be argued that retrospection does not in fact involve a breach with the relativism of the more typically impressionist modes of modern fiction. Neither the immediate verbal rendering of sense impressions, nor the later development of the stream-of-consciousness novel, has any certain basis in experience; after all, no one has ever seen an impression, let alone a stream of them, and life offers no model for putting them into words. Memory is somewhat closer to our consciousness; and the act of putting memories into words is a common and observed phenomenon. Retrospective narration, then, though one of the oldest forms of narrative, has as good a claim to represent actual experience as more modern methods; and the way Conrad uses Marlow is peculiarly adapted to showing the individual engaged in trying to understand what has happened to him.

Conrad's use of Marlow as the voice of retrospection, then, combines old and new narrative methods. Marlow's memories of his lonely experiences on the Congo, and his sense of the impossibility of fully communicating their meaning, would in themselves assign *Heart of Darkness* to the literature of modern solipsism; but the fact that Marlow, like Conrad, is speaking to a particular audience makes all the difference; it enacts the process whereby the solitary individual discovers a way out into the world of others. One can surmise that Conrad found the narrative posture of moral and social neutrality intolerable; and so under cover of Marlow's probing of the meaning of the past, Conrad smuggled in the ancient privilege of the narrator by the backdoor, and surreptitiously reclaimed some of the omniscient author's ancient rights to the direct expression of the wisdom of hindsight.

Edward Crankshaw has argued that "Marlow was invented so that Conrad could moralize . . . freely without ruining his illusion . . . which was dependent on his, the author's, aloofness and impersonality."[20] Through Marlow, Conrad can unobjectionably express the sort of moral commentary on the action which had been proscribed by Flaubert and the purists of the art of the novel, and which had seemed somewhat obtrusive when Conrad did it directly, as he had occasionally in *The Nigger of the "Narcissus"*, for instance. But Marlow is much more than a device for circumventing the modern taboo on authorial moralising; he is also a means of allowing his author to express himself more completely than ever before; through Marlow Conrad discovered a new kind of relation to his audience, and one which enabled him to be more fully himself.

The first Marlow story, "Youth," was also the first story which Conrad ever wrote with a particular group of readers—that of *Blackwood's*—in mind. This defined audience may have given Conrad the initial psychological impetus towards dramatising a fictional situation in which a narrator rather like Conrad addresses an audience rather like that of *Blackwood's*. Marlow's listeners comprise a company

director, an accountant, a Tory lawyer, and a primary narrator, all of them ex-
seamen; in effect they are a composite of the two audiences Conrad had himself
encountered—those at sea and those he now visualised as his readers. The connection between the two audiences probably had its roots in Conrad's early years
in London, and the friends there who had provided him with a transition between
his lives on sea and on land. In the years 1890 to 1892 Conrad had done a good
deal of sailing, and no doubt yarning, in the Thames estuary aboard a crusing yawl;
he retained its actual name in *Heart of Darkness*, the *Nellie*; and though he did not
give the name of its captain and host, the *Nellie* in fact belonged to Conrad's old
friend Hope, who was indeed a director of companies (*S W W*, 122-24). Marlow
himself, of course, is also a composite, combining the two main roles in life that
Conrad had experienced—the seaman and the writer; and the moral perspective
which Marlow's commentary endorses is very largely the professional and social
ethic that he shares with his immediate audience.

At all events, through the presence of Marlow's companions on the *Nellie*, the
old friendly commerce of oral storyteller and the listening group is restored. This
commerce had already been implicit in "Karain," a story published in, though not
written for, *Blackwood's*. There Conrad made his first full use of a participant
narrator, an unnamed character who occasionally raised questions about the meanings and motives which the story involved; on one occasion he even steps out of
the frame to wonder about the reaction of his audience: "I wondered what they
thought; what he thought; ... what the reader thinks?" (*T U*, 52). This active
interplay between narrator and immediate audience is itself an image of the further
interplay which Conrad imagined between his story and its public; and it creates an
intimacy between author and reader of a kind that is surely unique in modern
fiction.

This intimacy of communication is notably absent in Henry James's *The Turn
of the Screw*, which has been cited as a possible influence on *Heart of Darkness*.[21]
There both the "I," the primary narrator, and Douglas, who tells the main story to
its "compact and select auditory," completely disappear once the governess's tale
begins; she has no audience, and since her written diary belongs to the past, it has
the kind of cold unanswerable authority which is automatically conferred when the
source of a story is beyond recall.

Marlow's living voice, and the congenial setting which awakens it, profoundly
affect the atmosphere of all his narratives. Henry James, writing in 1914 about
Chance, described Marlow as a "reciter, a definite responsible intervening first
person singular." But, as he went on to emphasize, Marlow was not just a reciter;
there was a personal and spiritual "residuum"; and the effect of that "residuum," as
James wonderfully put it, was not merely that "of such and such a number of images
discharged and ordered, but that rather of a wandering, circling, yearning imaginative *faculty*, encountered in its habit as it lives and diffusing itself as a presence or
a tide, a noble sociability of vision."

The eclectic insouciance of Conrad's use of Marlow goes far to justify Garnett's view that Marlow came into being because he "saved trouble" and "came

natural" to Conrad (*E G*, xxx); one can understand James's distaste for the infinite pluralism of Marlow's narrative functions. Still, for all his fastidious objections to Marlow as a character and as a method, Henry James, like countless readers, is eventually won over by Marlow's "noble sociability of vision."[22] James's phrase in effect recognises that Marlow is a persuasive fictional voice for that movement towards human solidarity which Conrad had affirmed as his essential authorial purpose in the preface to *The Nigger of the "Narcissus"*.

NOTES

Nearly all page references for quotations from Conrad are taken from *Dent's Collected Edition of the Works of Joseph Conrad* (London: J. M. Dent, 1946–55). Abbreviations used in the text:

B   William Blackburn, ed., *Joseph Conrad: Letters to William Blackwood and David S. Meldrum* (Durham, N.C.: Duke University Press, 1958)

E G   Edward Garnett, ed., *Letters from Conrad, 1895 to 1924* (London: Nonesuch Press, 1928)

L L   G. Jean-Aubry, *Joseph Conrad: Life and Letters,* 2 vols. (London: Heinemann, 1927)

N   Zdzislaw Najder, ed., *Conrad's Polish Background: Letters to and from Polish Friends,* tr. Halina Carroll (London: Oxford University Press, 1964)

N L L   *Notes on Life and Letters*

S W W Norman Sherry, *Conrad's Western World* (Cambridge: Cambridge University Press, 1971)

T S   *The Sisters: An Unfinished Story,* by Joseph Conrad, With an Introduction by Ford Madox Ford, ed. Ugo Mursia (1928; rpt. Milan: U. Mursia, 1968)

T U   *Tales of Unrest*

Y   *Youth—A Narrative; and Two Other Stories*

[1] Letter of Conrad to Elise Hueffer, 3 December 1902 (transcript courtesy of Frederick Karl).

[2] Cited by Kenneth Cornell, *The Symbolist Movement* (New Haven, 1951), p. 97.

[3] Preface, *Le Livre des masques: Portraits symbolistes* (Paris, 1923), p. 13.

[4] *Henry James* (London, 1951), p. 281. See also Leon Edel, *Henry James: The Master, 1901–1916* (Philadelphia and New York, 1972), p. 46.

[5] Dated 16 October 1896. I am indebted to Frederick R. Karl for giving me a copy of this letter, and to the Academic Center Library at the University of Texas for permission to publish part of it.

[6] G. Jean-Aubry, *Joseph Conrad: Lettres françaises* (Paris: Gallimard, 1929), pp. 34, 77; also in dedication copies to James. For the later development of the friendship, see Edel, *James: The Master*, pp. 47–56, and my "Conrad, James and *Chance*," in *Imagined Worlds: Essays on Some English Novels and Novelists in Honour of John Butt*, ed. Maynard Mack and Ian Gregor (London, 1968), pp. 301–22.

[7] Ford Madox Ford, *Portraits from Life* (Chicago, 1960), p. 11.

[8] Joseph Warren Beach, *The Method of Henry James* (New Haven, 1918), p. 233.

[9] "Apology for Marlow," in *From Jane Austen to Joseph Conrad: Essays Collected in Memory of James T. Hillhouse*, ed. Robert C. Rathburn and Martin Steinmann, Jr. (Minneapolis, 1958), p. 276.

[10] "James and Conrad," *Yale Review* 35 (1945): 265.

[11] Thomas C. Moser, "From Olive Garnett's Diary: Impressions of Ford Madox Ford and His Friends, 1890–1906," *Texas Studies in Literature and Language* 16 (1974): 525. James thought "The End of the Tether" the finest of the three stories in the *Youth* volume; it was the only one using third-person narration.

[12] "Henry James: An Appreciation," 1905 (*N L L,* 18–19).

[13] Preface to *Roderick Hudson* (Henry James, *The Art of the Novel,* ed. R. P. Blackmur [New York, 1934], p. 5).

[14] See Elsa Nettels's fine recent study, *James and Conrad* (Athens, Ga., 1977), especially pp. 65–66.

[15] *The Turn of the Novel* (New York, 1966), p. 99.

[16] "Henry James and Rémy de Gourmont," *Make It New: Essays* (London, 1934), p. 287.

[17] *Art of the Novel*, ed. Blackmur, p. 321.

[18] Michel Raimond, *La Crise du roman: Des Lendemains du Naturalisme aux années vingt* (Paris, 1966), pp. 25–43.

[19] Most recently, Tzvetan Todorov, "Connaissance du vide," *Nouvelle Revue de Psychoanalyse* 11 (1975): 145–54.

[20] *Joseph Conrad: Some Aspects of the Art of the Novel* (London, 1936), p. 73.

[21] Edel, *James: The Master*, pp. 54–55; and Roger E. Ramsey, "The Available and the Unavailable 'I': Conrad and James," *English Literature in Transition* 14 (1971): 137–45. In view of James's resistance to *Heart of Darkness* there is a nice complementary irony in Conrad's unenthusiastic comment on *The Turn of the Screw:* it "evades one, but leaves a kind of phosphorescent trail in one's mind" (*L L*, vol. 1, p. 256).

[22] *Notes on Novelists, with Some Other Notes* (New York, 1914), pp. 347; 350–51.

Garrett Stewart

LYING AS DYING IN
HEART OF DARKNESS

It is indeed impossible to imagine our own death; and whenever we attempt to do so we can perceive that we are in fact still present as spectators.   —Freud, "Our Attitude towards Death"

Lying is dying. So says Marlow, and so Conrad is out to demonstrate, even at the expense of his own narrator. "There is a taint of death, a flavour of mortality in lies" (p. 27), [1] Marlow announces early in *Heart of Darkness,* but the final words he quotes from himself in the novel—his consoling statement to Kurtz's devoted fiancée that her lover expired uttering her name—constitute his own lie about a dying man's last words. Thus lie's fatal taint makes rot even of a man's deathbed integrity. It infects and cancels that unflinching power of speech at mortality's point of no return which Conrad calls in *Lord Jim* the "triumph" of expression "in articulo mortis" (p. 233; Ch. xli), his own expression evoking the English word "articulation" as well as the Latin idiom for "turning point." The full import of Marlow's self-indicting charity is bound to elude us if the imagery of death has not been carefully logged. *Heart of Darkness* is the deviously mapped quest for a sequestered space beyond geographical coordinates, a recessed sector of the soul to which only death, firsthand or secondhand, can guarantee passage. Negotiating the further transit from Kurtz's renowned deathbed utterance to Marlow's appended lie (itself, as I try to show, an indirect death scene), detecting the continuity between main plot and coda, is one of the most troublesome maneuvers in Conrad studies. Yet taking the scent of lie's taint, as it emanates from the symbolic corpses and metaphoric decay that litter the course of the story, is the best way of tracing Conrad's equation of death and deceit. Whether political, moral, or psychological, mendacity is the most mortal of sins, against ourselves and others. Although Marlow equivocates, Conrad is there behind him to warn us that the lies of Western idealism mislead us to death.

The plot of *Heart of Darkness* is in part a political autopsy of imperalist myths.

From *PMLA* 95, No. 3 (May 1980): 319–31.

A level-headed seaman named Marlow, teller of his own tale, journeys to the Congo as steamer captain for a European trading company; hears rumors about another agent of the company, an eloquent mastermind named Kurtz; later discovers that the man has submitted to, rather than suppressed, the natives' savagery, with its hints of cannibalism and sexual license; finally meets up with Kurtz, remaining by his side to hear the man's deathbed judgment on his own degeneracy and diabolism; and then returns to Europe to lie about Kurtz's "worthy" end in order to give the man's fiancée something to live for and with. Marlow's trek toward Kurtz, first by water, then by land, is made now in the wake of a generalized epidemic of death, now in the footsteps of walking specters: a dead march to the heart of a defunct and festering ideal of European superiority. Though the novel's "adjectival insistence,"[2] which so famously annoyed F. R. Leavis, centers nowhere more relentlessly than on permutations of "dark" and "deadly," "tenebrous" and "moribund," the effect is one not so much of morbid atmospherics as of moral asperity, an attack on death-dealing imperialist motives and the truths they obscure.

Heart of Darkness harkens back to origins. It suggests that a naked exposure of the human ego, unshielded by civilization and its self-contents, to a world of savagery presumed to be far beneath it is, in the long evolutionary run, only a baring of the soul to the most primally rooted human impulses. To plumb the native is to come up against the innate, apart from all cultural or racial demarcations. Even before Marlow begins his African narrative proper, he ruminates that the Thames, on which he and his fellow seamen are traveling, has also been, as far back as the Roman colonization, "one of the dark places of the earth" (p. 5). Apropos of the story to come, this initial sense of a primordial blackness triggers an association, more than gratuitous, with "death skulking in the air, in the water, in the bush. They must have been dying like flies here." In Roman England under the pall of colonization, yes, just as in Africa, where Marlow found everywhere "the merry dance of death and trade . . . in a still and earthly atmosphere as of an overheated catacomb" (p. 14), where trade rivers were "streams of death in life" (p. 79).

Beyond the sinister topography of the African landscape, which lays bare the inevitable brutality of imperialism as itself a mode of death, Marlow has also faced his own private demise in an embodied omen. On leaving the company offices in Europe, he must pass by those black-garbed, knitting women, the sibylline harpies and harbingers of death, to whom departing agents seem to sense as the appropriate valediction "Morituri te salutant" (p. 11). As one about to die, or narrowly to skirt his own death, Marlow shortly after encounters two European predecessors, predeceased, on his way to what he calls (recalling a metaphor from its grave) the "dead center" of Africa. First he hears reports of the anonymous Swedish captain who "hanged himself on the road" (p. 79)—no one knows exactly why, but no one is surprised—and later he learns certain details about an earlier Nordic fatality, the Dane Fresleven, who was Marlow's immediate predecessor in the post of company agent and who was conveniently murdered by a representative of the jungle so that Marlow could step "into his shoes" (p. 9). Marlow, sensing the mortal stakes in his adventure and unwilling to content himself with the mere report of Fresleven's death, searches out the corpse in the jungle, become by now a skeletal memento mori with grass growing through its ribs.

Marlow therefore achieves in life what the rest of us receive from such stories as the one he spins: he procures an intuition of his own end in the doom of a surrogate. Yielding us the "warmth which we never draw from our own fate,"[3] or in Conrad the chill of recognition, the death scene is art's perpetual bequest to life, though its insights may too easily be forfeited. One of the chief motives for a death scene in literature is thus in *Heart of Darkness,* and never more so than with the final death of Kurtz, devolved on a character within the fiction, indeed the narrator, who gravitates to the death of the Other, first with the nameless Swede and much more urgently with the murdered Fresleven and then twice later, as we will see, to savor the extremity otherwise unavailable to consciousness. The reader, through character—as Marlow, through rumored dooms, skeletons, finally dying men—comes within the safe proximity of his or her own end, a death by imaginative proxy. To vary Shakespeare, in art we ruminate our ruin at one remove, as Marlow's mortuary agenda so complexly exemplifies up to, and even after, his own feverish brush with death following immediately on the death of Kurtz.

Kurtz himself is introduced as the barely living fulfillment of the mortal fate of Marlow as contemplated through his double, Fresleven—though such thoughts hover at the level of mere foreboding, without as yet any explicit parallel between Marlow and Kurtz, except that they are both European agents in Africa. When Kurtz makes his long-delayed appearance Marlow describes him too, like Fresleven, as a skeleton, "the cage of his ribs all astir, the bones of his arms waving" (p. 60). In a scene that looks forward to the remarkable epiphany in *The Magic Mountain* where Hans Castorp sees latent within him, by way of an X ray, his own corpse, Kurtz as breathing skeleton keeps company with the remains of Fresleven as a death's-head memento mori. As Kurtz emerges from his blankets "as if from a winding-sheet" (p. 60), his moribund condition is also personally retributive, an oblique revenge on himself, as arch imperialist, for those untended dying natives in that "grove of death" (pp. 17–18) Marlow had earlier come on, all of whom were reduced to skeletal "bundles of acute angles." In tandem with this ironic reprisal for Kurtz—the witherer withered—is another symbolic pattern of poetic justice, for Kurtz has also been shriveled to an image of the precious corrupted element, the cold ivory, in which he has traded and debased his humanistic ideals. The mania for this dead bone strikes Marlow from the first as having a "taint of imbecile rapacity" like (as with lying for that matter) "a whiff from some corpse" (p. 23), and when Kurtz appears on the scene to personify that greed, his all-but-fossilized being seems like "an animated image of death carved out of old ivory" (p. 60).

Even before Kurtz's first onstage appearance a premature and precipitous description of him as a breathing corpse broke into Marlow's chronological narrative, providing a glimpse of the story's haunted destination. Marlow cannot keep down the need to tell his auditors in advance that the visionary encounter with genius he had gone in search of would never be more than spectral—the eviscerated Kurtz reduced, by the time Marlow first sees him, to a disembodied voice in a "disinterred body" (p. 49). Exploring Marlow's preoccupation with Kurtz *as voice* leads us to recognize the logic of such a premature intrusion, for it argues the deepest logic of the novel's first full-dress death, which frames this premonition, the wordless end of a subtly partial doppelgänger for Marlow and Kurtz together in the former's native helmsman. Marlow can share in Kurtz's slaying self-knowledge because "it"—what was left of the man, his neutered "shade" or "wraith" (p. 49)—"it could speak English to me. The original Kurtz had been educated partly in England." Thus Conrad quietly implicates England, and Marlow as Englishman, in Kurtz's European hubris and diseased idealism—and of course implicates himself, too, as British-educated master of nonnative English eloquence. I introduce Conrad's famed English, not just Marlow's expert storytelling, because the local stress on the risks and responsibilities of rhetorical power seems to broaden outward into a comment on the dark expressiveness that brings us the story in the first place.

Marlow admits that his grandiose expectations of Kurtz center on the man's vocal eloquence, for "I had never imagined him as doing, you know, but as discoursing. . . . The man presented himself as a voice," possessing as his only "real presence" the "gift of expression, the bewildering, the illuminating, the most exalted and the most contemptible, the pulsating stream of light or the deceitful flow from the heart of an impenetrable darkness" (p. 48). Marlow realizes the double nature of language, its power to illuminate and ennoble but also to corrupt, and he imagines Kurtz as a disembodied annunciation of this very duality. Kurtz's wasted person when finally encountered bears out this sense of him as language incarnate, for his flesh has withered to the bone, leaving only a speaking soul, a direct effluence from the heart of darkness. And it is a death scene, as so often in literature, that will finally put to the ironic test this power of eloquence. It is important to note, also, that we have a piece of transcribed as well as merely rumored eloquence that ties Kurtz not only to Marlow as a speaking "presence" but again to Conrad, this time as author. Before returning to the narrative of the trip upriver, Marlow slows to summarize a report Kurtz had written for the International Society for the Suppression of Savage Customs; even here the dangerous underside of rhetorical flourish is apparent: "It was eloquent, vibrating with eloquence, but too high-strung . . . a beautiful piece of writing. . . . It made me tingle with enthusiasm. This was the unbounded power of eloquence—of words—of burning noble words . . . the magic current of phrases." Kurtz exposes the danger of the verbal genius that delivers him to us as a prose incarnation, for at the end of his manuscript he had scrawled into view that darkheartedness which, like his greatness, is charged by the current of his magniloquence, though rendered now in a sudden truncation of all burning and burnished phrase: "Exterminate all the brutes!" Rhetorical sonority in a moral vacuum boils down to a curt, criminal injunction, and the dream of piercing eloquence that Conrad shares with Marlow, especially in this most "high-strung" and overwrought story, and that both share with Kurtz, an eloquence obsessively stressed in this digression, stands confessed in its essential emptiness. Voice must mean what it delivers, and even Marlow as narrator here—though not Conrad, who is an ironic step or two to the side—protests too much in his brooding reiterations.

To follow Conrad more deeply into the relation of voice to death and darkness, we must note the strategic location of this digression on Kurtzian verbal virtuosity. Closing off the intrusive reverie, Marlow writes: "No, I can't forget him, though I am not prepared to affirm the fellow was exactly worth the life we lost in getting him" (p. 51). He is referring to his murdered helmsman, a man of no words at all lanced to death in a native attack meant to keep the rescue party from removing Kurtz. "I missed my late helmsman awfully. I missed him even while his body was still lying in the pilot-house." Despite Marlow's deep-seated racism, death solidifies the sense of human commonality, for stabbed through the side, the otherwise negligible "fool-nigger" suddenly "looked at me over his shoulder in an extraordinary, profound, familiar manner, and fell upon my feet" (p. 46). It is the "familiarity" of a soul that knows its own death in the common body. The nameless savage, civilized only enough to enable him to serve the mechanical function of steering, has no English in which to voice the mysteries of his injury and his death. Yet even untutored mortality has its voiceless eloquence: "I declare it looked as though he would presently put to us some question in an understandable language, but he died without uttering a sound. . . . Only in the very last moment, as though in response to some sign we could not see, to some whisper we could not hear, he frowned heavily." Death speaks to, but not through, him an unspeakable something, the whisper of incommunicable revelation, and the resulting frown "gave to his black death-mask an inconceivably sombre, brooding, and menacing expression"—that last noun used in only one of its senses and awaiting completion in the articulate death of Kurtz. Kurtz too has his facial expressions carved in the death mask seemingly hewn of his coveted ivory, but he dies vocally transmitting, as well as receiving, the "whisper" from beyond. The moment of death for the helmsman is precisely marked by a transition in the prose across one of Conrad's most stunning flourishes of the "gift of expression." In this jungle world where death is so treacherously slurred with life, where the landscape itself evinces a Coleridgean "life-in-death," the syllabic momentum of Conrad's studied euphony smooths and blurs one noun into its stretched sibilant antonym, the stare of life into the blank of death: "The lustre of inquiring *glance* faded swiftly into vacant *glassiness*" (my italics). But one death, so vividly imagined and so final, immediately leans forward to become the preview of another.

Almost at once, by a deviously pertinent non sequitur, Marlow adds to the pilgrim at his side: "And, by the way, I suppose Mr. Kurtz is dead as well by this time." So begins the frenetic early digression on Kurtz and on the fear of a lost opportunity for an audience with him, imagined only as an audition of his voice in the aftermath of the helmsman's voiceless demise. Just as Marlow is changing the subject—or is he?—from one certain death to a probable one, he is tearing off the shoes filled with the blood of the helmsman who fell at his feet, imploring but mute, as if in a last brotherly supplication. Certainly we are to recall the dead Fresleven and Marlow, on that earlier captain's death, stepping "into his shoes." Now it would seem that Marlow's own life's blood has been shed into them in a symbolic blood brotherhood with his pilot that amounts to a sudden doubling at the point of death. If we assume Conrad is preoccupied with such secret sharing as part of a coherent symbolism in this story, we must begin to range and discriminate Marlow's dead or dying doppelgängers. At first almost a matter of statistical survey or impersonal backdrop, then slowly driven home, even internalized, the surrogate deaths gather step by step toward an excruciating revelation.

En route, the death of the helmsman is an important and rarely discussed middle term. Immediately after the conjecture of Kurtz's probable death, Marlow returns to the death of the pilot to suggest a closer tie than expected between himself and his helmsman: "... for months I had him at my back—a help—an instrument. It was a kind of partnership. He steered for me—I had to look after him" (p. 52). One is brawn, physical instrumentality, the other percipience and concern; one muscle, the other mind; and death serves to distinguish, but at the same time to bond, them "like a claim of distant kinship affirmed in a supreme moment."

When we note later that the same phrase, "supreme moment," is used for Kurtz's death (p. 71), we have the parallel unmistakably confirmed. Providing a cool head to Kurtz's tortured soul, Marlow pilots for Kurtz as the helmsman has done before for Marlow. The psychological crux here is a vexing crisscross of doubles that lingers in the imagination until it sorts itself into shape. Though allegory may seem too bald a term for the nested subtleties of Conrad's elusively apportioned psychology, some appreciation of pattern on our part is essential.

If Kurtz is the heart or soul of darkness repressed beneath the accretions and delusions of civilization, what is Marlow's relation, obsessive as it is, to Kurtz? As organizing and expressive consciousness, passionately desirous of the Kurtzian eloquence so as better to tell the Kurtzian secrets, Marlow is mind—we might say ego or even superego—to an id identified with those dark lusts in the jungle. When Kurtz tries to return to the jungle, Marlow must prevent him. Mind must detect and control the unconscious atavistic urges, repress the regressive. This is what Marlow indirectly admits when he has caught up with the escaping Kurtz in the underbrush: "Soul! If anybody ever struggled with a soul, I am the man" (p. 67). Of course many have had such conflicts, but usually with their own soul. In the psychic scheme of this novel, however, all things external seem to radiate from Marlow as percipient center, even the jungle incantation in this very scene, for "I confounded the beat of the drum with the beating of my heart, and was pleased at its calm regularity" (p. 66). But only Kurtz knows the true rhythms of that native darkness and embodies them symbolically as the objectified buried interior of Marlow's consciousness. In the introduction to a joint edition of this novel and "The Secret Sharer," Albert Guérard points out that Conrad's departure from such classics of doppelgänger fiction as Poe's "William Wilson" and Dostoevsky's *The Double* reflects a shift away from the pattern whereby "the second selves of the heroes are embodiments of the accusing conscience."[4] Instead, the Conradian double tends to embody a "more instinctive, more primitive, less rational self," a relation in which the helmsman certainly stands—and falls—to Marlow. So too with Kurtz in relation to Marlow, though at the last moment the unconscious life does seem to spew forth a voiced conscience, accusatory and horrible. Interested also in the doppelgänger, Richard Ellmann has suggested that we might go outside the narrative to see Kurtz as a shearing off of one part of Conrad, whose Polish name Korzeniowski abbreviates by transliteration to Kurtz.[5] When Conrad in *Heart of Darkness* decided to test such delvings and divisions of self against its ultimate cancellation in death, however, he inserted the helmsman as the middle term that would help render such death in its twin definition—physical mortality as well as the closure of consciousness—and thus augmented the allegory of his terminal partnerings.

The helmsman, Kurtz, and Marlow form a triangle of body and soul equidistant from the overseeing mind. A mere "instrument" of the white imperialist, yet a physical tool rather surprisingly missed when his awareness has vacated the body, the helmsman is the animal, or preconscious, side of Marlow, primitive but no more initiated into darkness, perhaps, than Marlow. His going is the death of the body, mortality at its lower common factor, in which the "distant kinship" claimed for the first time is merely the fraternity of those who, born for death, are thus, regardless of color, human. Death democratizes as it levels, the corpse of the Other becoming the body of a brother. First a skeleton in tall grass, now a bodied but speechless demise, soon the death throes of an almost incorporeal eloquence: these are the stages of Marlow's face-to-face confrontation with mortality, one on one, or one on naught.

For this confrontation, the "whisper" that registers as a glint in the helmsman's eye must eventually be given voice, even if it is "The horror! The horror!" that Kurtz "cried in a whisper" (p. 72). Since, in his murderour panic to remain behind, the ailing Kurtz must have seen his desperate unfitness for return both to civilization and to its curative ministrations, must have known that the life he lowered himself to in the wilderness had slain his European illusions and had spelled death all along, the final welling up into utterance of his self-denunciation is not only belated but posthumous. Like spiritual corpses before him in Dickens, George Eliot, and Hardy, Kurtz dies offstage just moments after his last words. (We must wait for the manager's black servant to stick his head in the cabin door and say—with "scathing contempt" but, because of his untrained grammar, without the verb of being that lends paradox to most predications of death—"Mistah Kurtz—he dead.") Direct representation of demise would be redundant for this "disinterred" wraith, whose terminal disease had long before done its worst.

The symptoms of Kurtz's jungle fever are, like the words that punctuate its final stage, a direct tapping of spiritual essence. Though understated in its allegorical causation, his is one of those classic deaths of the literary tradition whose etiology wavers between physiology and symbolism. Not only did he live a spiritual death, but the death he dealt to others returns to him with the gruesome suitedness of his physical end. We have watched allusions accumulate from the start to the traditional effect that as he has slain, so he is laid low; as he lusted, so death covets him. When we first see him he is wasted to the inanimate matter of his obsession, his face an ivory death mask; the maker of skeletons and corpses, he is collapsed now to a heap of bone. Morally as well as bodily the jungle has claimed him, and its endemic death now overmasters him by punitive reversal: Africa "had taken him, loved him, embraced him, got into his veins, consumed his flesh, and sealed his soul to its own by the inconceivable ceremonies of some devilish initiation" (p. 49). His terminal sickness is merely the pathological insignia of his soul's disease. Kurtz dies lingeringly of a fever contracted at the heart of the primordial. Something he encounters there meets no resistance, immunological or spiritual; it first inflames, then gradually emaciates him, eating him up from within. This contact is one of the overdetermined weddings of medicine and morality against which, once they become more than a literary figuration, Susan Sontag rails so passionately in *Illness as Metaphor*.[6] They are, of course, the very lifeblood of classic fictional dying, where dramatic sense must be made from the onset of mortal absence.

With just this purpose in mind, Marlow comes to the death of Kurtz with expectations fashioned by myth or literature or both: "Did he live his life again," Marlow asks in one of the clichés of extinction, "in every detail of desire, temptation, and surrender during that supreme moment of complete knowledge?" (p. 71). Kurtz himself has another mortuary formula haltingly in mind just before the end, not Marlow's "drowning man archetype" but another facile parallel between life and its end: "I withdrew quietly, but I heard him mutter, 'Live rightly, die, die...' I listened. There was nothing more." To such swallowed clichés has Kurtz's superb rhetorical gift dwindled. We struggle to recognize a stuttered version, caught in Kurtz's throat, of some balked orthodox formula like "Live rightly, die rightly"— sacred to religion as well as to all those nineteenth-century fictional deaths by aesthetic predestination. Only the converse (if any such formulaic correspondence) could be true for Kurtz, and full fictional honesty demands that, live however you have chosen to live, the fact is simply that you die, not crystallizing your raison d'être but canceling it. Kurtz, knowing this no doubt, cannot get beyond the predication of death—"die, die," the broken record of a broken soul. Yet he is still struggling to sum up in his scorching last words, "The horror! The horror!" The whispered repetition raises for us an even more teasing question: Why twice? Is there a thanatological recipe present here too? "He had summed up—he had judged. 'The horror!'" Both summation and judgment are comprehended in that single word, repeated in Kurtz's actual words once for each—the horror that has been perpetrated, the horror that descends as judgment, either in this pitiless and empty death or in whatever damnation there could be to come. Not until the coda of the novel, when the horror is deceitfully expurgated only to grin from the very depths of its denial, will the full doubleness of its reference be implicitly whispered.

Contaminated by the "horror," Marlow himself shortly falls ill and nearly gets himself buried along with Kurtz, but instead of focusing on his own near death, Marlow insists that "It is his [Kurtz's] extremity that I seem to have lived through" (p. 72). The idiomatic preposition "through" reminds us that only another's death can be undergone without finality, lived up to the moment of and worked past to its other side. And this is for Marlow, of course, not displacement or evasion, at least the first time around, for Kurtz's soul is not some phenomenon entirely removed from him. Allegorically, if we may say so, Kurtz *as soul* represents—below the level of the still-repressive consciousness for which Marlow *as mind* has stood—the buried anguish and guilt of Marlow's own soul, as the helmsman had earlier stood for, and in the stead of, Marlow's bodily self in his multistaged encounter with oblivion. In his book on Conrad's relation to autobiographical narrative, Edward W. Said suggests that *Heart of Darkness* exaggerates the entire first-person mode to a crisis point, where the reportorial or ruminative impulse no longer has the benefit of retrospect. Drawing on Schopenhauer, Said writes that the "only possible meeting between thought and action is in death, the annihilation of both. For the mind to accept death as a solution of the difficulty would be to accept the devastating irony that permits the destruction of the consciousness, the only faculty capable of enjoying the solution."[7] Conrad's early tales instead, according to Said, "posit a compromise in which the agent usually dies . . . and the reflecting mind continues still uncertain, still in darkness." The mind, miraculously sustained beyond the symbolic death of body and soul, remains puzzled with the potentially creative questioning of artistic distance. Again we must note the emphasis on voice, on the articulated end of experience that provides the matter of reflection. Kurtz's death before the eyes and especially the ears of Marlow is best read as the death not of a man alongside a man but of a tragic agonist in the presence of a receptive, if finally too timid, interpreter. One student of Conrad has suggested that Kurtz evokes "from the sensitive Marlow feelings akin to the traditional emotions of pity and terror."[8] Death is cathartic; it boasts the revelatory "compression" (Marlow's own term) of literature pitched to its "supreme moment," where the consciousness, of reader or audience or here "partner," can move, instructed but unconsumed, through the death of the Other.

If this weathering of death by a double were advanced as a *modus moriendi* in life, however, rather than in tragic art, a basic premise of existentialism, as phrased in emphatic italics by Heidegger, would be directly violated, for "*No one can take the Other's dying away from him*" (Heidegger's italics).[9] Death is undeflectably one's own, for its "end" has a teleological component that is irreducibly private, the coming from potential into presence, always final, of being's fullness—for Kurtz that complete, and completely recognized, "horror," a corruption damningly one's own even while universalized. Kurtz therefore projects the latent predilection of the human race for darkness, a prepossession that when ripened to completeness becomes the very definition of death, the end (to vary Heidegger's "being-toward-death") of a tragic being-toward-darkness. In a characteristic run of ontological argot, Heidegger sums up the principle of mortal individuality by saying that "coming-to-an-end implies a mode of Being in which the particular *Dasein* [roughly "Being"] simply cannot be represented by someone else" (p. 286). Yet what is true existentially, true to life, cannot be true to art, or art would fail us precisely where we most need the intervention of a shaping consciousness. Art's tragic figures must die for us, and for Marlow in our place.

The notion that Kurtz elicits from Marlow the "traditional emotions of pity and terror" that, say, Kurtz or Faust or any other tragic figure evokes in us as audience is developed at some length in Murray Krieger's valuable chapter on Conrad in *The Tragic Vision*. For Krieger, "*Heart of Darkness* is effective as an ideal archtype of the literature of the tragic vision, giving us an exemplary version of the relations between representatives of the ethical and of the tragic realms." By his "relation to Marlow," that is, Kurtz becomes in his fatally concentrated self-revelation "an allegory of the role that the visionary and the literature in which he figures are to play for those of us who are interested but not ourselves committed totally."[10] Marlow is entirely aware, too, of the role he has assigned to his articulate double as doomed visionary, even as we note how throttled and nihilistic is Kurtz's so-called tragic recognition. Death by proxy, terminal vantage through a ritual scapegoat, may be entirely a literary invention, but it is one Marlow tries hard to validate from his experience, for it alone offers him a model of death with understanding, however horrible, to contrast with the nonepiphanic pallor of his own approach to the brink:

> I was within a hair's breadth of the last opportunity for pronouncement, and I found with humiliation that probably I would have nothing to say. This is the reason why I affirm that Kurtz was a remarkable man. He had something to say. He said it. . . . True, he had made that last stride, he had stepped over the edge, while I had been permitted to draw back my hesitating foot. And perhaps in this is the whole difference; perhaps all the wisdom, and all truth, and all sincerity, are just compressed into that inappreciable moment of time in which we step over the threshold of the invisible.   (p. 72)

Marlow, the moral consciousness who dips into the heart of tragic darkness but returns on guard, thus embodies what Krieger calls "the ethical resistance to the tragic" in which "moral strength resides" (p. 155). I should like soon to qualify this statement, for the tragedy in *Heart of Darkness* and the irony seem more pervasive than Krieger believes, Marlow's admirable "restraint" more like repression and delusion. Nevertheless, Kriger's point about the central dichotomy between moral percipience and tragic vision is well taken. It suggests that the order of art attempts to soften existential extremity by molding it to understanding and, further, that death by proxy may be taken as a test case for the entire narrative and dramatic enterprise, the knowing voice transmitting visionary experience into the receptive mind as the essential transaction of all fictional tragedy.

If Marlow is no more than an eavesdropper on tragedy, our mediator between visionary depths and the everyday, then the considerable number of critics who find him receiving Conrad's unqualified assent, even in his supposedly benign final lie, would be correct. Marlow, who aligns lies and death in his own mind, knows better. On any reading of the novel, one understands Marlow's awe at Kurtz's deathbed pronouncement, but why should the Marlow of majority opinion be at all dismayed that he too, no more than nearing that "last opportunity" for statement, could not muster Kurtz's extremity of self-judgment? Why should a man of complex ethical sensitivity who has "kept his head" through demonic tribulations feel diminished by comparison with a life so singlemindedly surrendered to blackness that a reverberating disyllable, like Keats's "forlorn," can toll its retribution? Or we can put the question another way: In this allegory of "homo duplex"—to use the term that Edward Said fitly borrows from Conrad's letters[11]—how lightly can we afford to take a doubling of the climactic denomination, "The horror! The horror!"? Not only a dead echo within the soul but a resonance with the darkness outside, in another dichotomy not only summation but also judgment, this doubleness seems further to indict both parties at the scene, Kurtz as well as Marlow—passing judgment on the former's exaggeratedly depraved soul, but only as it concentrates the potential horror of "all the hearts that beat in the darkness."

And perhaps there is one final doubling of "the horror" to consider, when Marlow lies to Kurtz's Intended that "The last word he pronounced was—your name." That we never know her name, so awkwardly withheld from the reader, that indeed her title "Intended" seems to incarnate in her all the original Kurtz's best blind intentions, admits her even more readily than otherwise into the sphere of his searing universal revelation: the horror in me (as Kurtz might have said), the horror in all, even in her, the nameless abstract ideal. A lie that would liquidate the tragedy, Marlow's fib exposes the lie of idealism that generates it. Marlow himself, however, has a lesser motive in mind when he falsifies Kurtz's death. Criticism often senses something vaguely contaminating as well as consoling about this lie, but what is *mortal* about it goes undiscussed. As I hope now to show, Marlow's last words about Kurtz's last words are the death knell of his own tragic apprehension, the squandering of Kurtz's delegated revelation on a squeamish deceit. They signal, in fact, some measure of the very death of self Marlow thought he had slipped past, for that "flavour of mortality" in lies leaves its acrid taste throughout the last scene.

Given what we know of Marlow's ultimate attitude toward the Congo experience, the surprise is that criticism can so widely persist in thinking Marlow's whitewashing capitulation merely a white lie, a sacrificial violation of his own spiritual insight out of humanist charity. When he pontificates early on about lie's taint, the point is hammered home as a personal revulsion. Lying "appalls me"; it is "exactly what I hate and detest in the world"; it "makes me miserable and sick, like biting into something rotten would" (p. 27). One must doubt whether it could be simply for the solace of another that he later submits himself to his spiritual death. His strict ethical theorem, the equation of death with lying, is even in the early context no stray remark, for it threads untruth to death in the causal nexus of the European experience in Africa. What dying and lying have in common is that they both induce decay, the psychic moribundity and physical decomposition visible everywhere on that colonized landscape we traverse on our way to the death of Kurtz. The novel's largest lie is the one that premises its experience: the ultimately self-revenging hubris of imperial impulse. The question is what degree of collusion in this untruth Marlow, long its implicit critic, ultimately allows himself to take comfort in.

Against the muddied tide of critical opinion, Eloise Knapp Hay, writing about the political novels of Joseph Conrad, has helped us to see how the political self-deception of Marlow serves to discredit him as a morally reliable narrator.[12] For though we read the novel as a progressive disclosure of European delusions in

Africa, we must recall that Marlow's words of introduction are uttered from the vantage of retrospect, uttered and thus undercut. Having seen the darkness at the heart of Europe's colonizing onslaughts, he can still say, with a combination of political acuity and idealistic confusion: "'The conquest of the earth, which mostly means the taking it away from those who have a different complexion or slightly flatter noses than ourselves, is not a pretty thing when you look into it too much. What redeems it is the idea only. An idea at the back of it; not a sentimental pretence but an idea; and an unselfish belief in the idea—something you can set up, and bow down before, and offer a sacrifice to. . . .' He broke off" (p. 7). Despite his witnessing to the inevitable corruption that comes from white imperialism, Marlow would seem to be saying that without "selfishness" Kurtz could have succeeded, and yet the very claim is demolished by the religious imagery of bowing and sacrificing. Idealism degrades itself to idol worship, as we know from the perverse exaltation and adoration of Kurtz in the jungle, his ascent to godhead.

The inbred spoilage of an ennobling ideal was also sketched out with the first jungle victim we heard about in any detail, the Danish captain Fresleven, who began as "the gentlest, quietest creature that ever walked on two legs" (p. 9). Yet he was murdered by a native while "mercilessly" beating an African chief over some misunderstanding about two black hens. After all, Marlow says without surprise, "He had been a couple of years already out there engaged in the noble cause, you know, and he probably felt the need at last of asserting his self-respect in some way." Thus is the nobility of the white man's grand burden sapped and trivialized. Marlow's parenthetical "you know" (such things taken for granted by us far-thinking Europeans) teeters uneasily between sarcasm and apologetics; Marlow himself is unsure how to feel about his beloved idealism, however fine and selfless, when it can be so readily undermined, here and of course with Kurtz, by eruptions of the ego in sadistic self-assertion. Indeed Kurtz seemed at first the very embodiment of this "noble cause," but too much its incarnation in the long run, too little its acolyte. If Kurtz somewhere held to any glimmer of his original "idea," he must have lost sight of it entirely amid the blackness of his end. Does Marlow mean to imply, however, that Kurtz is the kind of "sacrifice" the idea deserves? Surely Kurtz died in the name of his idea's death, not its perpetuation, died at the hands of his own traitorous neglect of the ideal. There are, Marlow is so far right, purposes in themselves sublime, but when they are implemented by persons in power the danger is always that others will be sacrificed to the ghost of idealism's grandeur, cannibalized by its rhetoric and its personal magnetism. Bowing down, we tend to give up our vigilance. In line with the imagery of adoration, Marlow himself is twice described in the prologue as an inscrutable effigy, first with a posture and complexion that "resembled an idol" (p. 3) and later, just before his defense of imperialism, with "the pose of a Buddha preaching in European clothes and without a lotus-flower" (p. 6). His own person partially incarnates that idolatry masquerading as an almost religious truth—in another key. Kurtz's idealism turned demonic— which is the monitory center of his tale. Though Marlow knows the evils of white suppression at first hand, he represses them far enough from consciousness to leave continued space for the European idealism he still shares with "the original Kurtz."

Recognizing this, we are a far cry from the sympathetic treatment given Marlow's lie about Kurtz's sustained greatness in the most recent, and on this point not untypical, book about Conrad: "Marlow's lie to her, strain as we may, obstinately remains an ordinary white lie, a humane expression of compassion without devious moral implications and by no stretch of the imagination can we regard it as evincing a form of corruption of his part."[13] H. M. Daleski is thus taking direct issue, and he means to, with Conrad's own statement that in "the last pages of *Heart of Darkness* . . . the interview of the man and the girl locks in—as it were—the whole 30,000 words of narrative description into one suggestive view of a whole phase of life, and makes of that story something quite on another plane than an anecdote of a man who went mad in the Centre of Africa."[14] To side with Conrad against many of his critics in this is to note, for one thing, Marlow's often discussed view of women as cocooned dreamers whom a touch of reality would wilt. Though on the one hand this helps explain his eagerness to protect the Intended from the truth, on the other hand Marlow should have learned better—given another woman he has met—by the time he sees Kurtz's fiancée. When the Intended wails her disbelief in Kurtz's absolute absence, Marlow joins her silently in this faith in the man's perpetuity: "I saw him clearly enough then. I shall see this eloquent phantom as long as I live." But his specter is, to use Conrad's suggestive language, "locked in" also to Marlow's haunted vision of the Intended and of another dark woman superimposed on her image, Kurtz's black liaison from the jungle: ". . . and I shall see her, too, a tragic and familiar Shade, resembling in this gesture another one, tragic also, and bedecked with powerless charms, stretching bare brown arms over the glitter of the infernal stream, the stream of darkness" (p. 78). When this sentence is followed immediately by the Intended's ambiguous intuition about Kurtz's death, the feminie pronoun itself is rendered ambiguous by the narrative's overlapping of two spectral images, as if the black (or brown) soul mate is whispering a cryptic truth through the tremulous voice of the white woman's delusion. We have just heard about the tragic African shade, and then: "She said suddenly very low, 'He died as he lived.'" Two "she"s obtain, one obtruding from the past, to reinforce both the Intended's myth and at the same time the darker reality that Kurtz's "tenebrous" consort in the jungle had no reason to doubt as he was torn from her.

Marlow has seen two colors of the feminine heart and thus of the human heart artifically construed as Other. But the Intended carries her savage sister inside her, just as Marlow envelops Kurtz. Dark truth lurks beneath blanching delusion, and both women, copresent in the narrator's mind's eye, are ill-consorted emanations of Marlow as well as Kurtz. Marlow's early allusion to Brussels as "a city that always makes me think of a white sepulchre" (p. 9) comes entirely clear only after we have grown to recognize Kurtz as the personified corpse of the *civis* and its hypocrisy; Marlow, returned to the "sepulchral city" (p. 72) as if for entombment himself, washes it the whiter with the bleach of deceit in the course of his lying interview with the Intended. We now see his previous remark about defending female illusions more clearly too as the self-protective gesture to which he briefly admits even during his much earlier allusion to the Intended: "Did I mention a girl? Oh, she is out of it—completely. They—the women I mean—are out it—should be out of it. We must help them to stay in that beautiful world of their own, *lest ours gets worse*" (p. 49; my emphasis on Marlow's revealing afterthought). When Marlow reflects at the end, in his own final words to us, that the alternative to his lie "would have been too dark—too dark altogether," he is speaking not only on her behalf but on his own, in rebuttal to the tragic truth vouchsafed to him in Kurtz's death and repressed in Marlow's own approach to that end, as well as being repressed, by timid necessity, in his subsequent return to civilization.

Marlow repeatedly describes his experience in Africa, and especially with Kurtz, as a "nightmare," and this is never more telling a metaphor than in Marlow's drawing back from the ultimate fate of Kurtz. Psychological truism has it that we never dream our own death, even in the worst of nightmares—that we always wake to consciousness within an inch or so of the abyss. So with Marlow's nightmare. We can neither dream nor, according to Freud, even force ourselves to imagine with any cogency our own demise. Marlow, therefore, must wake up from another's fatal nightmare just in the nick of time's tilting over into eternity. Only later is the lie of idealism unconsciously resurrected from its own death scene in order to be traded on as the barter of return, the inevitably exacted price of repatriation to the European community. Kurtz's revelation is a sweeping death sentence, the end point of an asymptotic nightmare that Marlow holds off in order to come back and go on. Kurtz's abject but profound darkness dims to a "grey skepticism" in Marlow that is not only the trivialization but the very ticket of return.

If, back at the sepulchral hub of Europe, the Intended's dark counterspecter, that feminine apparition from our savage source, might only be held to a shadowy depth that does not impinge so remorselessly on consciousness, the woman of Faith might still manage to embody for Marlow an ideal he could "bow down before," offer his own misguided and mortal "sacrifice" to in the form of that deadly lie. As he said earlier of Kurtz: "I laid the ghost of his gifts at last with a lie." These gifts of insight into darkness must be laid to rest, or else Marlow would have nothing left to revere. Kurtz's revelation of "the horror" is fatally incompatible with genuflection. Since we know that Marlow's own idol-like person seems an outward sign of such internalized idealism, internalized at the expense of full truth, we sense the relfexivity: "bowing my head before the faith that was in her, before that great and saving illusion that shone with an unearthly glow in the darkness, in the triumphant darkness from which I could not defend her—from which I could not even defend myself" (p. 77). With devious valor, however, he attempts this self-defense, and by preserving such a feminine dreamworld he hopes to prevent his own from "getting worse," making good the grammatical and psychic parallelism in "defend her . . . defend myself." For Marlow (to risk again the boxing off of a more expressive complexity) is ultimately homo quadruplex, a wholeness reified into the mental powers of assimilation (as well as repression) played off against lower and would-be higher functions: mind against body in the helmsman, heart or soul in Kurtz, and finally a supervening and repressive Faith in the Intended. In this fourfold "allegory," eventually unfolded, she represents pure idealist intentionality preserved against the corrosive truth of experience, but preserved by being interred along with the buried truth in a sarcophagal unreality.

Daleski follows his critique of Conrad's coda with this sentence: "Consequently, it is difficult for us to make any meaningful connection between the lie and death" (p. 75). But we are now in a position to make this connection amid the metaphors of spiritual deadlines and posthumous defeatism that litter the coda as much as they do the tale itself. Marlow's untruth is lethal precisely because it kills the meaning of a death. There is a corollary to the proposition that lying is a kind of dying. Truth, even grapsed only in death, is a defiance of death, a notion hallowed in Britich fiction's treatment of demise. Kurtz's self-realization, about the "horror" his life and death would have epitomized, rendered his image deathless in the mind, a perennial admonishing phantom, except that the lie kills it. Partly to abet Marlow in this homicidal denial, two of the most trusted mortuary formulas of fiction, each a version of death by epitome, are invoked with some verbal and thematic deviousness in connection with Kurtz's death, one early, one late. When Marlow realizes that the name Kurtz, meaning "short" in German, is belied by the man's considerable height, he says—as if forgetting (because wanting to, no doubt) the cauterizing truth telling of Kurtz's last utterance—that "the name was as true as everything else in his life—and death" (p. 60). Marlow's own retrospective account seems colored, obscured, by the late meliorating lie eventually summoned to slay Kurtz's black epiphany. Marlow does, however, recognize the "true" consonance of Kurtz's life and death in another sense, for the persistent specter of Kurtz's ghost calls up this postmortem observation: "He lived then before me; he lived as much as he had ever lived ... a shadow darker than the shadow of the night" (p. 75). Ghostliness is at one with his ghastly aura in life. There is further evidence in the coda that Conrad, if not Marlow, has the mortuary tradition in literature specifically in mind, with its often rigorous equations between death and identity. When, hoping for solace, the Intended clutches at the time-tested heroic prescription, "He died as he lived," Marlow's mock iteration, "His end was in every way worthy of his life," not only secretly reverses the moral judgment implicit in her faith, even as he preserves some of that faith for her and for himself, but helps us see the additional irony to which Marlow, in the throes of untruth, is no doubt blinded. The epitomizing apothegm of death is traditionally phrased with a change in tense—"He died as he *had* lived"—with pluperfect brought to perfection (in the existential sense) in the preterit. The Intended, however, has unwittingly summarized the nature of a corrupt life coextensive with death and equivalent to it: the long-pending end of a man who, again, "died as he lived." Living a lie of moral superiority, lies being deadly, Kurtz died *while* he lived ("as" in this sense), his death scene true to life in its very deadliness. What Céline would call "death on the installment plan" is, however, a truth about Kurtz that is itself sabotaged and assassinated.

An equally mordant telescoping of tense arrests us in the most curious passage in this coda, where Marlow seems more than usually aware that his words may fail to capture his only half-glimpsed purpose: "For her he had died only yesterday. And, by Jove! the impression was so powerful that for me, too, he seemed to have died only yesterday—nay this very minute. I saw her and him in the same instant of time—his death and her sorrow—I saw her sorrow in the very moment of his death. Do you understand? I saw them together—heard them together" (p. 76). Her black-draped mourning is Kurtz's darkness visible; her untarnished faith is the lie overlaying his fatal eloquence. For her Kurtz died yesterday, while for Marlow, who somewhere knows the truth, he dies in the instant, every instant, of her deluded mourning, in which Marlow now colludes. The faith Marlow so sustains, in and through its feminine vessel, is a faith that kills, that denies the tragic content of the death scene—as if Kurtz himself had not inched over the edge into revelation. And so in Marlow's mind's-eye vision—a palimpsest of mourning superimposed on simultaneous death—Kurtz's *present* deathbed, symbol of the present murder of his very meaning, and the Intended's immolation on the bier of his memory are, after all, "locked together." They give us death's poisonous aftertaste in the mouth of untruth. If this is an even bleaker reading of the story's denouement than usual, at least it seeks to respect the tragic potential of the previous climax, the legacy of insight willed by a cruel but lucid death.

For in the Intended's dedication to Kurtz's misunderstood and idealized shade there is, we come finally to see, a heart-denying lie that is equivalent to the death it euphemizes, a lie that rests at the heart of the death it originally causes. In short, such faith in moral supermen breeds the death of its own heroic avatars in their all too human incarnations. Marlow cannot separate the black of Kurtz's end from that of his fiancée's mourning, because he uses her suffering as an excuse to deflect the full import of the former tragedy, reducing it to futile pathos. This vicious circle is imaged as an almost hallucinatory superimposition, her continuing grief over and above her idol's recurring death. And it renders sickeningly visible the link between death and delusion just before the sustaining lie is tendered. If we can answer affirmatively Marlow's "Do you understand?" then this appalling double image becomes the symbolic configuration of death as lie incarnate, corpse and killing delusion seen in line with the same vanishing point, spiritual negation zeroing in on a void.

NOTES

[1] Conrad, *Heart of Darkness*, ed. Robert Kimbrough (New York: Norton, 1963). Subsequent references are to this edition. The quotation from *Lord Jim* is also from the Norton Critical Edition, ed. Thomas C. Moser (New York: Norton, 1968).

[2] Leavis, *The Great Tradition* (London, 1948; rpt. New York: New York Univ. Press, 1964), p. 177.

[3] Walter Benjamin, "The Storyteller," *Illuminations*, ed. Hannah Arendt, trans. Harry Zohn (New York: Schocken Books, 1969), p. 101.

[4] Guérard, Introd., *Heart of Darkness* and *The Secret Sharer*, Signet Classics ed. (New York: New American Library, 1950), p. 11.

[5] Ellmann, *Golden Codgers: Biographical Speculations* (New York: Oxford Univ. Press, 1973), p. 18.

[6] Sontag, *Illness as Metaphor* (New York: Farrar, 1978).

[7] Said, *Joseph Conrad and the Fiction of Autobiography* (Cambridge: Harvard Univ. Press, 1966), p. 113.

[8] Paul L. Wiley, "Conrad's Skein of Ironies," originally published in Kimbrough, ed., p. 226.

[9] Martin Heidegger, *Being and Time*, trans. John Macquarrie and Edward Robinson (1927; rpt. New York: Harper, 1962), p. 284.

[10] Krieger, *The Tragic Vision: Variations on a Theme in Literary Interpretation* (New York: Holt, 1960), p. 155.

[11] Said, *Beginnings: Intention and Method* (New York: Basic Books, 1975), pp. 104, 130.

[12] Hay, *The Political Novels of Joseph Conrad: A Critical Study* (Chicago: Univ. of Chicago Press, 1963); see esp. Hay's treatment of Marlow's lie, pp. 150–54.

[13] Daleski, *Joseph Conrad: The Way of Dispossession* (London: Faber and Faber, 1977), p. 75.

[14] Letter to his publishers, William Blackwood, 31 May 1902; quoted by Daleski, p. 73.

Benita Parry

LORD JIM

Conrad's reference to *Lord Jim* as a free and wandering tale may seem an improbable description of a work that unsparingly engages with the ideological origins and political uses of moral precepts, but it is suggestive of the generous and inquiring outlook produced by the novel's expansive narrative structure. Within the matrix of the fiction's polymorphous discourse, an ethical debate between the sanctions upholding conventional mores and the entitlement of heterodox postures, and in which both sides assume the legitimacy of the given social order, is interpenetrated and transcended by an enveloping ontological discussion where the drive for an alternative condition is articulated and the idea of a differently constructed culture projected. Thus a consciousness fixed on problems of conduct within the existing social world meets with the utopian aspiration after realising other forms of value, and the visible triumphs of the performance principle are dwarfed by the hopes of the visionary imagination. The effect of this dialogue is to interrogate a range of assumptions fundamental to the official ethos; however, this tendency is arrested when the text legitimises imperialism's formal suppositions by locating the source of moral consciousness in obedience to the spirit of a mystically conceived homeland and seeking to identify the saving impulses redeeming a heartless and conscienceless project.

To this extent the novel remains connected with the dominant mode of thought; where it stands on independent ground is in revealing the concealed premises of imperialism's philosophical foundations, moral injunctions and authorised ways of seeing, for that which in *The Nigger of the 'Narcissus'* is consigned to the periphery of the fiction's vista and disallowed by the terms of its colloquy, is the subject of mediation in *Lord Jim*—the political functions of moral absolutes, the mutability of fixed standards, the urgent claims of natural impulses, the case for regarding the pursuit of an ideal condition as a spiritual imperative. When Marlow speaks out for those 'moments of awakening' that transform consciousness, he

From *Conrad and Imperialism: Ideological Boundaries and Visionary Frontiers* (London: Macmillan Press, 1983), pp. 76–98.

delivers a protest against the repression of sensibility and the atrophy of vision which in *The Nigger of the 'Narcissus'* would have resounded as a call to rebellion, eliciting the execrations of the narrative voices and causing Marlow to be cast in the role of a seditious intruder. This affirmation of areas of experience disparaged by the other work is transmuted in the dichotomous imagery of light and dark where the sunshine displays the meanings acquired through rational cognition, and the dim light of moon and stars illuminates the realms of unconscious being, and if Marlow in conformity with his inherited beliefs and professional training denigrates the last for giving 'a sinister reality to shadows alone' (p. 246), he also, when analysing his paradoxical response to Jim, endorses the necessity of embracing both domains: 'He appealed to all sides at once—to the side turned perpetually to the light of day, and to that side of us which, like the other hemisphere of the moon, exists stealthily in perpetual darkness' (p. 93). It is this rejection of the severance between reason and instinct, thought and feeling that it transfigured in the protean form of Patusan's hills which from one aspect appear separated by a deep fissure and from another can be seen to be a single formation split in two by a narrow ravine 'with the two halves leaning slightly apart' (p. 220).[1]

Yet any interpretation of the novel as a univocal critique of imperialist ideology[2] must overlook the multiple and incompatible meanings that can be constructed from a text which dramatises the conflicting demands of constraint and freedom, conformity and individual conscience, responsibility to the laws of order and progress and fidelity to an unlicensed visionary faith, allegiance to tradition and commitment to a restructured future. In the absence of one omniscient viewpoint the interlocution of narrative voices constitutes the fiction's organising principle, and within the development of the moral and philosophical arguments, the eponymous anti-hero who, although he neither originates an alternative ethic nor incarnates the utopian imagination yet generates discussion of both, is the object of speculation rather than a participating intelligence. Through the perceptions of other protagonists who act as his judges or confessors, his motives and actions are expounded from a spectrum of subjective positions on matters of theory and belief, so that what Jim *is,* and the fiction is concerned to present him as an enigma to be decoded through the exercise of an innovatory system of analysis, is not the same as how he is seen, and it is how he is seen that is of significance. This distinction between his opaque essence and his apprehensible image is conceded by the scrupulous Marlow, who apologises to his audience for telling them so much about his own 'instinctive feelings and bemused reflections': 'He existed for me, and after all it is only through me that he exists for you' (p. 224). Such an admission of a personal and therefore qualified perception of Jim contrasts with the ostensibly objective record of Jim's origins, history and present circumstances provided by the first and anonymous narrator, whose introduction, despite the air of reliable detachment it affects, turns out to be enmeshed with prejudice.

Although like Marlow he can speak cynically about the clergy as the officially appointed custodians of morality whose function it is to manipulate piety and faith as a means of social control ['Jim's father possessed such certain knowledge of the

Unknowable as made for the righteousness of people in cottages without disturbing the ease of mind of those whom an unerring Providence enables to lie in mansions' (p. 5)], he looks on Jim's person and situation from the standpoint of one who consents to the imposition of regulations that will ensure the uniformity, cohesion and equilibrium of existing social arrangements. For him Jim's failure to acquire 'perfect love of work' and his passing infatuation with the Eastern promise of eternal peace, is evidence of a moral flaw that separates him from those of his own kind who had been successfully moulded by discipline, and from the pilgrims sustained by an austere and exacting faith and whose trust he betrays. His derision of Jim's hunger for the unattainable is spoken as a warning on the dangers of imagination and the fatal distraction of longing for the ideal, and his admonition of Jim's failure to comply with an established norm of conduct makes no assessment of the premises or purposes of that code. All the same his sententious version of a problematic situation allows that there is more to Jim's case than can be explained by the 'facts' the official Inquiry demands, and when he hands the narration over to Marlow, it is an acknowledgment that his outlook is insufficient for a task that requires other ways of seeing. Thus despite this narrator's privileged role as the first voice, his choral function is undeveloped and he speaks merely as one of a group of communicants adhering to ratified views and therefore expressing adverse opinions about Jim, and whose composite image of him is subtly and irrevocably altered by the substance of Marlow's mediation.

If the opening out of a wide perspective on Jim allows for many angles of vision, then both his critics and his protectors agree that he is an outsider by temperament and now an outlaw by conviction, a misfit rather than a rebel, who despite estrangement from his immediate family and displacement amongst the larger body of the merchant navy, is recognisably the product of imperialism's Service Classes. His idiom is reminiscent of a Boy Scout, his demeanour that of a disgraced subaltern eager for the chance to prove his true worth, and the youthful dreams which had set him apart from his more tractable companions on the training ship are taken chapter and verse from popular colonial fiction, retaining intact the veneration of endurance and leadership native to the genre. Jim's fantasies of surpassing heroism both ironically anticipate his abysmal failure and preview his magnificent achievement, the first violating his nation's imperialist creed and the other realising its colonial dream, and it is because he overturns expectations and blurs accepted discriminations by committing an iniquitous deed without himself being vicious and while continuing to profess fidelity to the traditions he has traduced, that he induces the reappraisal of old moral certainties and stimulates the construction of other standards of evaluation. It is Marlow's function to conduct this discussion, and in his narration Marlow, an older and more disenchanted avatar of the protagonist met with in *Heart of Darkness,* and one possessed of greater self-awareness and a larger degree of self-doubt, enacts his own passage from confidence in received ideas and authorised values to an uneasy agnosticism about both.

What his exchanges with the other voices demonstrate, is a passage fraught with doubts, hesitations and retreats, from reliance on 'a few simple notions you must cling to if you want to live decently and would like to die easy' (p. 43),[3] to a moral vision cognisant of grey areas and intractable problems that customary wisdom cannot even recognise:

> I felt the risk I ran of being circumvented, blinded, decoyed, bullied, perhaps, into taking a definite part in a dispute impossible of decision if one had to be fair to all the phantoms in possession—to the reputable that had its claims and to the disreputable that had its exigencies. I can't explain to you who haven't seen him and who hear his words only at second hand the mixed nature of my feelings. It seemed to me that I was being made to comprehend the Inconceivable—and I know of nothing to compare with the discomfort of such a sensation. I was made to look at the convention that lurks in all truth and on the essential sincerity of falsehood.   (p. 93)

This passage with its finely balanced antinomies and deliberated dissonances articulates Marlow's shock at recognising the arbitrariness of rigid moral categories and rehearses the essence of the inadmissible evidence he is obliged to examine, testimony he is initially predisposed to obfuscate and that ultimately colludes in transforming his personal theology. At the outset inclined to join in the general censure of Jim, whose improper professional conduct threatens 'the honour of the craft' to which Marlow belongs, and discomforted by a sense of 'the infernal alloy in his metal', 'the subtle unsoundness' of one who would put his disgrace before his guilt, Marlow is at the same time drawn to Jim's familiar and congenial features: 'I liked his appearance; I knew his appearance; he came from the right place; he was one of us' (p. 43).

It is a measure of Marlow's re-education that what he comes to value in Jim are those qualities at variance with his outward image as the very model of colonial manhood—his romantic conscience, his innocent individualism, his yearnings after an ideal, and in allowing that the two 'jumps' marking the definitive discontinuities in Jim's history were not the results of conscious will and rational decision ['I had jumped...It seems...I knew nothing about it until I looked up' (p. 111), is Jim's recollection of leaving the shop, just as he remembers his flight from imprisonment in the Rajah's compound and to the safety of Doramin's Settlement as having been executed 'without any mental process as it were' (p. 253)] and that cowardice does not adequately describe the one nor courage the other, Marlow is himself transported to a new vantage point from which he can command a wider view of the mainsprings to human action and exercise a greater tolerance of deviations from the statutory norm. Although Marlow is the fiction's principal narrator and its central intelligence, his viewpoint is itself the subject of scrutiny, and as a voice that is both sardonic and earnest, self-deprecating and self-righteous, Marlow acts not only as the communicator of the text's unquiet conscience about 'fixed standards', but as the means through which the remaking of a consciousness is revealed. As Marlow defies and submits to 'the power of merciless convention', defends the exigencies of the disreputable and advances the claims of the reputable, so does his struggle with the prerogatives of antagonistic principles and the pull of contradictory feelings introduce inconsistencies into his testimony and exegesis.[4]

In a novel which has as its 'Epigraph' the quotation 'It is certain my conviction gains infinitely the moment another soul will believe in it', uncertainty is the key-note of Marlow's address, one that seems calculated to involve his audience in his perplexity rather than to convert them to his now endangered convictions. His narration, in contradistinction to the official Inquiry which wants only facts, takes the form of an investigation into the credentials of those meanings and values morally binding on members of his social order, and since Marlow's findings discredit the postures of his complaisant interlocutors and imperil the tenets of his own per-suasion, his delivery has need of oxymoron to communicate the sense of dislocation at finding no fixed and invariable points of reference, and confronting the necessity of inventing an alternative epistemology:

> I cannot say I had ever seen him distinctly ... but it seemed to me that the less I understood the more I was bound to him in the name of that doubt which is the inseparable part of our knowledge ... It was a strange and melancholy illusion, evolved half-consciously like all our illusions, which I suspect only to be visions of remote, unattainable truth, seen dimly ... I have that feeling about me now; perhaps it is that feeling which has incited me to tell you the story, to try and hand over to you, as it were, its very existence, its reality—the truth disclosed in a moment of illusion.   (pp. 221, 323)

Marlow's use of illusion to signify the prefiguration of a truth not yet grasped and not its negation, marks a departure from his accustomed habits of thought and registers an acknowledgement that the familiar vocabulary of empiricism is inade-quate to comprehend the quality of his new perceptions. That the long-standing adherent of positivism finds himself reaching after 'absolute Truth, which, like Beauty itself, floats elusive, obscure, half-submerged, in the silent and still waters of mystery (p. 216), and employs the language of metaphysics to register this ambi-tion, intimates the dimensions of his crisis and suggests a context for his concerted and elaborate mystification of Jim's person.

Since Jim's unspeakable act is not commensurate with his appearance, manner, origins and training, Marlow spontaneously obscures that which he does see but cannot admit, and his view of Jim observed through fog, haze and mist[5] registers the opacity of his vision and not the intrinsic unintelligibility of the person perceived: 'He was not—if I may say so—clear to me. He was not clear ... I cannot say I had ever seen him distinctly ... I am fated never to see him clearly ... For me that white figure in the stillness of the coast and sea seemed to stand at the heart of a vast enigma' (pp. 177, 221, 241, 336). Inevitably Marlow, whose sense of reality had hitherto derived from the assimilation of observable facts and the recognition of unqualified moral distinctions, consigns Jim to a place in the crepuscular light; but when he demands that attention be paid to Jim's 'shadowy ideal of conduct,' he is obliged to step outside 'the sheltering conception of light and order which is our refuge' (p. 313) and allow that the dark is an inseparable part of reality and not its annulment. In his search for Jim's 'truth', Marlow negotiates a path through the realms of empirical observation and intuitive insight, signposting his route with images of sun and moon and designating positive qualities to the first and negative properties to the other.

> There is something haunting in the light of the moon; it has all the dispassion-ateness of a disembodied soul, and something of its inconceivable mystery. It is to our sunshine, which—say what you like—is all we have to live by, what the echo is to the sound: misleading and confusing whether the note be mocking or sad. It robs all form of matter—which after all, is our domain—of their substance and gives a sinister reality to shadows alone.
>
> (p. 246)

All the same Marlow is troubled by what the dark holds ['What is it that moves there?' he asks on gazing into a deep well', 'Is it a blind monster or only a lost gleam from the universe?' (p.307)], and out of discontent with the conventional schema he still continues to reiterate, he not only posits the light as a pragmatic utility rather than a sign of an epistemological truth, a sanctuary from 'the chaos of dark thoughts' that shuts off 'a view of a world that seemed to wear a vast and dismal aspect of disorder' (p. 313), but rescues from disrepute and derogation the aspects of reality denied by his culture. Thus because Marlow is conceived as a protagonist able to distance himself from current orthodoxies and contemplate dissident alternatives, he is equipped by the fiction to do battle for the reputation of the outcast Jim and in doing so to interrogate an aspiration vilified by the official spokesmen of im-perialist civilisation.

The debate between traditional values and heterodox ideals is dramatised in the course of Marlow's implicit dissociation from the negative evaluation made of Jim by the first narrator, and his direct confrontations with the doctrinaire views advanced by those protagonists whose unbending disavowal of the renegade obliges him to clarify the terms of his own eccentric allegiance. In the opinion of the skilled, courageous and ostensibly self-assured Captain Brierly, the epitome of Service and Honour, the disclosure of Jim's disgrace defames the public image of the maritime community and he wants nothing so much as that Jim should disap-pear, leaving the noble features of the merchant navy in pristine condition. Marlow can easily dispose of a stance dependent on keeping up formal appearances and devoid of moral content, and his bald and neutral reference to Brierly's suicide soon after the reported conversation draws attention to the fragility of the man's rigid adherence to a practice that is not rooted in moral conviction. Here Marlow discloses a shift in his own attitudes that serves to moderate his initial judgement of Jim, and by the time of his meeting with the French Lieutenant who had years earlier been a member of the boarding-party gone to the aid of the stricken *Patna*, Marlow had allied himself with Jim, while still seeking a sound basis for this com-mitment and needing reassurance on the fitness of his anomalous loyalty.

Hence he eagerly invites the stalwart old seaman, scarred by wounds that

display past valour, possessed of an inert placidity and a dispassionate demeanour
that speak of emotional restraint, to join him in taking a 'lenient view' of Jim's case,
a miscalculation which obliges Marlow to witness the manner of his companion
change from that of a tolerant village priest, accustomed to confessions of sin,
suffering and remorse, to that of a cold and formal judge: 'He drew up his heavy
eyelids ... I was confronted by two narrow grey circlets, like two tiny steel rings
around the profound blackness of the pupils. The sharp glance, coming from that
massive body, gave a notion of extreme efficiency, like a razor-edge on a battle-
axe' (p. 148). The dominant imagery of weaponry in Marlow's recollection establishes a connection between iron self-discipline and the repression of sensibility, and
when the decent old sailor, to escape the discomfort of Marlow's outrageous
suggestion, gets to his feet 'with a ponderous impetuosity, as a startled ox might
scramble up from the grass' (p. 148), while punctiliously declaring his inability to
contemplate the worth of existence when honour has been lost, he shows himself
in speech and deportment to be one of Marlow's benighted who 'go through life
with eyes half shut, with dull ears, with dormant thoughts' (p. 143), and is remembered by him as having spoken his verdict 'in the passionless and definite phraseology a machine would use, if machines could speak' (p. 159). Marlow is
discomposed by the man's relentless rectitude, but his representation of the encounter acts to alienate affection from this impeccable practitioner of the tradition
of the sea, by his making space for a sympathetic hearing to the cause he is pleading
on behalf of one who has profaned that custom.[6]

The last antagonist to Marlow's heretical commitment, and the one who
musters the most sophisticated arguments, is the only member of his original
audience who was later and by letter 'privileged' to learn about the outcome of
events concerning Jim, a man wholly devoted to those doctrines underpinning
imperialism which on Marlow's expanded horizon are now visible as epistemologi-
cally unsound and morally suspect. Without dissenting from the dogmas of his
correspondent on the necessity for colonial actions to be based 'on a firm conviction in the truth of ideas racially our own, in whose name are established the order,
the morality, of an ethical progress' (p. 339), or for colonialism's servants to fight
in the ranks if their lives are to count—indeed by dissembling with the disclaimer,
'I affirm nothing'—Marlow vindicates the integrity of one who had defected from
the mission and yet remained faithful to principles, and whose subsequent gallantry
intimates his confessing 'to a faith mightier than the laws of order and progress'
(p. 339). Just as Marlow is an active agent in Jim's fate, so does the relationship with
Jim destroy his confidence in the platitudes solemnly spoken by the unnamed
'privileged' man, and it is with some bitterness that he reflects on the smallness of
his own achievement in having kept his place in the ranks of an insignificant multitude. Where Marlow's interlocutors regard the rules governing their particular
social order as objectively validated and permanently valid moral imperatives, he,
because of responding to the imponderables in Jim's situation, is disturbed by 'the
most obstinate ghost of man's creation ... the doubt of the sovereign power enthroned in a fixed standard of conduct' (p. 50), misgivings which, in one who had

sought to rely on the moral guidance provided by a guild, signify a critical juncture in his construction of an alternative ethic. His sardonic estimate of Jim's pious father, who is convinced that the existing system is the best of all possible worlds and regards the social utilities of his inequitable society as ethical axioms, has the authority of the lapsed believer looking back on those few simple notions he had once trusted as adequate to direct and sustain a worthy existence, and coming to terms with the need to discover or devise an ultimate authority for morality commensurate with dynamic historical circumstances and variously orientated value systems: 'The old chap goes on equably trusting Providence and the established order of the universe . . . Virtue is one all over the world, and there is only one faith, one conceivable conduct of life, one manner of dying' (p. 341).

Because for Marlow the real significance of crime is that it breaks faith with the community of mankind, he cannot but admit that Jim in deserting his fellows stands accused of more than professional misconduct. Yet without abandoning this definition, he seeks for wholly other standards by which Jim's self-evident flaws and obvious qualities can be measured, and he finds these in an aspiration outside and hostile to the authorised commandments of imperialist society—in the pursuit of visionary desires that unfit the dreamer for fulfilling socially appointed functions which serve to perpetuate the existing order. Having instinctively condemned Jim as a traitor to his calling, Marlow, in response to a feeling wider than the fellowship of the craft, forges a bond of intimacy with the apostate, and while he demonstrates in his concern for the living Jim and his epitaph to a dead comrade is a disinterested love for a friend or a child that survives, and is strengthened by, the detestation of the conformist and the obloquy of those who guard the established order of society. But Marlow does more, and where the first narrator automatically expels Jim from the community of his own kind, he examines the roots to moral precepts and the ethical foundations to socially ordained action in an effort to prove that despite his culpability, Jim remains 'one of us'.

It has so far been argued that the discourse in Lord Jim produces a critique of imperialism's official ethos; all the same there are compelling reasons for reading it as a novel that manifestly has not cut the umbilical cord connecting it with the dominant ideology. In the 'Author's Note' appended almost two decades after the work was published, Conrad wrote that on conceiving the person of Jim, it had been his wish 'with all the sympathy of which I was capable, to seek fit words for his meaning. He was "one of us" ' (p. ix). The generality of this last phrase leaves it open to a number of constructions, and common to the possible interpretations which the text can support is the notion of a closed and elect group (the club, the regiment, the religious order, the guild, the masonic lodge), a concept critically different in sentiment from the ecumenical embrace signified in the quotation used as the 'Epigraph' to Youth: A Narrative and Two Other Stories, the volume which includes Heart of Darkness, and that could as appropriately be inscribed on the tombstone of the Marlow met with in Lord Jim: ' . . . But the dwarf answered: "No; something human is dearer to me than the wealth of all the world" '. Because

Conrad in his retrospective preface is addressing a readership deemed capable of identifying the unspecified aggregate, just as Marlow tells his tale to cronies connected with colonial trade who would share an idiom and whom he includes as belonging within the undefined fraternity, it is easy to suppose that the incantatory refrain to which Marlow time and again returns implies Jim's membership of the merchant navy and more broadly, the British Service Classes. Certainly when first assessing Jim's person and milieu, Marlow salutes that company from which the Empire recruited its servants as an aristocracy of the trustworthy and the valiant: 'He stood there for all the parentage of his kind, for men and women by no means clever or amusing, but whose very existence is based upon honest faith, and upon the instinct of courage' (p. 43).

But as Marlow does not see himself as belonging with 'that good, stupid kind we like to feel marching right and left of us in life, of the kind that is not disturbed by the vagaries of intelligence and the perversions of—of nerves, let us say' (p. 44), and is in rebellion against those who have immunised themselves against 'the intensity of life' and blinded themselves to new ways of seeing, it would seem that the identity of this society needs to be sought elsewhere; and in a fiction which discovers the ultimate sanctions for moral consciousness to reside in the indwelling essence of the nation and the race, the words 'one of us' can be seen to take on a more portentous and precise ideological meaning. If by using the phrase 'community of mankind' Marlow infers the existence of one international and indivisible human collective, then the universality of this concept is countermanded by his paean to a Homeland perceived as the guardian spirit giving guidance and shelter only to its own:

> I was going home—to that home distant enough for all its hearthstones to be like one hearthstone, by which the humblest of us has the right to sit. We wander in our thousands over the face of the earth, the illustrious and the obscure, earning beyond the seas our fame, our money, or only a crust of bread; but it seems to me that for each of us going home must be like going to render an account. We return to face our superiors, our kindred, our friends—those whom we obey, and those whom we love; but even they who have neither, the most free, lonely, irresponsible and bereft of ties,—even those for whom home holds no dear face, no familiar voice,—even they have to meet the spirit that dwells within the land, under its sky, in its air, in its valleys, and on its rises, in its fields, in its waters and its trees—a mute friend, judge, and inspirer . . . But the fact remains that you must touch your reward with clean hands, lest it turn to dead leaves, to thorns, in your grasp. I think it is the lonely, without a fireside or an affection they may call their own, those who return not to a dwelling but to the land itself, to meet its disembodied, eternal, and unchangeable spirit—it is those who understand best its severity, its saving power, the grace of its secular right to our fidelity, to our obedience. Yes! few of us understand, but we all feel it though, and I say *all* without exception, because those who do not feel do not count. Each blade of grass

has its spot on earth whence it draws its life, its strength; and so is man rooted to the land from which he draws his faith together with his life. I don't know how much Jim understood; but I know he felt, he felt confusedly but powerfully, the demand of some such truth or some such illusion.

(pp. 221–2).

To read in this eulogy the yearnings of an author who had known the deracination of exile is a necessary but insufficient observation, for while it does describe the emotions that inform the passage, it avoids engaging with the function of the speech within the text, which is to designate the nature of the compact uniting a moral community, and as a consequence, to establish that in this commonwealth Jim, who had forfeited his mariner's license, had not lost his place.

Because the fiction's argument can find no final authority attesting to the truth of fixed and invariable standards, and concludes that the official ethic is determined by utilitarian imperatives and institutional needs, the historical determinants of moral concepts are established, and it becomes necessary to seek for the source and arbiter of exemplary conduct outside the confines of the pragmatic rules governing any particular and mortal social order, and beyond the bewildering plurality of diverse faiths and incommensurable value systems. With his nostalgia for stable and integrated social formations where there had existed both an identity of public role and individual desire and a coherence of moral thinking, and which he knew had been shattered by historical changes in the West, Conrad in Lord Jim recovers the idea of a moral consensus and locates this as immanent in the idea of the eternal nation, where a continuing tradition embodied in unchanging mores commanding fidelity to agreed purposes is binding on all classes and through the ages. It is loyalty to such an unwritten, uncodified and ahistorical ethos that the fiction proffers as the valid basis of solidarity, and since Jim never ceases to pay homage to the precepts of this commonwealth—'The thing is that in virtue of his feeling he mattered' (p. 222)—he remains by that definition and by Marlow's valuation, 'one of us'. A conscience mirroring the 'soul' of his homeland and a consciousness of having broken faith with a due obligation to serve its will admit Jim to a universe from which a specified group of the fiction's other wanderers are forever exiled—the skipper, mate and engineer of the Patna who deserted the ship out of cowardice and then justified their flight, the degenerate mariners frequenting the eastern seaports, seduced and enslaved by a life of ease, the lawless latter-day buccaneers hungry for excitement and gain, the depraved Chester and Robinson obsessed with a scheme for wrenching wealth from a waterless guano island. In the context of Marlow's deference for the tutelage provided by home, it becomes apparent that the function of these peripheral characters, all of whom are connected with colonial service, trade or adventure, is to display that they violate the moral consensus of their cultural community by traducing the spiritually inspired colonial impulse. With the violent intrusion of Gentleman Brown as the fiction's archetypal antagonist to all morality and the mythic perverter of imperialism's positive intent, the boundaries of the moral republic are delineated to incorporate those whose unwavering allegiance is to the dominant aspiration of the nation, and this in the world of the novel is incarnate as imperialism. Thus a reading of Marlow's key speech, one which is spoken in the voice of the exiled colonial servant and addressed to an immediate audience who are participants in the same experience, will reveal the presence of our old friend the redeeming idea and will show that what Marlow is concerned to prove is how Jim's fidelity to imperialism's saving ideals establishes him, despite his defection, as 'one of us'.

That variable meanings can be constructed from Marlow's peroration on home and his repeated use of the phrase 'one of us', points up the text's equivocal relationship with received ideas, for on its simplest level his words can legitimately be construed as a patriotic eulogy and an affirmation of ethnic solidarity delivered without irony by a protagonist possessed of a rich sardonic vein, and who on the other occasions derides the ignorance of chauvinism and the arrogance of racism. Such an interpretation of Marlow's meaning, and one which shows him as an ally of the 'privileged' man, suggests that the elusive community is none other than those who serve imperialism's cause in foreign parts, a proposition given credence by Marlow's view of Jim amongst the people of Patusan as 'a creature not only of another kind but of another essence' (p. 229), existing in 'total and utter isolation' from 'them'. This representation suggests the possibility of 'one of us' being a term of racial identification distinguishing the colonialists from the alien world of the other.[7] Marlow's most powerful impression is of Jim's dissociation from his foreign environment, and despite his elegaic recall of him 'dominating and yet in complete accord with his surroundings—with the life in the forests and with the life of men' (p. 175), it is only by placing him mentally in his father's rectory and amidst his serene and unconscious family where he stands out as an incongruous presence, that he can at last see him whole, 'returned at last, no longer a mere white speck at the heart of an immense mystery, but of full stature, standing disregarded amongst their untroubled shapes' (p. 342). In fashioning this image, Marlow communicates a belief in inalienable racial roots which forever fix even the alienated in the soil of their native culture, and it is this concept that he articulates in emphasising Jim's dubious relationship with Patusan: 'all his conquests, the truth, the fame, the friendships, the love—all these things that made him master had made him a captive, too . . . Jim the leader was a captive in every sense . . . Every day added a link to the fetters of that strange freedom . . . he was imprisoned within the very freedom of his power' (pp. 247, 262, 283). The contrast between the passionate asseveration of home as mute friend, judge and inspiration, and the regretful depreciation of Jim's enslavement to Patusan, cuts across the commendation of Jim's achievement and acts to foreground the fundamental flaw in the position of white rajahs.

Here Marlow enacts a dual function as iconographer and iconoclast of the colonial myth; by hailing Jim's triumph in bringing peace and prosperity to Patusan as evidence of the white man's energy, enterprise and ingenuity, he represents Jim as heir to the tradition of colonial chivalry; and in emphasising Jim's cultural autonomy and his estrangement from the foreign society that has given him his 'chance',

Marlow denies himself the possibility of commemorating the legend. For he shows that it is not from his Malayan comrades and vassals that Jim seeks confirmation of his redemption, but from his peers back home, addressing his pledge of fealty to their codes and their ideals. So committed is the fiction to the power of patriotism and the sustenance afforded by the sense of national identity, that endorsement is given by an unexpected source; even Stein in whom the fiction sketches a portrait of proto-internationalist, and whose preoccupation is with formulating the nature of the human vocation binding on the species rather than with the origins of the moral consensus uniting a community, appears to suffer a sense of territorial banishment. Having found refuge and fortune in the East, he bequeaths his renowned collection of beetles and butterflies to the small German town of his birth, 'Something of me. The best' (p. 205), a sentiment that echoes the yearnings of Jim sick for a home that he will not again see: 'I shall be faithful . . . I shall be faithful . . . Tell them . . .' (pp. 334, 335). Such uncontradicted articulations of devotion to the nation and the race which is insensible to the ethical values cherished by either, draws *Lord Jim* back into the orbit of traditional imperialist ideology from which the fiction's discourse on matters moral and metaphysical struggles to escape.

Impinging on the foregrounded ethical argument about the foundations of moral principles and the sanctions for principled conduct, is the surrounding and elliptical philosophical discussion which considers the mainspring and ends of action and resituates problems of social value within the larger conceptual context of a human telos. With the opening out of this discourse, the proposition maintained by the overt narrative voices in *The Nigger of the 'Narcissus'* that the good of any practice is inherent in the activity itself and derives from the successful completion of any given task is overtaken by a view discriminating between forms of performance and assigning worth only to those acts motivated by ideals and striving after the realisation of distant, millennial goals. Standing outside the utilitarian tradition fostered by imperialist civilisation is the posture represented by Stein, who enters the fiction as the *deus ex machina* in Jim's fate and stays to fulfill a yet more portentous function as the prophet of utopian aspiration, for it is his testament that rescues the claims of imagination and visionary anticipation from the contumely of ideologues teaching the necessity of a safe positivism. But even the text premonitions and echoes of his articulate refusal to accede to the repression of desire and the banishment of the dream. Marlow himself speaks out eloquently for the validity and nobility of ruling passions when he chastises the sober and successful men of affairs listening to his tale for having starved their imaginations to feed their bodies, and applauds the 'bizarre obstinacy of that desire' more powerful than greed which had induced the seventeenth-century traders to defy unknown seas and death in their zeal for pepper: 'To us, their less tried successors, they appear magnified, not as agents of trade but as instruments of a recorded destiny, pushing out into the unknown in obedience to an inward voice, to an impulse beating in the blood, to a dream of the future' (p. 227).

He is joined in his avowal of ontological expectation by the first narrator who, although initially scornful of Jim's hunger for the unattainable, recounts with sympathy the dissatisfactions haunting the 'privileged' man now retired to the comfort and security of a London flat: 'No more horizons as boundless as hope, no more twilights within the forests as solemn as temples, in the hot quest of the Ever-undiscovered Country over the hill, across the stream, beyond the wave' (p. 338). Both Marlow and the primary narrator speak in praise of the ardour impelling the colonial adventurers of old to heroic feats, but their acclaim is animated by their honouring the liberating effect of the inspiration rather than the immediate objects of their desire, and the ventures themselves serve as metaphors of the pursuit of the future, and not as instances of illustrious colonial achievement. However, it would be alien to the fiction's dialectic if the doctrine of hope were to be uncontradicted, and the passionate advocacy of utopian desire as a spiritual necessity is moderated by the doubts that are made to accrete around the person and teachings of Stein and, more dangerously, by the negative form of the visionary impulse incarnate in Gentlemen Brown's rage to initiate the apocalypse. Although Stein is introduced by Marlow as wise, trustworthy and humane, a man of both physical courage and intrepid spirit, the substances of his theories as well as the manner of his address arouse Marlow's suspicions, an uneasiness that he communicates in a constellation of allusions to Stein as a shade, a ghost gliding through a twilight world, 'a shadow prowling amongst the graves of butterflies' (p. 214), occupying an uninhabited and uninhabitable house, 'a crystalline void', silent as a crypt, with dark, empty rooms, dead exhibits and an atmosphere of catacombs. But if these mortuary images undermine Stein's standing as a guru able to guide the living through the perplexities of the concrete world, then what he has to say does all the same have authority as a statement of a dissident ontological outlook, and even though his gnomic utterances seem impossible of semantic explication, the spirit rather than the letter of his words does issue as a coherent declaration of faith in hope as the means of realising the human vocation, and the creation of an alternative world as its authentic end.

Ian Watt accounts for the contradictions in Stein's parable by pointing out that the sentence, 'A man that is born falls into a dream like a man who falls into the sea', had originally read 'A man that is born is like a man who falls into the sea'.[8] Yet it could be argued that the final wording, despite its greater opacity, expresses more exactly the import of Stein's belief that in the face of this generic dilemma, the human purpose is achieved through the exercise of imagination, the capacity for abstract thought, the ability to construct mental images, the urge to envisage the shape of the future, powers which distinguish the species from the magnificent butterfly that 'finds a little heap of dirt and sits still on it' (p. 213). It is Watt's contention that the main reason why Stein's parable resists any consensus of analysis is 'the patent asymmetry of its basic metaphor: there is nothing that can stand as a satisfactory opposite to the sea, and thus give some measure of concreteness both to the individual's struggle in the water, and to its different outcomes. This has been the main stumbling-block in most interpretations of "in the destructive element immerse" ' (op. cit., pp. 327–8). But such an antithesis does exist and is a focus for the fiction's representation of the dream as the source of ontologically significant action, since Stein's use of the swimmer-sea metaphor to communicate dynamic human will recurs in Marlow's trope of the sea as 'the very image of struggling mankind . . . with its labouring waves for ever rising, sinking, and vanishing to rise again' (p. 243), and this last has as its contrary 'the immovable forests rooted deep in the soil, soaring towards the sunshine, everlasting in the shadowy might of their tradition, like life itself' (p. 243). When Stein completes his self-interrupted exhortation with the words, 'In the destructive element immerse . . . That was the way. To follow the dream, and again to follow the dream—and so—*ewig*—*usque ad finem* . . .' (p. 214–15), the metaphors of sea and dream, travail and visionary longing come together to signify his belief in the arduous and continuous pursuit of the ideal; and ultimately it is this stance which the fiction develops as the true expression of the species' destiny, for the creed teaching passive deference to time-honoured custom, that is immanent in the primal landscape of unreconstructed nature, is disclaimed as a negation of the human essence.

Stein, who is the heir to German romanticism and a European tradition of political idealism that had led him to participate in the 1848 Revolution and forced him into exile after its defeat, is shown to be a paradigm of the effective romantic who had translated his aspirations into reality, dissolving in his own history as youthful radical and later as honourable adventurer and confidant of native rulers in the East, the artificial dichotomy between imagination and performance. Significantly, when he prepares to give Marlow his answer to the question he has framed as 'how to be', he uses the past tense—'That was the way'—by this alluding to his own abandonment of a practice that he continues to enjoin on others, since he had in old age capitulated to the division between the prose and the poetry, mechanically overseeing his extensive commercial empire while deriving spiritual fulfillment from the lonely study of lepidoptera. Stein's pronouncements should therefore be read as a declaration of commitment to an idea spoken by one who, although personally disillusioned, continues to affirm the urge to envision and implement a transfigured human order. Thus even as he is in full verbal flight his speech is arrested, as if his inspiration has been destroyed by his move from the distant shadows of his dark room into the circle lit by the lamp, from the obscurity where fancy is bred, to the brightness where empirical fact is evident as the only truth. For Marlow this transition from confident delivery to murmured hesitancy appears as proof of his having no answers, or worse, that his advice is fraught with dangers:

> The whisper of his conviction seemed to open before me a vast and uncertain expanse, as of a crepuscular horizon on a plain at dawn—or was it, perchance, at the coming of the night? One had not the courage to decide; but it was a charming and deceptive light, throwing the impalpable poesy of its dimness over pitfalls—over graves. His life had begun in sacrifice, in enthusiasm for generous ideas; he had travelled very far, on various ways, on strange paths, and whatever he followed it had been without faltering, and therefore without shame and without regret. In so far he was right. That was the way, no doubt.

> Yet for all that the great plain on which men wander amongst graves and
> pitfalls remained very desolate under the impalpable poesy of its crepuscular
> light, overshadowed in the centre, circled with a bright edge as if surrounded
> by an abyss full of flames.   (p. 215)

Marlow's dissatisfaction with Stein's philosophy rests on its avoidance of practical
difficulties, its romantic embrace of the hazards and failures associated with quixotic
ventures; all the same the images in which he couches his mistrust communicate
contradictory signals, some discrediting Stein's solutions as perilous and incapable of
consummation, and others acknowledging that acolytes of utopianism must and will
endure risk and defeat in pursuit of transcendent goals.

Thus although doubt does attach to Stein's prescriptions, his posture is not
repudiated by the fiction and is even given oblique validation in Marlow's elegy to
Jim, which offers in his death a triumph denied to Brierly's demoralised suicide, for
this lament is irradiated by esteem for Jim's sacrifice to the dream, his fidelity to a
shadowy ideal of conduct, his surrender to the claim of his own world of shades.
Because Jim's passion is mediated by Marlow, who against the grain of his creed acts
as a witness for ideas that are not his own, the 'impossible world of romantic
achievement' (p. 83), whose realisation must be deferred to a future time, survives
in the text as an emblem of the will to initiate a transfigured tomorrow. Yet
because the fiction's discourse generates its own antithesis, an opposite form of the
utopian inspiration manifests itself, one that is also motivated by a refusal of the
here and now, and in Gentleman Brown, 'a blind accomplice of the Dark Powers'
(p. 354), an archetypal figure of the non-rational will that pits itself against the
established order and defies history, exults in destruction and looks on the world
as its prey, the fiction produces the enemy of hope and the architect of cosmic
cataclysm:

> There was in the broken, violent speech of that man, unveiling before me his
> thoughts with the very hand of Death upon his throat, an undisguised ruth-
> lessness of purpose, a strange vengeful attitude towards his own past, and a
> blind belief in the righteousness of his will against all mankind, something of that
> feeling which could induce the leader of a horde of cut-throats to call himself
> proudly the Scourge of God.   (p. 370)

It is this embodiment of the exterminating angel, a being 'moved by some complex
intention' (p. 353) in his ambition to strew the earth with corpses and envelop it in
flames, who stands as a warning of the dangers to the messianic imagination and
serves to redefine the contours of a positive millenarianism.

In a fiction that is disillusioned in a creed of action from which the question of
goals beyond immediate necessity is expunged, and converted to the conception of
activity as a means to the realisation of ideal ends, the dialogue is between incommensurable western ideologies and the introduction of a foreign code negating the
principle of performance and orientated towards Nirvana engenders no power to

challenge the terms of the discussion. If the quest for repose and the annihilation of desire which lies at the heart of eastern metaphysics and is peripheral to all religious systems is allowed a voice, it is repudiated as a denial of the ultimate human ends projected by the fiction. Marlow's tolerance towards episodic lapses into the longing for peace is inseparable from his conviction that it signifies an abandonment of hope and with it abdication from the human vocation: 'Which of us here has not observed this, or maybe experienced something of that feeling in his own person— this extreme weariness of emotions, the vanity of effort, the yearning for rest?' (p. 88). The dream in its negative form as narcosis is embodied in the representation of Patusan, and if it does exist in the fiction as a highly articulated form of hierarchical and ritualised social existence, it is primarily a metaphysical landscape whose every feature departs from western conceptions of form, norm and value: 'do you notice how, three hundred miles beyond the end of telegraph cables and mail-boat lines, the haggard utilitarian lies of our civilisation wither and die, to be replaced by pure exercises of imagination, that have the futility, often the charm, and sometimes the deep hidden truthfulness of works of art?' (p. 282).

While Marlow's disenchantment with pragmatism does cause him to look with favour on a place still uncorrupted by technology, and through a balancing of antinomies to augur a validation of its immanent meanings, the ultimate vision of Patusan is realised in a configuration of negatives: it is timeless, immobile, a land without a past, one of the earth's lost, forgotten places, where the smells are primeval, the air stagnant and the old trees and old mankind exist in their original dusk of being:

> A brooding gloom lay over this vast and monotonous landscape; the light fell on it as if into an abyss. The land devoured the sunshine ... It remains in the memory motionless, unfaded, with its life arrested, in an unchanging light ... I had turned away from the picture and was going back to a world where events move, men change, light flickers, life flows in a clear stream, no matter whether over mud or over stones ... I breathed deeply, I revelled in the vastness of the opened horizons, in the different atmosphere that seemed to vibrate with a toil of life, with the energy of an impeccable world.
>
> (pp. 264, 330, 331)

In communicating his hostile perceptions of an alien and estranging world and confirming the worth of his own culture, Marlow returns to the conventional connotations of the dark and invokes the established dichotomy between the error of inertia and the good of action, for whereas to him the people of Patusan appear to exist 'as if under an enchanter's wand', Jim 'lives', a contrast between passivity and volition that signifies respectively human purpose denied and enacted; and while he recoils from the pristine and featureless vistas of the unreconstructed East, he takes delight in Stein's artificial gardens where the local vegetation had been brought together in a fluted grove of exquisite beauty and grace. With this the fiction invites its audience to applaud initiative, creative imagination and the will to transform the environment as victories against the stasis of repetitive custom, unvarying habit and immemorial usage, and since the contrast is embodied in the polarised structures of West and East, the West is rescued from the onslaught made by the text on its contemporary ambitions and terms of seeing.

But if no salvation is discovered in the rival goals of another civilisation and the text produces eccentric versions of dominant conceptual categories, *Lord Jim* does dramatise a radical critique of imperialist ideology that is directed against a spiritually repressive culture demanding unreflective obedience to the laws of order and progress, misrepresenting social utilities in the service of class interests as moral axioms and restricting the definition of knowledge to exclude meditations on alternative human conditions. Yet the novel itself begets no prefigurations of the content to the dreams of the future, nor how these are to be given corporeal form, and this absence can be adduced to the discontinuity between the significations of past historical circumstances which is the subject of the narrative, and a political and theological critique of a contemporary ethos, between the regretful demystification of the legend about colonial romance, and the determined censure of the utilitarian philosophy inspiring the imperialism of a later epoch. Because the fiction locates the manifestations of idealistic intent and significant action in the past, and interprets this bygone age as if the succeeding era were not already visible and the future there-fore still unknowable, the death of Jim and the frustration of his hopes necessarily leaves the political horizon empty, for the consummation of promise cannot be presented by a triumphant imperialism that has been disavowed by the text. Thus in a novel which rescues victory from a tale of total defeat, the fiction's vatic impulses are constrained to issue as illuminations of the human need to anticipate and possess the future, but without intimations of who the architects of the new age will be or what it is they are striving to construct.

NOTES

References are to the Medallion Edition 1925–28 which has the same pagination as the Uniform and Collected Editions of *The Works of Joseph Conrad* (Dent).

[1] Cf. Dorothy Van Ghent, who sees in the fissured hills an image of Jim's condition: 'He is not only an outcast from his own kind but he is also an outcast from himself, cloven spiritually, unable to recognise his own identity, separated from himself as the two halves of the hills are separated'. *'On Lord Jim'* in *Twentieth Century Interpretations* of Lord Jim: *A Collection of Critical Essays*, edited by Robert E. Kuehn (New Jersey: Prentice-Hall, 1969), p. 75; essay first published in *The English Novel: Form and Function* (New York: Holt, Rhinehart and Winston, 1953).
[2] See Stephen Zelnick, 'Conrad's *Lord Jim:* Meditations on the Other Hemisphere', *The Minnesota Review*, No. 11 (Fall 1978). Even if Zelnick does interpret the novel too exclusively as a critique of imperialism, his essay remains essential reading on a work that has too often been emptied of its historical meanings in critical discussions.
[3] This is an obvious example of how Conrad's fictions interrogate bald declarations made in his prose writing—cf. 'Those who read me know my conviction that the world, the temporal world, rests on a few very simple ideas; so simple that they must be as old as the hills. It rests notably, among others, on the idea of Fidelity'. 'A Familiar Preface' to *A Personal Record,* p. xxi.
[4] Irving Howe writes: 'In the contrast between what Marlow says and what he tells, lies the distance Conrad can allow between the stoical norm and the romantic deviation; which is to say, between the desire to cling to moral formulae and the recognition that modern life cannot be lived by them, between the demands of social conscience and the freed fantasies of the idyllic or the dangerous, between the

commandments of one's fathers and the quandries of exile'. 'Conrad: Order and Anarchy', *Politics and the Novel* (New York: Horizon Press, 1957), pp. 81–2; essay first published in *Kenyon Review* (Autumn 1953) and (Winter 1954).

[5] For Albert Guérard, in *Conrad the Novelist* (Harvard University Press, 1958), the fog, mist and moonlight in which Jim is seen signifies Jim's self-deception and not Marlow's perception.

[6] The tendency in critical discussion to see in the French Lieutenant one of Conrad's intended exemplary figures is hard to maintain in the light of the equivocal representation.

[7] Jeremy Hawthorn, *Joseph Conrad: Language and Fictional Self-Consciousness* (London: Edward Arnold, 1979), argues that one meaning of 'one of us' is the solidarity of colonialists in their relationship to the colonised.

[8] Ian Watt, *Conrad in the Nineteenth Century* (Chatto and Windus, 1980).

Mark Conroy

PARAGON AND ENIGMA: THE HERO IN *LORD JIM*

Charlie Marlow is a curious blend of storyteller and embryonic novelist. He combines the desire for clear moral counsel and straightforward narrative with bafflement in the face of a narrative and moral frame that are anything but straight-forward or clear. It will soon be plain that in the case of *Lord Jim,* which of course he narrates, this bafflement is often strategic: the story may have counsel neither Marlow nor his audience/readership would wish to heed.

For the moment, it can be said that this odd mix of clarity and obscurity characterizes nothing of Marlow's more aptly than his vision of the figure of Jim. Indeed, the gap between Jim's vivid persona and what if anything may be behind it forms a major reason for Marlow's almost morbid preoccupation with Jim's case. In one famous passage, for instance, Marlow relates to his colleagues his impression of Jim from their dinner at the Malabar House, where they have their lengthy conversation about the *Patna* incident. All that time, says Marlow, "I had before me these blue, boyish eyes ... this young face, these capable shoulders, the open bronzed forehead ... this appearance appealing at sight to all my sympathies: this frank aspect, the artless smile, the youthful seriousness. He was of the right sort; he was one of us." [1] This description of Jim forms a vision of surface, and one which emphasizes "appearance" in all its "frank aspect" and ingenuous simplicity. But it is also an evocation of ineffable depths, as the following lines suggest: "He talked soberly, with a sort of composed unreserve, and with a quiet bearing that might have been the outcome of manly self-control, of impudence, of callousness, of a colossal unconsciousness, of a gigantic deception. Who can tell!" (p. 78).

The immediate appeal of Jim to "all [Marlow's] sympathies" is thus marked by a profound ambiguity, a sense of depth sinister and beyond reach. In fact, this fatal ambiguity may be the richest source of Marlow's dread fascination with Jim. The way in which this ambiguity situates itself in the narrative and the means by which the ambiguity produces the resonance of Jim for Marlow and the reader both arise as issues in this vision of Jim—issues that prompt us at the outset to consider the

From *Modernism and Authority: Strategies of Legitimation in Flaubert and Conrad* (Baltimore: Johns Hopkins University Press, 1985), pp. 99–117.

basis of Jim's appeal to Marlow's sympathies. What can it mean to be "one of us"?

For Marlow's description inscribes a vision not only of Jim but also of a community in which he is placed. What can "one of us" refer to, though? One could read the phrase as meaning that Jim is a kind of Everyman, part of the human community or the great family of man. While this reading may not be contradicted by the narrative, it would probably be more useful to start with a more specific reading of the phrase. After all, when the reader is told that Jim has blue eyes, capable shoulders, and fair hair (also mentioned by Marlow), and that he is "of the right sort," the social and racial determinants are clear. One sees that much of Marlow's concern for Jim's case is rooted in an identification with Jim's social and professional role as a member of the British merchant marine and, more broadly, as a representative of British colonialism.[2]

Marlow's commitment to the code of the merchant marine was, incidentally, shared by his author, who as late as 1918 stoutly defended his old profession at great length against the casual remark of an obscure British M.P.[3] Marlow's desire to retain a belief in the efficacy of the merchant marine code must be understood, because it is responsible for much of the story's impact. Furthermore, the audience for most of Marlow's yarn is no anonymous gathering; they are members of the merchant service as well. Jim's "failure of nerve" must be of especially acute interest to this audience because it is invested in the code that Jim seems to represent so well out serves so poorly at the crucial point.

The contradictions of this code imply the larger question of the British Empire itself, but that problem—a problem of legitimation—is at first muted, crepuscular. Surely nobody knows better than Conrad that the smaller and the larger questions are of a piece. These connections will become clear as the narrative weaves them, but their strands will entrap Jim from the very start, despite his belief in his own isolation.

It is ironic, in a sense, that Marlow envisions this role for Jim in the first place (that of bearer of merchant marine values), since Jim considers himself totally set apart from the rest of the crew of the *Patna*, the ship to which he is assigned. Schooled in light holiday literature, Jim joins the merchant marine because he "saw himself" as "always an example of devotion to duty, and as unflinching as a hero in a book" (p. 6). In addition to this slight case of *bovarism*, Jim is isolated from the crew as well by a certain contempt and a distaste for associating with them, such as in an argument between crew members in which Jim takes no part, continuing only to smile "at the retreating horizon; his heart was full of generous impulses, and his thought was contemplating his own superiority" (p. 23). Jim is consistently presented as one who is studiedly ignorant of the conditions in which he works. He is ignorant finally on two counts: that of his own dependency on the other crew members and the necessity of working with them; and that of his complicity in the larger British commercial trading network that uses the service of the merchant marine to ship its goods.[4] Jim's ignorance is not simply incomplete understanding: it is a necessity of survival, and his self-deception, like the self-deception of Marlow, is the fate of good men attempting to keep faith with a dubious cause.

Yet, Marlow takes the very circumstances of Jim's isolation from the actual community of mariners and places him at the center of an ideal or virtual community of mariners; and this validation is based, interestingly enough, not on what Jim actually does, but rather on his aspect or image. The appeal is always to Jim's physical appearance, as though this in itself provided the evidence of superiority. Jim sees himself in splendid isolation, whereas Marlow places Jim in the center of the mariners' tradition. However contradictory of each other, both visions are equally deluded, at least on the evidence of the *Patna* incident itself. At the crucial moment, Jim joins the crew whose membership he sought to shun (and who are not at all eager to have him, either). Since he was paralyzed by his disdain for his crew and his unavoidable complicity with them, "he had preserved through it all a strange illusion of passiveness, as though he had not acted but had suffered himself to be handled by the infernal powers" (p. 108). It is Jim's inability to recognize his own complicity with the other crew members—even after his jump—that renders him incapable in turn of understanding his action as an action. He experiences it—or at least speaks of it to Marlow—as something thrust upon him. "I had jumped . . . it seems" (p. 111).

The question thrown into the starkest relief by Jim's actions involves the bedrock of values that the merchant marine code of conduct is supposed to be. Marlow speaks of "those struggles of an individual trying to save from the fire his idea of what his moral identity should be, this precious notion of a contention, only one of the rules of the game, nothing more, but all the same so terribly effective by its assumption of unlimited power over natural instincts" (p. 81). If Jim, who represents for Marlow the highest aspirations of that virtual community of the merchant marine, can join the actual community of the *Patna* crew who desert their ship, then what of any attempt to see the marine as based on codes of conduct deeper than expedience or pecuniary motive? The fact that the merchant marine derives its functions from the larger pursuit of empire does not suffice to justify its existence; it only increases the ambiguity of its status. It is worth nothing that the above citation can refer equally to Jim and to the narrator Marlow; for if Jim fails to perform according to the code of conduct, who is to say that this failure might not be contagious?

The code of conduct assumes for Marlow's narrative a kind of talismanic function, as a way of fending off the contamination of moral failure or paralysis of will. The character in the early part of the novel who serves as the cautionary figure for Marlow and his listeners in this respect is Montague Brierly, of whom Marlow says: "He had never in his life made a mistake, never had an accident, never a mishap, never a check in his steady rise, and he seemed to be one of those lucky fellows who know nothing of indecision, much less of self-mistrust" (p. 57). The implacable Brierly is compared to a rock whom the sting of life would only scratch like a pin, and his "self-satisfaction [at the inquiry into the *Patna* incident] presented to me and to the world a surface as hard as granite." (Marlow adds laconically, "he committed suicide very soon after" [p. 59].)

As he proceeds to discuss Brierly, Marlow presents the contamination more explicitly by saying that, while he was examining Jim, "he was probably holding silent inquiry into his own case," and that he must have found himself guilty because "he took the secret of the evidence with him in that leap into the sea" (p. 58). When Brierly, during the trial, denounces the publicity and asks Marlow "Why are we tormenting that young chap?" and "Why eat all that dirt?" the latter surmises that "at bottom poor Brierly must have been thinking of himself" (p. 66).

In Brierly's view, it is all a question of professional trust and confidence:

> "We are trusted. Do you understand?—trusted! Frankly, I don't care a snap for all the pilgrims that ever came out of Asia, but a decent man would not have behaved like this to a full cargo of old rags in bales. We aren't an organized body of men, and the only thing that holds us together is just the name for that kind of decency. Such an affair destroys one's confidence."
>
> (P. 68)

Even in the course of defending his "decency," Brierly reveals much of the reason why it fared so poorly on the *Patna:* the merchant marine and the traders it serves make little distinction between the people they transport and a cargo of "old rags in bales." Brierly's hope is to give Jim two hundred rupees to clear out of town; in proposing this, though, he reveals his own susceptibility to the cowardice Jim has shown in jumping ship in the first place. Clearly, he has reason to fear for his confidence.

Brierly's suicide enacts a sinister inverted parody of Jim's abandonment of the *Patna;* only his peculiar retreat is from internal guilt rather than external circumstance. His mate recalls that "four iron belaying-pins were missing round the mainmast. Put them in his pockets to help him down, I suppose.... Maybe his confidence was just shook a bit at the last" (p. 61). The small narrative of Brierly and his demise is a warning exemplum, presenting the danger of contamination that Jim's story contains. This danger, unspoken by Marlow, haunts his narrative nonetheless. For if the man whose role is that of exemplary model for gentlemen seamen deserts his ship and the code of the sea, surely this suggests a vacuum into which more and more seamen will be drawn, like the "everlasting deep hole" Jim falls into when he jumps—a vacuum the more fearful because it seems to figure an inner emptiness (p. 111). Whether Marlow's narrative is a remedy for the disease or itself a poison depends in part on whether Jim's failure of nerve is unique to himself, susceptible of explanation only in metaphysical or psychological terms, or whether his story is synecdochic for an already existent, if latent, epidemic. Marlow's own obsession with Jim's case suggests the latter explanation; yet the rhetoric of Marlow's tale suggests the former. The dissonance between these two views of Jim will persist as we proceed, for this tension is crucial to the narrative. What seems to implicate Marlow's audience in Jim's behavior is constantly changed into inscrutable fate or caprice of individual temperament. But could Jim's fate be inscribed in the conflicts of his position in the social and material world of his seaman's trade? If that is the case, his story indeed becomes a cautionary tale to Marlow's mariner audience.

The code of conduct to which Marlow and Jim both have recourse is essentially aristocratic in origin; the seamanship invoked implies a military model that is preindustrial. Yet the function of the merchant marine at this time was very much a part of industrial society: to ship men and goods from port to port. The pilgrims on the *Patna* are human cargo to the British crew; the notion of "stewardship" and the solidarity of crew with vessel it invokes are inappropriate for these conditions. The split between the pilgrims and their stewards is also racially coded, and this racial connotation to the incident deepens the conflict and the subsequent shame of Jim's actions in joining the crew. Albert Guérard focuses this problematic in treating the "Malay helmsman" Conrad fleetingly alludes to in the course of the *Patna* narrative:

> "The two Malays had meantime remained holding to the wheel"—only thoughtless, immobile figures, not even part of our moral universe.... [But our attention is directed by the information that the ship didn't sink.']
>
> We then move away from the *Patna* to the inquiry, where the two helmsmen were questioned, as for relief.... The first helmsman, when asked what he thought of matters at the time, says he thought nothing. The second "explained that he had a knowledge of some evil befalling the ship, but there had been no order;... why should he leave the helm?"
>
> Marlow refers to the helmsman rightly as an "extraordinary and damning witness." [5]

Guérard is correct to stress the significance of these Malay helmsmen in the drama of the *Patna,* not only because their heroism throws Jim's protestations of heroism into unpleasant contrasts but also because their race emphasizes the cultural identity of those who abandoned the *Patna,* as opposed to those abandoned. It is their dual function, as victims of the *Patna* incident and as the sole adherents to the code of the sea, which redoubles the indictment of Jim and the crew and contributes mightily to Jim's shame.

This failure of stewardship and the accompanying shame set in motion the search for rehabilitation. The result is the second major story of the text, involving the island of Patusan. Patusan becomes for Jim the place of atonement, the arena where high intentions can be transmuted into action rather than, as in the *Patna,* case, alibis for action. In that connection, it is worthwhile to note that the "artistic necessity" of the Patusan episode is a part of its thematic interest for this question of good intentions. If, as some have contended, *Lord Jim* is a short story that overstayed its welcome, then that claim rests in some measure on the belief that the second major narrative development—Jim's attempt to establish a separate community in Patusan—says nothing new, that it is simply a matter of Jim's trying and failing once again. To deal with that objection, it is well to examine the thematic connotations of the Patusan section and to suggest ways in which it complicates and enriches those of the *Patna* section.

That there is a relationship between the merchant marine and the larger economic thrust of empire is clear; yet this relationship is not immediately germane to the incidents related in that first story but subsists only as a haze around the narrative's glow (to borrow Marlow's famous metaphor in "Heart of Darkness" yet again). One can argue many of the implications of the *Patna* incident without engaging those matters, and critics have generally done so. This becomes more difficult in the Patusan chapters, as the resonances widen in concentric fashion to embrace the larger complex of the British project of empire and the "white man's burden" ideology of stewardship for which Jim is such a splendid figure. For at issue in *Lord Jim* is the legitimation of empire: not legitimacy, which is more in the nature of a *donné,* or established fact, but legitimation, which is the process of establishing that fact. The Patusan narrative makes explicit the problems of legitimation that were only implicit in the *Patna* affair; for now the matter of governance is fore-grounded in the logic of the narrative itself, in the second chance Jim is offered.

It is part of Jim's desire to do right by the indigenous people as a compensation for his failure of stewardship. This opportunity is granted him when Stein, a mer-chant friend of Marlow's, assigns him to his trading post in Patusan; it seems at the time a way of gaining back the honor lost on the *Patna.* At the same time, of course, Jim does go into Patusan as heedless of the nature of the colonial project that engages him as he was on the deck of the *Patna.*

No doubt the Jim of the Patusan chapters is a more active soul than the Jim of the *Patna,* but the illusory relation of actor to deed still operates—arguably, to even more deadly effect. Jim still views his deeds as self-generated, uncontaminated by an outside. Just as the absolute split of inner and outer allowed Jim to treat his jump as if he really had nothing finally to do with it, so it now allows him to attribute his temporary success in Patusan to his own high-minded activity, and that alone. More than once, Marlow notes the obverse side of this coin in the form of Jim's unwitting reliance on the community of Patusan for his own validation. He points out that "all these things that made him master had made him a captive, too. He looked with an owner's eye at the peace of the evening, at the river, at the houses, at the everlasting life of the forests, at the life of the old mankind, at the secrets of the land, at the pride of his own heart: but it was they that possessed him" (pp. 247–48). The very way in which the particulars of Patusan's history and geography demonstrates how thoroughly Patusan becomes for Jim a specular space, whose image entraps him as Narcissus was entrapped in his own reflection. It is not only the land itself that possesses Jim in this remark of Marlow's, it is also the pride of Jim's own heart.

But his reliance on this space for his self-definition is not a relation he has consciously appropriated. Perhaps this is at the base of the paradoxical "contemp-tuous tenderness" that Marlow sees in Jim's entire attitude toward Patusan. The contempt is Jim's response to the local people, who needed an outside force to bring order into their chaos; the tenderness an unacknowledged but firm depen-dence on Patusan as the reflection of his own handiwork—indeed, of his very soul. When Dain Waris is described, this bond of specularity is again evoked: "If Jim took the lead, the other [Dain Waris] had captivated his leader. In fact, Jim the leader was a captive in every sense. The land, the people, the friendship, the love, were like the jealous guardians of his body. Every day added a link to the fetters of that strange freedom" (p. 262). That Dain Waris's "function" has been filled by Jim as his double and that this situation further fetters Jim becomes obvious by the conclusion of the novel.

Unlike the situation on board the *Patna,* it is evident that here Jim's obsession with self has by no means paralyzed him to act. To the contrary, in subduing Tunku Allang and in keeping him at bay, Jim displays much courage. It is not in action or inaction per se, but rather in the fantasized relation of self to action that the ideological moment resides; and this relation continues to hold sway, even though Jim seems at first to do quite a bit of good in Patusan. The lack of a conscious grasp of the social conditions of his actions in Patusan leads Jim to seek isolated realms where his powers can be fully realized and reflected in the arena of action, with no external contaminants. Royal Roussel has put the matter this way:

> Patusan is a world where Jim's "word was the one truth of every passing day" ... and associated as it is with his voice, Jim's control suggests the absolute power the consciousness of the artist exercises over the world he has brought into existence. Yet because this power results from the fact that this world ... is self-contained, a world apart from the life of men, the creation of such a world inevitably involves the limitation of the consciousness of the artist. His power is only good in this fixed area.[6]

In addition, Jim's failure fully to realize his power in the fixed setting of Patusan arises less from his imprisonment in his own handiwork than it does from his inability to accept that Patusan never was his handiwork in the first place; it was already "contaminated" by an outside, just as Jim's actions are in turn already contaminated by the imperial apparatus that calls them into existence.

This contamination of Jim's world, or rather this preexistent situation that only seems a contaminant, goes to the heart of the legitimation question. Avrom Fleishman has argued in *Conrad's Politics* that Conrad was in most essentials the inheritor of a nineteenth-century English organicist tradition of political thought, in which the indigenous state is "the ultimate political norm and is conceived ... as a *nation,* the community of people bound together by organic ties derived from their historical tradition and sense of place, their continuity in time and space."[7] The terms of the organicist model tend to meld together familial and political modes, so that political legitimacy comes to resemble (sometimes more than metaphorically) that of a son to a father. In his reign at Patusan, then, Jim is caught between two lines of filiation, from both of which he attempts to draw legitimacy.

In the first place, he partakes of a line of merchant-traders which extends back from the Portuguese Cornelius, through the Bavarian Stein, to the Scotsman M'Neil. It is Cornelius whom Jim at once displaces and represents in the Patusan trading post. In the second place, he rules Patusan as the displacing representative of Dain Waris, who is the blood-son of Doramin. Jim is therefore caught between two systems of authority: the Patusan system, which is based on a straightforward blood tie, and the European system, which is based on a chance concatenation of interests (and nationalities) and which only parodies an organic line of filiation. Jim's uneasy position, lodged as it is between these two loyalties, prepares the way for his fall.

To clarify what the first line of filiation really signifies one must also ask what these landless European interests are. The fact that Jim is described as building a fort with the labor of ex-slaves, planning his coffee plantation, and obtaining a monopoly on the gunpowder in Patusan indicates it clearly enough. These are commercial interests. Conrad's exposition of the connection between colonial expansion and pecuniary motive is consistent, running from "Heart of Darkness" through *Nostromo* to *Victory*. This commercial skein is also woven in *Lord Jim*, but in a peculiar way: as something to be defined, ignored, willed out of existence. This tale is Marlow's to tell, and his tendency (as much as Jim's) is to find reasons for empire which are noble and good. Just as the audience for Marlow's after-dinner story was significant for the narrative, so the addressee for the bundle of letters which tells the last part of the story provides a clue to its implications. Marlow writes to this man:

> You said ... that "giving your life up to them" (*them* meaning all of mankind with skins brown, yellow, or black in colour) "was like selling your soul to a brute." You contended that "that kind of thing" was only endurable and enduring when based on a firm conviction in the truth of ideas racially our own, in whose name are established the order, the morality of an ethical progress.   (P. 339)

To Marlow's correspondent, it is not love of gain but contact with the savages that makes colonialism shameful; still, Marlow agrees with his essential contention that the so-called British idea could redeem the imperial adventure from taint of whatever type. The notion of trusted stewardship and altruism is part of Marlow's creed—and perhaps proof to him of racial superiority as well. This belief in the British idea ("racially our own") informs Marlow's mode of description in evoking his last vision of Jim on the island of Patusan. As his ship departs,

> two half-naked fishermen had arisen as soon as I had gone; they were no doubt pouring the plaint of their trifling, miserable, oppressed lives into the ears of the white lord, and no doubt he was listening to it.... Their dark-skinned bodies vanished on the dark background long before I had lost sight of their protector. He was white from head to foot, and remained persistently visible with the stronghold of the night at his back.... That white figure in the stillness of coast and sea seemed to stand at the heart of a vast enigma. The twilight was ebbing fast from the sky above his head, the strip of sand had sunk already under his feet, he himself appeared no bigger than a child—then only a speck, a tiny white speck, that seemed to catch all the light in a darkened world.   (P. 336)

This passage, the conclusion of Marlow's first tale and an account of his last glimpse of the protagonist, is nothing if not chiaroscuro, where this "white speck" in a "darkened world" is the white lord and protector of the "dark-skinned bodies" around him. Like the code of the sea, this language of patronage also has recourse to the preindustrial codes of lord and vassal (especially ironic since Jim has earlier abolished formal feudalism in Patusan). This stewardship of the sovereign, imaged in Marlow's final glimpse of Tuan Jim, hearkens back to the vision of a personal social order; an order that appeals both to Jim and to Marlow, and whose strong cultural symbolism is used both to neutralize the racial collision brought about by imperialism (as Jim listens patiently to the fishermen's complaints) and also, paradoxically, to suggest the innate superiority of the race whose exemplar Jim is (as he alone captures all the light in a darkened world). White "from head to foot," in contrast to the scarcely dressed fishermen who blur into the wilderness background, Jim is the helpmeet of these "trifling, miserable, oppressed" peoples because he saves them from themselves. There are undercurrents of doubt even here. If Jim stands at "the heart of a vast enigma," is that enigma Patusan, or is it Jim's existence and motives? In other words, is he, like Kurtz in "Heart of Darkness," himself the enigma at whose heart he stands? Despite these darker shadings, and despite the odd detail that Jim increasingly resembles a child as he grows distant, it is nonetheless accurate that Jim is here cast in imagery far removed from the cloudiness Marlow so often bestows on him. Whether he is clearly seen in Marlow's last rendering, he is without question brightly seen; the blinding light he radiates here demonstrates just how much the narrator shares in Jim's own fantasies of nobility.

Given the symbolic freight that this vision of Jim carries, where by synecdoche his project comes to stand for the process of colonization itself, a character like Chester, for instance, who wants to put Jim to work for him, inspires the most profound shock and revulsion in Marlow. It is the British idea itself, in all its altruism, which Chester threatens to contaminate. A "West Australian," Chester "had discovered—so he said—a guano island somewhere," which he considers as "good as a gold-mine" (p. 161). He argues that Jim's conduct before the board of inquiry proves he is the man for his operation, because "he can't be much good" (p. 166). He states that "I'm going to dump forty coolies [on the guano island]—if I've got to steal 'em. Somebody must work the stuff. . . . Let him take charge. Make him supreme boss over the coolies. . . . Surely he wouldn't be afraid of anything forty coolies could do—with two six-shooters and he the only armed man, too! It's much better than it looks. I want you to help me to talk him over" (pp. 166–67). Marlow indignantly refuses. What startles in Chester's scenario is how closely it resembles Jim's subsequent position in Patusan as "supreme boss" over the indigenous population, gathering to himself as much gunpowder as possible. Chester's scenario for a man he sees as "no earthly good" is a strangely inverted version of the role Jim actually assumes—though he assumes with it the altruism that is supposed to make all the difference between a "supreme boss of the coolies" and the white lord and protector Jim has become for Marlow in his closing glimpse.

The potential for Chester to infect the hero is contained because Marlow himself puts a stop to it, and Jim is not asked to enlist his services in the pursuit of his schemes. Yet, Chester is not the only figure in Lord Jim who personifies greed in search of opportunity. Gentleman Brown, eventually an agent of Jim's downfall, is himself the fullest image of the crass materialism prefigured by Chester.

Brown is a more formidable contaminant than Chester because, whereas

Chester must get Jim's active acknowledgement and help in order to succeed, Brown needs only his acquiescence or paralysis. Chester's plan requires Jim's certitude that the two of them are in some way alike; Brown only needs Jim's uncertainty as to whether the two are so very different. In any event, Brown's appearance—unannounced and unthinkable—proves a fatal contaminant to Jim in his new role of feudal patron in Patusan.

Critics have argued endlessly over what it is that causes Jim to cave in to Brown. Some emphasize racial factors, others Brown's status as a kind of double for Jim.[8] These are finally not contradictory reasons for Jim's paralysis; in fact, they feed on each other rather well when the psychological leverage needed (and obtained) to produce the paralysis and uncertainty Brown uses to advantage is considered in more detail.

Brown at least is motivated by clear, if unsavory, purpose; his project is, if anything, too painfully apparent, and its goals are simple. The fuzziness that so frequently accompanies idealistic motivation is not his problem: "I came here for food. D'ye hear?—food to fill our bellies. And what did *you* come for? (p. 382). Jim's ambiguity of motive is what most handicaps him against Brown. After all, there is a strength, an integrity, in Brown's opportunism which Jim's high-mindedness lacks. Brown seems cognizant of his position in the social and material network of self-interest much more than Jim does. Similar as Jim and Brown may be in their complicity in the exploitation of others, Jim does not really acknowledge this complicity—to himself above all. Brown, on the other hand, accepts this fact of life and glories in it. As a result, Brown knows with firmer resolve who his friends (or accomplices) really are: "This is as good a jumping-off place for me as another. I am sick of my infernal luck. But it would be too easy. There are my men in the same boat—and, by God, I am not the sort to jump out of trouble and leave them in the d———d lurch" (pp. 382–83). This could, of course, be just more of Brown's talk, but its power derives from the fact that Brown credits his identity with and reliance upon the other members of his crew; the contrast with Jim of the *Patna* is sharp, to say the least. The scabrous integrity of Brown draws its strength from his firm knowledge of his own entrapment in imperialism's commercial motor. Both men are trapped, in a sense; but Brown understands the contours of that confinement, while Jim can only apparently guess at them.

As the narrative unfolds, one sees that despite his search, Jim never really found who "his people" were. For better or for worse, Brown knows who his people are, and he is stuck with them. But that very weakness is the psychological strength that beats his antagonist, whose supposed freedom from mere self-interest in turn becomes a prison of self-deception. Roussel says that "Jim, like the artist, who creates such an enclosed work, finds that he has become the prisoner of his own creation. He finds, in the words of Marlow, that he is 'imprisoned within the very freedom of his power.'"[9] This is a fair statement of the case, with the proviso that Jim is not finally the prisoner of his own autotelic creation so much as of an island and the preexisting human community on whom he still relies for his validation.

Chester and Brown are thus figures of contamination, not to mention that all-pervasive source of contamination, Cornelius, Jim's abject and constantly lurking sidekick. These contaminants are all heavily invested with the thematic of raw capital accumulation and greed, and they all threaten Jim either because they recognize a similarity in Jim's position to their own (as with Chester or Brown) or because they "go with the territory" as a part of Jim's role (as with Cornelius). Yet these figures, though dangerous to Jim's "integrity," are straightforwardly so. The merchant Stein is a more insidious contaminant, perhaps the most fateful one, in large part because his motives are good. Stein's place is therefore the locus of some of the most telling structural ambiguities of this tale.

If Jim seems to evince the delusion that he can separate his individual heroics from the material social structure that makes them possible, then Stein's must be to think that effective idealism can be promoted and sustained by imperialism's cash nexus. In line with this delusion, Stein sends Jim to Patusan in the first instance, seeing it as the "practical" thing he can do as a favor to Jim, to give him an "opportunity." In a famous passage, Stein says to Marlow:

> A man that is born falls into a dream like a man who falls into the sea. If he tries to climb out into the air as inexperienced people endeavour to do, he drowns—*nicht wahr?*... No! I tell you! The way is to the destructive element submit yourself, and with the exertions of your hands and feet in the water make the deep, deep sea keep you up.   (P. 214)

This admonition can be read as Stein's formula for a romanticism that comes to be tempered by its very contamination. By trying to fulfill his ideals—by "following the dream," as Stein goes on to suggest—Jim will learn to endure the reality that will confront him in his attempts. It is a neat formula, though flawed in some signal respects. Even Marlow has his doubts: "The whisper of his conviction seemed to open before me a vast and uncertain expanse, as of a crepuscular horizon on a plain at dawn—or was it, perchance, at the coming of the night? One had not the courage to decide; but it was a charming and deceptive light" (p. 215).

Like Chester, Brown, and Cornelius, Stein's primary motivation in coming to Asia was capital accumulation. The mentality that accompanies the merchant instinct is surely not alien to him, though neither is political activity as Marlow relates. But the naked greed whose aura clings to the others does not attach to Stein. For one thing, he is presented as more interesting psychologically than the others. For another, there is a temporal displacement at work, since Stein's active exertions on behalf of wealth are long since finished. He has, so to speak, made his pile, and it is only atop that pile that Stein can convince otherwise sensible critics that he is some sort of *raisonneur* in the *Lord Jim* drama.[10] It should be clear, though, that in addition to commenting upon the action, Stein is himself an agent in the drama. Some sense of his role can be gleaned from an unlikely source: his butterfly collection.

The famous butterflies Stein collects have admittedly been subject to innumerable symbolic readings, but one irresistibly suggests itself to the reader mindful of his past career. Pursued by Stein and pinned to his board, they are part of the process by which he has pursued wealth in all its varieties. Indeed, they are analogous to those living, breathing men whose labor Stein has taken and converted into storable capital. In concert with the larger colonial structure, Stein can take the activity of men, transform that activity into a fixed object, and store it; and the pinning down of the butterflies enacts, as in a sacrificial ritual, the way Stein converts this labor into money. When, at the close of the major sacrificial ritual in the book, Jim's death, Stein is described as sadly waving to his butterflies, how, in the light of the above interpretation of those butterflies, is that gesture best read?

I dwell upon the death of Jim because it brings to a head the contradictions in the ideology of sacrifice that grounds imperialism as a legitimate form of rule. Everyone, Marlow, Brierly, Jim, and even Marlow's anonymous correspondent—who decries it—takes it for granted that the British mission of empire is profoundly altruistic. Many readers of the novel, taking similar assumptions for granted, choose to read Jim's acquiescence in his execution as his fullest moment of recognition and a voluntary sacrifice of self before the community of Patusan. Thus, Conrad commentator Avrom Fleishman states:

> In the final analysis, colonization is a viable—the only viable—form of imperialism, not so much because it ameliorates the worst conditions of native life but because the commitment to social progress allows the individual to discover himself in the community formed and improved by his efforts. He can then egoistically surrender himself to the community, wearing, as Jim does, "a proud and unflinching glance." [11]

Leaving aside the larger question of colonialism as viable governance, one notes that Jim's decision to have Doramin put him to death is less an admission of personal guilt than a concession to local custom; this suggests that the egoism Fleishman remarks is not in the surrender to a community that reflects Jim's handiwork, but rather in fatal alienation from that community. He shows no remorse and in fact repeats again his frequent statement "Nothing can touch me"—fitting words for a man incapable of admitting any contamination, much as he formally accepts his guilt. His gesture of sacrifice—performed, as usual, by another "priest" than himself—contains within it the recognition that, in the view of his adopted community, he has done wrong; it also serves to show the community and himself that he can, the *Patna* incident to the contrary, overcome the fear of death. But atonement for felt guilt, as the "proud, unflinching glance" attests, is not at issue for Jim. What seems at first glance to be the act of profoundest altruism, the sacrifice, is really the moment of greatest egotism. In this respect, the climactic scene recalls a paradox that bedeviled Marlow when Jim took his medicine and testified at the *Patna* hearings: it soon became clear in that instance that he did so less out of eagerness to admit his mistakes than out of stubborn refusal to see them as mistakes. Furthermore, as Roussel points out, this willingness to die represents a reneging on his commitment to Jewel never to leave her—Jewel, who is his surest claim to legitimacy in the Patusan native line—and in that sense, his decision is, if anything, the opposite of altruism. [12]

It is nonetheless accurate for Ian Watt to state that "Jim does something which no other hero of a great twentieth-century novel has done: he dies for his honour." [13] He has, finally, little choice but to be true to what Marlow calls the "shadowy ideal of conduct." And despite its narcissistic overtones, Jim's death is still a sacrifice of a sort: a sacrifice on the altar of Stein's good intentions. The "opportunity which, like an Eastern bride, had come veiled to his side" is, in this inverted wedding imagery, not Jewel but death itself, and the bride is unwittingly given away by Stein (p. 416). His plans for Jim are to be ways of uniting the mix for a time, becoming at once proprietor of a thriving trading post and enlightened leader of the Patusan people. But the presence of Cornelius is at once the emblém for the impossibility of this alliance and a crucial factor in bringing about the death of Dain Waris, a direct cause of Jim's ultimate downfall. This structural ambiguity within Jim's position makes a quandary of the sort occasioned by Brown almost inevitable. [14] For all his talk of the "destructive element," Stein does not acknowledge the dissonant lineages built into Jim's position as the adoptive heir of both Doramin and Stein: dissonant claims that Jim must live up to as the representative for both Dain Waris and Cornelius at once. The sea of Patusan is supposed to bear Jim up, but somehow he only drowns in it.

Jim's failure to act in this second part of the narrative is a failure of legitimation for this adoptive son in a way the *Patna* incident was not. His position is one of direct governance here; the reader and Jim himself both see the people whose lives are affected by what Jim does, whereas in the early chapters the pilgrims are on the periphery of vision. More importantly, Jim's conflict in the first section involved whether to admit he was a spiritual member of his crew. In the Patusan crisis, his loyalty, however furtive or unacknowledged, to one class of people is in active opposition to his loyalty to another class. Like his indecision on the *Patna*, his indecisiveness in Patusan only makes matters worse, and the inevitable split in loyalty destroys him. He comes to resemble one of Stein's butterflies in his very victimization by the situation Stein has presented him. We recall here one very potent symbol of the fragile union of opposites entailed in Jim's position: the silver ring of Doramin's that Stein confers upon Jim as his first introduction to Doramin, and which rolls against Jim's foot as Doramin rises to shoot him. Watt points out the silver ring's curious status as talisman of the brittle marriage of interests between colonizer and colonized; he even notes how the ring seems to be "an ironic variation on the folk-tale motif of the poisoned gift." [15] Watt does not elaborate upon how this ironic gift motif, if accurate, could be presumed to reflect on the giver; but then perhaps elaboration is not needed. The "poisoned gift" may speak for itself.

Jim is not completely victim, however. Although a clash between the indigenous peoples and other interests was sooner or later likely, Jim's inaction makes him a collaborator in his own destruction beyond the requirements of the situation, as if to display, despite himself, his a priori contamination by what he thought could never touch him. For like the ideology he takes with him, Jim was always already contaminated by the larger colonial structure that he sought at once to justify and to deny. Indeed, when Marlow describes him as a "disembodied spirit astray amongst the passions of this earth, ready to surrender himself faithfully to the claim of his own world of shades," we are tempted to read it as a definitive sign that Jim is an embodiment of ideology itself—an insubstantial mirage existing uncomfortably among brute material and social facts.

What Marlow has in mind, though, is something much more metaphysical, and—usually the case with Marlow—more mysterious. Jim's sickness, as Marlow represents it, is ontological rather than historical; and the language Marlow uses when he reflects upon Jim's malaise consistently seeks the high ground of opaque subjectivity. In fact, the logic of the narrative as sketched here is systematically elided by Marlow, who at crucial points takes refuge in two realms: the inscrutable workings of fate and the murkiness of individual motive. When Marlow reflects, the thematic accent is on ambiguity at times everything seems, like Jim, to be "inscrutable at heart," "under a cloud." Marlow's despairing remark "I am fated never to see him clearly" can be said to reflect upon the viewer as well as the object viewed.

In the first section of the story, concerning the *Patna,* the obsession with subjective motive predominates. Marlow's evocation of mood in going to dine with Jim sets the tone for the revelations: "The views he let me have of himself were like those glimpses through the shifting rents in a thick fog—bits of vivid and vanishing detail, giving no connected idea of the general aspect of a country. . . . Upon the whole he was misleading" (p. 76). As the novel progresses and Jim becomes further dogged by the consequences of the *Patna* incident, the emphasis becomes less "existential" and shifts rather toward the unfolding of ineluctable fate: "A clean slate, did he say? As if the initial word of each our destiny were not graven in imperishable characters upon the face of a rock" (p. 186). And when Jim makes the crucial decision to allow Brown passage, Marlow says: "There's no doubt his mind was made up that Brown should have his way clear back to the sea. His fate revolted, was forcing his hand" (p. 391). Indeed, this stress laid upon fate has led many critics to argue, however incorrectly, that the novel has a tragic overtone, or that Jim is a tragic hero."[16]

To a large extent, then, the reading of *Lord Jim* pursued here, prompted though it is by the narrative logic, is denied systematically by the narrative voice, as if Marlow (or his author) were trying to halt the synecdochic logic of the narrative terms and put them in "quarantine" to stop the contamination; as if (perhaps in the wake of Brierly's example) something must be done to stop the expanding concentric circles that widen from the plot incidents to implicate Marlow himself and his reader.

Like any novel, *Lord Jim* is not so much a document recording a world as it is a way of construing values to itself and to its culture. In that signifying role, *Lord Jim's* rhetorical function is to present a possibly devastating threat to specific assumptions of Conrad's audience—assumptions Conrad seems to have shared, at least in part—and to resolve the resultant contradictions in such a way as to reaffirm those values. For those purposes, it is not enough that Jim be a romantic idealist; his romantic idealism, as I have indicated, must be of a sort consistent with the British idea. It is his status as the carrier of British public-school values and colonial ideology which makes him a source of identification and interest for Marlow and for the virtual audience of the narrative, yet the results of Jim's attempts to realize the British idea prove too damaging to be resolved on their own terms without breaking too many ideological constraints. To retain its implicit "pact with its audience," to reaffirm the endangered values, the text occludes the historical generalizations about imperialism and its mission which are suggested by the very terms used to make the readership concerned with the story in the first place; instead, the narrative moves to a thematic level that pointedly drops the implications of the narrative for its larger historical moment, at those instances where the narrator reflects upon the events.

The gap between the narrative logic and the thematic metaphysics is the rhetorical space that Marlow creates and from which he speaks: it measures the extent to which the "white man's burden" ideology has become, by the time of *Lord Jim,* very fragile indeed. As a further step in the fathering contamination, Jim's final tragedy in Patusan becomes for Marlow what the *Patna* incident was for Brierly: a danger to be warded off. Marlow must make Jim's fate into either the totally individual drama of an isolated man or else the ritual emblem for the human condition, rather than admit his own more immediate entanglement in the larger whole of which Jim was a part. By making Jim's story a pure emblem—and emblem of mystery at that—Marlow has erected a talisman of metaphor which should be proof against the spreading contagion of the narrative's more direct causal (or metonymic) implications. The metaphysics of doom and fate here have the paradoxical effect of helping to rescue the British idea from the taint of Jim's failure.

On the ashes of the narrative's own logic, Marlow attempts to reconstruct a community of identification for Jim. One should recall Marlow's initial meeting with Jim in the Malabar House in reading his farewell lines:

> He is one of us—and have I not stood up once, like an evoked ghost, to answer for his eternal constancy? Was I so very wrong after all? Now he is no more, there are days when the reality of his existence comes to me with an immense, with an overwhelming force; and yet upon my honour there are moments, too, when he passes from my eyes like a disembodied spirit astray amongst the passions of this earth, ready to surrender himself faithfully to the claim of his own world of shades.   (P. 416)

He sums Jim up in a characteristically ineffable line: "Who knows? He is gone, inscrutable at heart" (p. 416).

The community of "us" in which Marlow places Jim, the "us" from whose shifting locus Marlow speaks, has a much different resonance from that first community Marlow evokes when describing Jim in the Malabar House. That Jim in the Malabar House is above all "of the right sort": he has a mission, is exemplary of a particular nation and class, and embodies public-school ideals. It is in this narrower sense that this specific Jim can be called "one of us." In the closing evocation Jim retains his typicality—but of what has he become typical? Of everyone and, in a sense, of no one; and he is typical primarily by virtue of his inscrutability. Even the times when Marlow professes to see Jim clearly, as the closing remarks suggest, it is the force of his existence, some kind of mythic quantum, which is felt—and not any generalizable notions derived therefrom. Even when Jim shines brightly, he is obscure. The more specific freight of symbolism he starts out with—public school, the British idea, and so forth—are stripped from him at crucial moments in the narrative, and only his murkiness is allowed, finally, to remain.

Again, it is not so much that this shift in Jim's allegorical weight is somehow wrong or intrinsically absurd; the rhetorical point would be that, strategically, the shift is just right. It is symptomatic because it is an elision of the text's own narrative logic. One is initially drawn to Jim's story by the assumption that it may have something to reveal about the legitimacy of the merchant marine and the British project of empire, and that the story would provide clues to the viability and fate of that larger project. Yet, as the story reaches its conclusion, those specific historical dimensions are ignored in Marlow's reflections in the favor of the abstractly metaphysical and the unknowable. But this turning-away is a pointing-toward, symptomatic of a profound unease with the imperialist project which gains increasing currency with both authors and audiences in Britain, as witness later, more full-blown "thesis novels" on the British in Asia, such as E. M. Forster's *A Passage to India*.

Marlow's oscillation between his own narrative's logic and thematic ambiguity is an indication of the way Conrad has fashioned a narrative by taking over the prevailing ideology of the "white man's burden" and transforming it. This ideology has been pushed close to its limit by the narrative, and that ideology's failure inscribed in the consequences of Jim's very actions. That Marlow must then have recourse to the metaphysics of ambiguity in reflecting upon that failure is only a measure of the extent to which *Lord Jim* has exposed the limitations of the historically based values that were its raw material. To read the attempt to retrieve the British idea from the consequences of its own failure is to measure the gap that is Marlow's space of enunciation, and this doomed effort that he speaks. Or which speaks him.

NOTES

[1] Conrad, *Lord Jim* (New York: Doubleday, Page & Co., 1924), p. 78. All subsequent references to this work are noted in the body of the text.

[2] Robert F. Lee makes a similar argument in *Conrad's Colonialism* (The Hague: Mouton, 1969), pp. 35–39. Curiously, though Lee isolates the "us" of "one of us" quite precisely, he still seems anxious to conclude that Conrad's essential view of the "us" is affirmative.

[3] See Conrad's article "Tradition," which attacks a British M.P. for intimating that the merchant marine lacked a tradition of courage, despite the generally eulogistic character of the remarks as a whole. Cf. *Notes on Life and Letters*, in *Collected Works* (Garden City, N.Y.: Doubleday & Co., 1924), p. 195.

[4] A figure who ignores the social and material conditions of his own work and who views himself as the hero in a book could well be interpreted as the carrier of ideology, and this is indeed the way Jim's character is encoded. If Louis Althusser is right to say that ideology, like the Freudian ego, is a *fonction de méconnaissance*, then Jim is the ideological character par excellence, the man whose image of his own mission—and, by extension, that of his nation and race—is a noble fiction, subtended by the social and

material elements it strains always to ignore. On Althusser's relay between the Freudian ego and ideology as two forms of the *fonction de méconnaissance*, see *Lenin and Philosophy*, trans. Ben Brewster (New York: Monthly Review Press, 1971) p. 172, pp. 218–19, et passim.

[5] Albert Guérard, *Conrad the Novelist*, (New York: Atheneum, 1967), pp. 155–56.

[6] Royal Roussel, *The Metaphysics of Darkness* (Baltimore: Johns Hopkins University Press, 1971), p. 100.

[7] Avrom Fleischman, *Conrad's Politics* (Baltimore: Johns Hopkins University Press, 1967), pp. 58–59.

[8] Lee emphasizes the "subtle appeal to their common blood" that Brown allegedly makes to Jim in *Conrad's Colonialism*, p. 105. Guérard, despite his earlier belief that race is the decisive factor, comes to decide that Brown's role is a kind of *semblable* for Jim: a mirror-image that brings forth memories of Jim's own disgrace on the *Patna*. Discussing this theory in *Conrad the Novelist*, p. 150, he credits it to Gustav Morf.

[9] Roussel, *Metaphysics of Darkness*, p. 101.

[10] Tanner, "Butterflies and Beetles—Conrad's Two Truths," *Chicago Review* 16, no. 1 (1963): 123–40. Tanner recognizes the contaminating role played by Cornelius, Chester, and Brown, although he ignores the subtler but more effective contaminating agent that Stein becomes.

[11] Fleischman, *Conrad's Politics*, p. 111.

[12] Roussel, *Metaphysics of Darkness*, p. 93. Just as Jim relies on the people of Patusan for his own sense of worth—just as "they possessed him," rather than the reverse—so he now relies upon the community for the opportunity to display his gesture of "exalted egotism," although undoubtedly he sees the community as somehow his creation. To the end, Jim apparently ignores the bonds of dependence which make his great gesture possible.

[13] Ian Watt, *Conrad in the Nineteenth Century* (Berkeley and Los Angeles: University of California Press, 1979), p. 356.

[14] This ambiguity in Jim's line of legitimacy is at least sensed by Watt when he remarks that "Jim cannot possibly reconcile all the just claims upon him" during his tenure on Patusan (ibid., p. 348).

[15] Ibid., p. 347.

[16] Robert B. Heilman, in his introduction to *Lord Jim* (New York: Rinehart, 1957), suggests this line of interpretation on p. xxiii. This shift from subjective psychology to ineffable fate is partly attributable to an increased tendency in the narrative for Jim's tale to be told not by himself but by other witnesses: "It is through the eyes of others that we take our last look at him," says Marlow (p. 339). It is partly owing to the larger ritual setting of Jim's final fall from grace, as well. Both modes for evoking ambiguity are retained throughout, though, and both elide much that the narrative logic itself has built up. The imagery surrounding Jim's story alternates between subjective motive and public, inevitable fate—both shrouded in the Marlovian mists of inscrutability.

Kenneth Simons

THE LUDIC IMAGINATION: "YOUTH"

It is this very feeling of being a hero which one of our best authors has well expressed in the famous phrase *"Es kann dir nix g'schehen"* It seems to me, however, that this significant mark of invulnerability very clearly betrays—His Majesty of Ego, the hero of all day-dreams and all novels.   —Freud, "The Relation of the Poet to Day-Dreaming"

Young Marlow: Actions That a Man Might Play

The best reason for supposing the idea of the ludic is of some importance to "Youth" is that the story begins with an anticipatory denial of play. Marlow's five listeners all "began life" in the merchant service and so share "the strong bond of the sea," "the fellowship of the craft" which is "life itself" (Y 3). Enthusiasm for yachting or cruising on the other hand is merely "the amusement of life" and implicitly issues only in imitative, ersatz versions of these. Let us assume for the moment that Conrad's overt directives for interpreting the story and the categories they impose are shored around the problem of play—which in a story about youth he cannot avoid, but from which he is also compelled to divert attention. The first question, then, is what Conrad would like the reader to understand as the constituents of "life itself."

The most striking fact about the story is the perfectly symmetrical alternation of natural forces and the symmetry of the human responses they elicit. To stay afloat, the *Judea's* crew desperately pumps water out of the leaking hold, at first continuously and then two hours in every four. When the decision is made to put back to Falmouth, the heavy winds which had exacerbated the leak now swing around directly into their faces, thus stabilizing the ship but also stymieing their retreat. Once in port, the extreme duress of the episode collapses into unbroken

From *The Ludic Imagination: A Reading of Joseph Conrad* (Ann Arbor, MI: UMI Research Press, 1985), pp. 1–10.

boredom and languid inactivity. When on the ship's last passage out the coal begins to burn, they pump water back into the hold with the same total expenditure of energy, this time eight men working while four rest. Clearly, the structure of experience in the story is such that the negative aspect of one situation becomes, in retrospect, the absent positive aspect of the next; recall that while fighting the fire, Mahon wishes only that the now well-caulked ship would again "spring a tidy leak" (Y 21). Yet the flooding and burning of the hold are the donné of existence, fixed extremes which alternate but never coalesce. In effect, the men are drawn into the dialectic of experience by taking upon themselves the role of the absent positive element; in both extremes, and at every point, outward reality negates their intentions, thus forcing them into the distinctly human function of creating, or rather being—point for point—the positive countervailing force.

This, presumably, is the thematic armature of the story wherein Conrad finds, and would like the reader to find, "a symbol of existence" (Y 4). Conrad's sense of "existence" is expressed in the reductive simplicity and exaggerated completeness with which the barely maintained equipoise between contending forces seems to fill out the whole of life. Marlow is symbolically situated between Beard (age) and Mahon (pronounced "Mann"). The most strenuous exertion can only hope to protract the vital balance of forces, never establish them permanently; life provides you with just enough strength and leeway to counterbalance death, and no more. The interlinking of necessity and work, demand and response, is absolute. Human purpose and work are synonymous ("A man is a worker," Conrad says in one of his essays "If he is not that he is nothing. Just nothing—" [NLL 190]), and the poignancy of the human condition as it is modeled on the *Judea* arises from the fact that what seems most purposeful in life is surrounded and conditioned by an abiding futility. In a somewhat simplified form, these are the thematic generalities that bulk large in the narrative as the ones Conrad would like the reader to pursue.

The problem, however, is that unlike Captain Beard, Marlow does not feel the metaphysically claustrophobic situation as one of entrapment. On the contrary, it evokes for him the sharpest and most vivid sensation of being alive, and for just that reason is the appropriate vehicle for his story. Moreover, his formulation of the airtight juncture of necessity and response as being most evocative of that vitality is thoroughly imbued with the sense that it is fun.

Our argument is that existing across from the alternation of physical forces, and the thematic categories they carry, is a parallel alternation in the perception of those events. Marlow selectively incorporates elements of external reality into an imaginative schema which antecedes the events themselves; thus he is able to see fatality as adventure, and all action, regardless of its content, gives rise to a sense of promise or possibility. Beard, of course, sees fatality for what it is, as possibilities closing down. Insofar as he attempts to transform an inner will into an outer material achievement, his character is defined by a process opposite to Marlow's. Where Marlow seems to perform an action for its own sake, as an end in itself, Beard does it for the sake of a goal not immediately inherent in the actions themselves. For him, action is fruitful only it if realizes a particular set of intentions.

The basic stuff of Marlow's youthful egotism can be seen in terms of the primacy of subjectivity which actively shapes reality and subordinates it to the self. Psychologically, his position is invulnerable; able to transform outward negativity into what is imaginatively positive, he is beyond the reach of humiliation or failure. Beard's orientation toward even the most humble objective achievement is precisely what lays him open to these and, ultimately, sees him shaped by reality and entirely subordinate to it. Beneath the obviously contrasting qualities of youth and age are the basic elements of the distinction between ludic and nonludic behavior, play and work. Within the unimaginative, morally austere universe of work and duty where actions "count" is the open-ended ludic universe of youth, and at the outset we are interested more in the identity than in the conflict between the two spheres.

Beginning with the work at the pumps, Marlow's mood oscillates throughout the story between the sentiments of romance and responsibility, adventure and duty. Coming on deck to take his watch, he catches a glimpse of their "weary, serious faces."

> "We pumped all the four hours. We pumped all night, all day, all the week— watch and watch.... There was for us no sky, there were for us no stars, no sun, no universe—nothing but angry clouds and an infuriated sea. We pumped ... for dear life; and it seemed to last for months, for years, for all eternity, as though we had been dead and gone to a hell for sailors.... The sails blew away, she lay broadside on under a weather-cloth, the ocean poured over her, and we did not care. We turned those handles, and had the eyes of idiots. As soon a we had crawled on deck I used to take a round turn with a rope about the men, the pumps, and the mainmast, and we turned, we turned incessantly, with the water to our waists, to our necks, over our heads. It was all one."   (Y 12)

We then swing back to the individual response, the more deeply held subjective impression:

> "And there was somewhere in me the thought: By Jove! this is the deuce of an adventure—something you read about; and it is my first voyage as second mate ... and here I am lasting it out as well as any of these men, and keeping my chaps up to the mark.... I would not have given up the experience for worlds. I had moments of exultation."   (Y 12)

This perceptual pattern in which "romance" corresponds to subjective impressions, and "responsibility" corresponds to objective participation, exists across from the alternation of fire and water as the most salient characteristic of the narrative. While youth itself models the interaction of the work and play spheres, it is untroubled by an awareness of the duality. Both evoke the same response, both are felt with equal verve. Responsibility, for example, is "romantic"; "Fancy!" he says, "Second mate for the first time—a really responsible officer!" In the ship's "Do or Die" motto he finds a "touch of romance" that "took [his] fancy immensely" (Y 5). The East itself, "ruled by kings more cruel than Nero the Roman, and more splendid than Solomon the Jew" transcends the threadbare categories of the spirit; the appeal of the "hebraic" professional ethos of duty and the appeal of the pagan East, means and ends, are undifferentiated.

The sequence repeats itself when the coal begins to burn. Having "never noticed so much before how twisted and bowed" Beard is, Marlow first observes his "hollow eyes and sunken cheeks" (Y 22). Undaunted by Beard's spectral appearance, Marlow is "as pleased and proud as though [he] had helped to win a great naval battle" when it appears briefly that the fire is extinguished. The subsequent explosion of the coal dust does not dim his exultation:

> "You should have seen them! Some were in rags, with black faces . . . like sweeps, and had bullet heads that seemed closely cropped, but were in fact singed to the skin. Others, of the watch below, awakened by being shot out from their collapsing bunks, shivered incessantly, and kept on groaning even as we went about our work. But they all worked. That crew of Liverpool hard cases had in them the right stuff. . . . we stumbled, we crept, we fell, we barked our shins on the wreckage, we hauled." (Y 25)

Bewildered by the violence of the explosion and apprehensive that the charred masts will topple over, the crew retreats aft. Marlow, on the other hand, thinks "Now, this is something like! This is great. I wonder what will happen" (Y 26). Just prior to the abandonment of the ship the image of the naval battle appears once again. Each man "had the marks as of a naval battle about him—bandaged heads, tied-up arms, a strip of dirty rag round a knee" which, in the light of the flames, leads him to a further analogy with a "band of desperate pirates," "those reckless sea-robbers of old making merry amidst violence and disaster " (Y 33).

The most significant instance of this wavering between objective and imaginative participation occurs when Marlow is given command of his own "cockleshell." The *Judea* has to be abandoned, although he feels neither regret looking back nor trepidation looking forward; requisite fidelity in seeing the last of the old ship and the prospect of his own command are equally "fine." This episode is the point at which the major forces of the story, here symbolized chronologically, cross-sect. As Beard is losing his first command, Marlow is gaining his. Exasperated with the delay and seeing no reason why they should not leave at once, Marlow clambers aboard and finds Beard sleeping like a child with "his legs drawn up and one arm under his head" (Y 32). The reversal of their respective positions is reflected in the reversal of Marlow's tone. From pirates to pragmatism is evidently a short step: countering Mahon's apology for Beard's weariness with an "indignant" reply ("there will be no life boats . . . if you fool around much longer"), Marlow initiates the abandonment among the lingering crew members and nudges Beard from the ship.

Beard orders the boats to stay as close together as possible in case of bad weather:

> "And do you know what I thought? I thought I would part company as soon as I could. I wanted to have my first command all to myself. I wasn't going to

sail in a squadron if there were a chance for independent cruising. I would
make land by myself. I would beat the other boats."   (Y 34)

To that end he jury-rigs a sail and soon outdistances Beard and Mahon. In the same
sense that he "invents" a sail, he creates the entire episode; sighting a ship on its
outward passage, he says nothing to his men, wary that it might be bound back to
Europe and so deprive him of both his "first command" and his "discovery" of the
East. After voluntarily declining to be rescued—a decision, it is important to note,
he makes for the men as well—Marlow incongruously redirects the reader's attention to the degree of physical punishment he endured in the lifeboat. The
pattern he finds in duress here is qualitatively indistinguishable from that on the
Judea; rain squalls keep them "baling for dear life" but, in filling the water cask,
quench the thirst the work creates. Upon making land, Marlow "exults like a
conqueror" (Y 38), but again this is only one of the set of terms he has reserved
all along to assess his experience. During the voyage he found in the *Judea's*
ungainliness an analogy to the "men of old who, centuries ago, went that road in
ships that sailed no better, to the land of palms, and spices . . ." (Y 18), "the East of
the ancient navigators, so old, so mysterious . . . living and unchanged, full of danger
and promise" (Y 41).

The men do not share the exultation of his vision. "Blind with fatigue" they fall
off the thwarts to sleep. The arrival of Beard's boat three hours after his own
completes the pattern of the episode by evoking Marlow's "professional" concern.
The mood of his warning to "mind the end of that jetty, sir" brackets the episode
and sets off sharply the content it encloses. In much the same manner, the two
steamships *Miranda* and *Celestial* bracket the story as a whole. The gruff voice
issuing from the *Miranda* after it collides with the *Judea* in port is intensified in the
volley of abuse ("It began by calling me Pig, and from that went crescendo into
unmentionable adjectives—in English" [Y 39]) which hurtles from the *Celestial*
mistaking Marlow's boat for a native craft. Before sleep, Marlow's "little life" is
rounded with abuse; ultimately the choice he has to make is not between romance
and responsibility, but between the compound he creates of both and the reality
represented by the steamships.

The adventure impulse, dominant in the instances cited above, should in some
way be contrasted with the "professional" attitude of duty and responsibility to
which Marlow so often alludes. Early in the story a sea washes over the *Judea,*
completely submerging Marlow and his watch at the pumps and shattering the deck
house "as if a shell had exploded inside." "As soon as I got my breath I shouted, *as
in duty bound* [my emphasis], 'Keep on boys!' " Later, when the coal dust explodes
and sends Marlow hurtling through the air, Beard (also dazed by the explosion) asks
him where the cabin table is: "I found my voice, and stammered out *as if conscious
of some gross neglect of duty,* [my emphasis] 'I don't know . . .' " (Y 24). As he is
sent sprawling into the afterhatch, Marlow sees the burning cargo below. His is the
most direct experience of the "hell for sailors"; at both points it is he who lives most
immediately and directly the fate of the ship, and at both points the sentiment of

duty is imaged as an almost unconscious response, embedded at the threshold of life itself.

Where the explosion is the occasion of Marlow's exultation, it is the scene of Beard's destitution, corresponding to the burst of energy and the vacuum it leaves. The polished table around which Marlow's listeners are assembled reflects their faces (Y 3, 42); so too the disintegrated cabin table reflects Beard in his entirety. Appropriately, the explosion occurs while he is winding the ship's chronometers. "Where we had our breakfast that morning he saw only a great hole in the floor. This appeared to him so awfully mysterious, and impressed him so immensely, that what he saw and heard on deck were mere trifles in comparison" (Y 24–25). In the midst of the vision of chaos and self-extinction, Beard takes the helm to get the "smouldering shell of a ship" back on course, and gently insists that the men square the foreyards.

Marlow's elaboration of the response is far more significant. He claims that there was not a man among the lot of "battered and bandaged scarecrows" who, while aloft, did not think the weakened mast would fall over with them on it. "Do you see the lot of us there, putting a neat furl in the sails of that ship doomed to arrive nowhere?"

> What made them do it—what made them obey me when I, thinking con-
> sciously how fine it was, made them drop the bunt of the foresail twice to try
> and do it better? What?   (Y 28)

For later reference, note should be taken that he formulates their motivation as something "secret," that "hidden something . . . that makes racial difference, that shapes the fate of nations" and, rather oxymoronically, as "something solid like a principle and masterful like an instinct" (Y 28). Both of his ideas evidence a fusion of the biological and the ideological, operative, for instance, in Marlow's "uncon-scious" sense of duty above. More immediately, however, we sense that his musings spin away from the central impression of the scene. The moment the sense of duty is articulated or appreciated outside of its integral relation to necessity, it takes on a deeply egoistic coloring. Thus the feeling here is that the quality of his self-awareness and the actual content of the moral imperative he observes cancel each other out, that the ideal of an unconscious sense of duty is belied by the highly self-conscious appreciation of selflessness. Accusing Marlow of cloaking his egotism behind the appreciation of professional morality, or of genuine maliciousness in putting the satisfaction derived from an idea before the lives of his men ("Fancy! Second mate for the first time—a really responsible officer!") would be overly severe because it ignores the simultaneity of the work and play moods. Thus we can recognize an underlying consistency between his behavior here while cele-brating professional selflessness, and in the lifeboat where the men are props in an imagined scenario, for whom he can choose severe and extended physical punishment so that he might "discover" the East, and then, unaware of any in-congruity, punch and kick them out of the state of exhaustion he has created in order to row out to the *Celestial* and ask for a passage away (Y 38). Moreover, just as his physical actions symbolically epitomized the life of the ship, so here he emerges as its ideological exemplar. The crew's obedience (ostensibly his subject) and Beard's rather pathetic order fall away to either side of him. It is he, and not Beard, who is concerned with a further aesthetic perfection in the midst of danger; and thus it is he, and not the crew, who is most graceful under pressure. It simply cannot be gainsaid that when we scratch the surface of these diverse episodes, they all have in common the fact that Marlow is the superlative of the virtue which the episode defines; at the pumps he is most dutiful, he is the instigating force of the abandonment, in the lifeboat the strongest, aloft the most courageous.

The censoring of the play element takes the form of Marlow's attempting to cast the import of what he is saying onto a theme that does not exist. Stepping outside of the dramatic sequence, and therefore straining to make his point, he reminds his listeners that he was only twenty and that the East was "waiting" for him (cf. Y 4, 12, 15). In the midst of the delays, detours and cul-de-sacs that comprise the life of the *Judea* he wants to remind them that the main thread of the narrative is the desire to get to the East, this being symbolic of the "romance of illusions" which has "passed unseen, in a sigh" like his youth. Yet Marlow quite explicitly declines to relinquish these "illusions." In the purple passage following the lifeboat episode he says that "I have seen its secret places and have looked into its very soul; but now I see it always from a small boat ... blue and afar ..." (Y 37). The vision of the East remains private, out of time, held aloof from political denigration in the contrast of real and play conquerors—one given to profanity and the other to poetry. The very saccharine quality of his apology for those of "the conquering race" who fall prey to the East's stealthy Nemesis indicates that public terms of evaluation have no bearing on the experience; "for me the East is contained in that vision of my youth. It is all in that moment when I opened my young eyes on it" (Y 42). This major inconsistency is a function of a deeper contrariety of intentions which runs throughout the work. The evocation of this entire thematic complex—the lure of the East, the association of Marlow's sense of romance with it, the consequent dispelling of illusions—diverts attention from the fact that romance is not a function of the East, the largely incidental goal, but rather of the multiple forms the play mood takes within the experience on the *Judea* itself. "Illusions" (from *illudere,* "in play"), consonant with ludic fantasy, are displaced onto the East, away from the actor and the more immediate forms of his playing.

Given this, Marlow's notion that the episode is a "symbol of existence" is strangely shallow. If it is that, then one renounces one's youthful illusions and recognizes that the *Judea,* not Bankok, is the promised land, or at least all that "men born to trouble, to leaky ships, and to ships that burn" will ever see of it (Y 31). But the underlying issue, again, has very little to do with illusions about the East, whether considered as a repository of adventures or as a symbol of death. These are a thematic patina laid over the problematic implications of Marlow's desire to play, and perhaps over the absence of a genuine conviction that the futility of warring with opposing forces on the *Judea* is life itself. The atmosphere Marlow creates rests finally on the sense that the episode retains the same appeal in the present as it had in the past, that youthful illusions are not undercut, but romanticized in retrospect.

For these reasons Marlow's apostrophes to his lost youth and his contrapuntal intrusions of "pass the bottle" ring hollow. Both are mechanically and imperfectly grafted onto the fact that to the extent that he declines to relinquish his illusions, he declines to relinquish the sensibility of youth. "To me," he says of the *Judea*, "she was not an old rattle-trap carting about the world a lot of coal for a freight—to me she was the endeavour, the test, the trial of life" (Y 12). The tone in conjunction with the past tense "was" again tries to force a distinction where none exists. Actually the ship is never perceived as a rattle-trap, never seen as it is. It was seen symbolically then, and it is seen symbolically now ("a symbol of existence"), a presumption without which there would be no story. Marlow's insistence that he loved the ship's commonness and decrepitude has to be taken with equal circumspection. "I would just as soon have abused the old village church at home for not being a Cathedral" (Y 18), he says; yet if the old rattletrap is the endeavor of life, then in what sense is the old church *not* a cathedral? The ship becomes the vehicle for hieratic fantasies of exploration, naval battles and pirates, for which its decrepitude is precisely the point of analogy, and it is just this secret feeling that Marlow is intent on protecting from the derision of the boys in port who row around the *Judea* chiding its "pretensions" to get to Bankok. The implicit equation of seeing symbolically with being naive ("O Youth!... the imagination of it!") raises serious questions about where Marlow's categories for reading the story are intended to take us, as well as a question about how great the ironic distance between the teller and the tale really is. In short, the story finds Marlow in an attitude of genuine ambivalence toward his own childishness. The essential validity of its imaginings lays a claim on him that he cannot entirely reject.

The objection might well be raised that he does throw an ironic light on his experience with the "O, Youth!" interjection. When the narrative swings toward his subjective impression of work-as-play, however, the emphasis follows that this remains the vital element of the episode which is not denied by time. To Wells, Conrad acknowledged that "Youth" was an honest story: "the feeling ... which induced me to write that story was genuine (for once) and so strong that it poked its way through the narrative ... in a good many places." [1] We might say then that each time his youth refuses to remain confined to the past and the truth of his feeling surfaces, Marlow's comment puts a cap less on the ludic nature of his behavior than on its honesty. Should the latter be openly acknowledged, "Youth" would cease to be serious fiction. The element in Conrad which prompted Leavis to group him with Henry James and George Eliot is, put simply, the presence of characters in whom imaginative energy must in some sense be denied, constrained, made responsible. The fictional imagination comes back to a negation of itself in that it is responsible to the higher purpose of recreating the very factors that delimit and contain it, primarily in terms of the strictures reality places on the personality. Yet nowhere is the impulse to resist that self-negating quality more evident than in "Youth," where the core tension between the affirmation of childishness and its tepid denial creates the story.

Marlow's interjections, intended to create the impression that the responsibility of the narrator encompasses the irresponsibility of the actor, are patches over the split between the unaltered emotional appeal of the episode and the thematic element tacked onto it. Briefly, the latter is built around a straightforward chronological metaphor which identifies the process of aging with the spontaneous combustion of the coal, the glowing mass of coal in the hold being the "triumphant conviction of strength, the heat of life in the handful of dust, the glow in the heart that with every year grows dim ..." (Y 37). The speed of the *Somerville's* towing fans the flames: the *Judea's* progress is such that destination and destruction draw together and finally coalesce.[2] However poignant, these thematic categories cut across the grain of the entire atmosphere of the work. Marlow would have us believe that only physical strength is lost with youth, that the only thing to regret about its passing is that "a chance to feel your strength" (Y 42) passes with it. In this case, it is not, as he calls it, a "deceitful feeling" but the only truth. The most ephemeral of values becomes the most cherished. It allows him to know in the lifeboat "how good a man he is," and, if this is an illusion, then the story collapses entirely. What Marlow seeks to recover, or recreate, is not just strength but the psychological absence of any independent opposing force to it, the absence of real negation, the insensitivity to death and ironically to the meaning of his own story, since it is the energy of his headlong rush to the East that singles out him, and not Beard, as "death's fool." "For youth," Conrad said, "all is reality in this world ... since it apprehends so vividly its images behind which a longer life makes one doubt whether there is any substance" (NLL 146). Yet by implication this absence of doubt and of divisive factors in experience generally is synonymous with egoistic self-absorption: "I find myself too sensitive," he once remarked to Lenormand, "I've lost all innocence."[3] What is lost for Marlow is precisely this feeling of self-sufficiency inherent in the ability to pretend, and in seeking to recreate the sense in which youth is out of time, he is naturally drawn to the ludic consciousness as both example and vehicle.

NOTES

All direct quotations are from *The Complete Works of Joseph Conrad*, 26 vols. (Garden City, N.Y.: Doubleday, Page, 1924). Citations in the body of the text are followed by page number, and are abbreviated as follows: *Notes on Life and Letters:* NLL; *A Personal Record:* PR; "Youth": Y.

[1] G. Jean-Aubry, *Joseph Conrad: Life and Letters*, vol. I (London: William Heinemann Ltd., 1927), p. 248.
[2] In *A Personal Record* Conrad writes at some length about his "Shakespearean associations" with the years he spent as second mate on the *Palestine* (September 1881 to March 1883) which form the biographical armature of "Youth." He cites reading *Two Gentlemen of Verona* to the accompaniment of caulkers' mallets while the ship was in Falmouth dry dock (cf. PR 72, Y 16), but conspicuously avoids

mentioning a number of the sonnets as sources for the dominant image patterns of the story. The last quatrain of sonnet seventy-three is the most obvious among them:

In me thous seest the glowing of such fire
That on the ashes of his youth doth lie,
As the deathbed whereon it must expire,
Consumed with that which it was nourished by.

[3] H. R. Lenormand, "Note on a Sojourn of Conrad in Corsica," *The Art of Joseph Conrad: A Critical Symposium*, ed. R. W. Stallman (Michigan State University Press, 1960), p. 6.

Fred Madden

MARLOW AND THE DOUBLE HORROR IN *HEART OF DARKNESS*

Joseph Conrad's contemporaneous production of *Lord Jim* and *Heart of Darkness* furnishes the distinct possibility that elements contained in one novel might provide means for the interpretation of the other. In fact, a passage at the beginning of *Lord Jim* has profound bearing on *Heart of Darkness*:

> I mean that inborn ability to look temptations straight in the face—a readiness unintellectual enough, goodness knows, but without pose—a power of resistance, don't you see, ungracious if you like, but priceless—an unthinking and blessed stiffness before the outward and inward terrors, before the might of nature, and the seductive power of men—backed by a faith invulnerable to the strength of facts, to the contagion of example, to the solicitation of ideas.
>
> (27)

The "outward and inward terrors" in this passage suggest the possibility that Conrad intended distinct and separable meanings for each of the "horrors" in Kurtz's cry. By its use of parallel construction, the passage from *Lord Jim* offers associations between the "outward terror" and "the might of nature" and between the "inward terror" and "the seductive power of men." These associations furnish directions toward an understanding of the two "horrors" of *Heart of Darkness*.

Marlow's growing awareness on his journey up the Congo of "outward horror" deriving from "the might of nature" and "inward horror" emanating from "the seductive power of men" forms a major pattern of the novel's development. For Marlow, the outer horror manifests itself in the decaying, diseased, and tainted atmosphere of the jungle and the inner horror in the merciless, mercenary colonizers. This awareness develops as he journeys up the Congo and becomes more and more firmly attached to Kurtz as his "choice of nightmares." The "choice" both helps Marlow to perceive the overwhelming presence of these two "horrors" and to form the bond with Kurtz which Marlow ultimately must break in his interview with Kurtz's Intended. In the interview, Marlow understands his own, personal

From *Midwest Quarterly* 27, No. 4 (Summer 1986): 504–17.

relationship to the two horrors—an understanding which forces him to part company with Kurtz's "ghost."

Behind his attachment to Kurtz and his final rejection of this attachment is Marlow's attitude toward corruption. In fact, the extensive forms of corruption Marlow encounters on his journey can be seen to form a literary definition of the various manifestations and meanings of this word. "Corruption" as it is usually defined has two main senses: one physical, the other moral or spiritual. Although it is not within the scope of this paper to make an exhaustive study of the use and definition of the word "corruption" in *Heart of Darkness*, a few examples in regard to these two main senses might suggest both the extent to which this word is bound up with the fabric of the text and its importance to interpretation.

"Corruption" in its physical sense includes disintegration or decay, infection or contagion, and decomposition. An atmosphere of physical corruption is apparent when Marlow arrives at the first station. He sees "pieces of decaying machinery"; an overturned railway truck, "like a carcass of some animal"; and "imported drainage pipes," not one of which "was not broken." Further on, Marlow discovers natives dying from "disease and starvation" and then an "upcountry agent" dying in the company bookkeeper's hut. Reports of men plagued by fever pervade the novel, and Kurtz's death, as well as Marlow's near death, results from disease. The tainted and decaying environment of the Congo created by examples of, and imagery relating to, decay and disease is reinforced by graphic descriptions of decomposition. The rotting presence of the jungle; the smell of dead hippo meat; "the stuff like half cooked dough, of dirty lavender colour" resembling human flesh and consumed by the natives on the riverboats; Marlow's account of the decayed corpse of the former captain; and the human heads deteriorating on stakes in front of Kurtz's hut contribute the disturbing presence of corruption in *Heart of Darkness*.

But if anything, physical corruption is less sinister and less repulsive to Marlow than the moral and spiritual corruption displayed by members of "the Company," *including Kurtz*. Through Kurtz and the manager especially, Marlow suggests varying shades of moral and spiritual corruption. If Kurtz deteriorates to moral depravity, the manager never rises above it. Both have "evil natures"; the manager is "a weak-eyed devil" while Kurtz is a "lusty red-eyed" one. The manger is continually aware of the advantages of bribery and courting favor; whereas Kurtz wants to succeed by self-aggrandizement rather than by petty managerial in-fighting. Both corrupt purity; Kurtz debases the idealistic side of his self, while the manager uses the morally neutral, external environment to further his own squalid, ambitious ends.

Although Marlow makes distinction between the two and picks Kurtz as his "choice of nightmares," both the manager and Kurtz are corrupt. Marlow makes this choice because there is nothing morally redeeming (or even interesting) in the manager's conduct. On the other hand, Marlow hears that Kurtz, at least, professes to have some ideals and a sense of morality. Conrad certainly means the reader to view Marlow's choice as "the lesser of two evils," but the choice is an important one because, in his "unholy kinship" with Kurtz, Marlow initially develops a perspective on his experiences; a perspective which he later finds he must discard before he can come to a larger realization.

On the journey upriver, Conrad carefully develops Marlow's growing identification with Kurtz through Marlow's interest in Kurtz's influence, artistic ability, and eloquence. Marlow increasingly desires to meet Kurtz, who, he feels, might offer some alternative to the avaricious and conniving practices of the company. When the two finally meet, Kurtz certainly does provide Marlow with an alternative, but one with which Marlow is hardly pleased since he judges Kurtz as a man whose soul "knew no restraint, no faith, no fear, yet struggling blindly with itself" (68).

Marlow's distaste for Kurtz's overwhelming egotism is not sufficient to allow him to escape Kurtz's influence, however:

> I had turned to the wilderness really, not to Mr. Kurtz, who I was ready to admit was as good as buried. And for a moment it seemed to me as if I also were buried in a vast grave of unspeakable secrets. I felt an intolerable weight oppressing my breast, the smell of damp earth, the unseen presence of victorious corruption, the darkness of an impenetrable night.... (63)

This passage offers a paradigm of Marlow's trapped situation in the novel. First, although he believes that he has turned away from Kurtz, Marlow has not escaped him. The images of burial still connect the two by foreshadowing Kurtz's death and Marlow's near death. Secondly, although Marlow feels that he has turned away from the kind of corruption which Kurtz embodies, the corruption in "the wilderness" is ultimately inescapable and oppressive.

"The wilderness" is steadily associated with physical corruption throughout the novel. But its physical corruptive presence can also be used for morally corrupt ends as the uncle of the manager recognizes:

> I saw [the uncle of the manager] extend his short flipper of an arm for a gesture that took in the forest, the creek, the mud, the river—seemed to beckon with a dishonouring flourish before the sunlight face of the land a treacherous appeal to the lurking death, to the hidden evil, to the profound darkness at its heart. (33)

In this physically corrupting environment the manager and his uncle hope to advance rapidly because, in the Congo, rivals for managerial power "die so quickly." Ironically, these two relatives, steeped in their moral depravity, are blessed with an iron constitutions resistant to physical corruption.

The above passage also suggests "the hidden evil" and "profound darkness" inherent in the wilderness itself. Although the idea of inherent "evil" seems to come from Marlow's speculation on the gesture of the manager's uncle, in a later passage Marlow directly proposes similar ideas about the wilderness's relationship to Kurtz:

> The wilderness had found [Kurtz] out early and had taken on him a terrible vengeance for the fantastic invasion. I think it had whispered to him things about himself which he did not know, things of which he had no conception. (59)

This passage presents the image of a naive youth "whispered to" by an agent of moral corruption. In fact, Kurtz's own moral depravity is linked in a reciprocal manner to the wilderness itself. When Kurtz escapes from the boat, it is "the heavy, mute spell of the wilderness" which draws him "to its pitiless breast" to awake "forgotten and brutal instincts" and "the memory of gratified and monstrous passions" (67). The composite image of these lines suggests the way in which an experienced temptress might corrupt innocence and awaken sexual desire in a youth. The wilderness, it seems, tempts Kurtz into moral depravity.

It must be remembered, however, that the description of the wilderness as an agent of moral depravity is presented from Marlow's point of view. Marlow often imbues the wilderness with menacing presence, but perhaps endowing it with a spiritually corrupting influence is suspect. It is true that the wilderness is physically responsible for Kurtz's deterioration to "an animated image of death carved out of old ivory" when Marlow first describes him. The "lurking death" in the wilderness also brings about Kurtz's death. But surely the wilderness is not ultimately responsible for Kurtz's behavior. Marlow emphasizes the "menacing" wilderness because he *needs* it to be "brooding" and corruptive. In order to protect his own self-image, egotism, and feelings of superiority, Marlow needs to see *all* the causes of corruption as outside himself, and this need lies at the very center of *Heart of Darkness*.

But before the implications of Marlow's attempt to avoid corruption can be confronted directly, it is necessary to see what Marlow feels he is escaping. In a passage quoted earlier, Marlow "turns away" from Kurtz only to become aware of "the unseen presence of victorious corruption" and "the darkness of an impenetrable night" (33). For Marlow, there is not simply a relationship between "darkness" and "the wilderness" but also a number of associations between "darkness," "the wilderness," and "corruption," associations which act to define one of "the horrors" in *Heart of Darkness*.

This associative definition of "horror" is tentatively presented by Marlow as a means of interpreting Kurtz's final words. But Marlow's understanding also depends upon Marlow's interpretation of Kurtz's final stare. Both the final words *and* the stare are closely linked in Marlow's description of Kurtz's death:

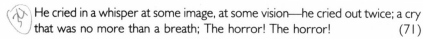
He cried in a whisper at some image, at some vision—he cried out twice; a cry that was no more than a breath; The horror! The horror!   (71)

At first Marlow feels that these final words are "a judgment upon the adventures of Kurtz's soul on earth." Later, however, after nearly dying of an illness himself, Marlow begins to find meaning in Kurtz's final stare:

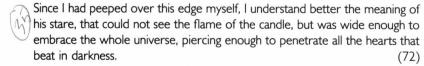
Since I had peeped over this edge myself, I understand better the meaning of his stare, that could not see the flame of the candle, but was wide enough to embrace the whole universe, piercing enough to penetrate all the hearts that beat in darkness.   (72)

Marlow's interpretation here widens the extent of Kurtz's judgment from "his own soul" to "all hearts that beat in darkness" (72).

When Marlow leaves the Congo and returns to Europe, his interpretation of Kurtz's stare and words continues to change. In Belgium, as he stands in front of the house of Kurtz's Intended, Marlow remembers Kurtz's stare again:

> I rang the bell before the mahogany door on the first floor and while I waited he seemed to stare at me out of the glassy panel—stare with that wide and immense stare embracing, condemning, loathing all the universe.   (75)

At the time that Marlow first saw Kurtz's stare, he indistinctly described it as resulting from "some image" or "some vision" (71). On the doorstep the stare is "wide and immense." But more, "the glassy panel" presumably reflecting Marlow's own countenance stares back with Kurtz's stare. This reflection seems to indicate Marlow's growing identification with what he feels is Kurtz's judgment. But there is the further possibility: that the "immense stare" is not just Kurtz's but Marlow's as well.

Through identification with Kurtz on his trip upriver, Marlow becomes sensitive to the pervasiveness of corruption and the necessity of a judgment condemning it. When he nearly dies on his journey downriver, Marlow experiences "a vision of greyness without form filled with physical pain, and a careless contempt for the evanescence of all things" (71). In contrast to Marlow's "death-bed revelation," Kurtz's words seem preferable:

> Better his cry—much better. It was an affirmation, a moral victory paid for by innumerable defeats, by abominable terrors, by abominable satisfaction. But it was a victory.   (72)

Kurtz's cry is a condemnation, and Marlow would like to identify with it because by repudiating corruption, Marlow can hope to deny his own involvement in it.

It is during his interview with Kurtz's Intended Marlow that loses his ability to separate himself from corruption and finally reject his role as observer of others to become a participant in their experience. The change which Marlow undergoes in the interview that brings him to this participation represents the thematic, imagistic, and structural culmination of *Heart of Darkness,* a culmination which takes part in four stages. The initial stage occurs when Marlow enters the house of Kurtz's Intended:

> The vision seemed to enter the house with me—the stretcher, the phantom-bearers, the wild crowd of obedient worshippers, the gloom of the forests, the glitter of the reach between the murky bends, the beat of the drum, regular and muffled like the beating of a heart—the heart of a conquering darkness. It was a moment of triumph for the wilderness, an invading and vengeful rush which, it seemed to me, I would have to keep back alone for the salvation of another soul.   (75)

The association of "the heart of a conquering darkness" with a "moment of triumph for the wilderness" imagistically suggests the presence of corruption which is not confined to the Congo but is present in Brussels as well. What Marlow begins to realize is the prevalent and unavoidable nature of corruption and its attendant darkness.

Secondly, this passage acts as another indicator of Marlow's feeling of superiority; he feels that he will be able "to keep back alone" the "invading and vengeful rush" of darkness "for the salvation of another soul," no doubt a reference to the "soul" of Kurtz's Intended. But, two pages later, Marlow begins to realize that he has been deluding himself in his belief that he can remain untouched by "the darkness":

> "Yes, I know," I said with something like despair in my heart before that great and saving illusion that shone with an unearthly glow in the darkness, in the triumphant darkness from which I could not have defended her—from which I could not have defended her—from which I could not even defend myself.   (77)

Here is a distinct change in Marlow's attitude. At the beginning of this passage, he treats ironically "that great and saving illusion" of Kurtz's Intended, but Marlow himself suffers from an equally great illusion in his feeling of superiority.

Yet, even after his momentary realization concerning his own inability to "defend" himself against corruption, Marlow reasserts pride in the superiority of his intellectual knowledge by sarcastically and cynically telling Kurtz's Intended half-truths about her financée:

> "His words, at least have not died."
> "His words will remain," I said.
> "And his example," she whispered to herself. "Men looked up to him—his goodness shone in every act. His example—"
> "True," I said; "his example too. Yes, his example. I forgot that."
> . . . She said suddenly very low, "He died as he lived."
> "His end," said I, with dull anger stirring in me, "was in every way worthy of his life."   (78)

Certainly Marlow's contempt for the naiveté of Kurtz's Intended bristles in this passage, but this contempt also reveals Marlow's condescension in his judgment regarding and condemning her. Conrad in this passage does not simply undercut the idealistic naiveté which blinds Kurtz's Intended, he more bitingly undercuts Marlow's smug, judgmental attitude, since Kurtz's Intended can only be seen, at best, as a minor character.

When Kurtz's Intended murmurs that she "was not with [Kurtz]" when he died, Marlow cannot maintain his feeling of superiority and his "anger subsided before a feeling of infinite pity." Here, for the first time in the novel, Marlow displays a heart-felt moment of compassion for another human being instead of contempt. In his pity for Kurtz's Intended, Marlow relinquishes his stance as observer to become sympathetically involved in the suffering of another person.

In addition, Marlow describes his pity as "infinite." This adjective reminds the reader of Kurtz's "wide and immense stare embracing, condemning, loathing all the universe" (75). But with his new emotion, Marlow parts company with Kurtz, "his choice of nightmares." The adjective "infinite" suggests an emotion not simply elicited in response to Kurtz's Intended but one indicating Marlow's realization that no one can escape corruption and the suffering it entails, something imagistically reinforced by the increasing darkness associated with the room and Kurtz's Intended herself.

After this feeling of "infinite pity," a feeling that is not confined to Kurtz's Intended but that also recognizes the inevitable corruption of everyone, Marlow can no longer maintain his stance as "observer." Consequently, he loses his ironic distance and blurts out that he heard Kurtz's last words which Kurtz's Intended immediately wants to hear. Her request leads Marlow into a dilemma. On the one hand, if Marlow repeats the last words, he will have to reveal Kurtz's moral depravity, the knowledge of which will corrupt the idealistic illusions of Kurtz's Intended, and Marlow will act as an agent of corruption. On the other hand, if he lies to Kurtz's Intended, Marlow must accept "the flavour of mortality" and "taint of death" that, throughout the journey, he has associated with lying and has attempted to avoid. If he lies, he must finally admit his own mortality and his inevitable spiritual, moral, and physical corruption. In short, Marlow has to choose between becoming an agent of corruption or admitting to himself that he is corruptible and mortal.

The choice is difficult for Marlow, and when he lies, he fears dire consequences:

> It seemed to me that the house would collapse before I could escape, that the heavens would fall upon my head. But nothing happened. The heavens do not fall for such a trifle. (79)

Marlow, who has continually avoided admitting the possibility of his own mortality and eventual corruption, is so caught up in his feelings of self-importance that it seems to him as if the heavens might fall when he lies to Kurtz's Intended. But by the act of lying, he admits to himself that he is corruptible and, by implication, mortal. Although Marlow's realization of his corruptibility and mortality terrify him, this recognition is a truthful assessment of his place in the human condition. Realizing one's own mortality can produce terror, but at the same time such a realization might be considered "a trifle" since mortality is, of course, inescapably a part of being human. Up to this point in the novel, Marlow has been denying not only his own mortality and eventual corruption, but also his humanity. By finally recognizing his own inability to escape corruption, Marlow discovers what, for Conrad, is the first "horror" of existence.

However, in lying to Kurtz's Intended, Marlow is able to escape the second "horror," one which is Kurtz's, not Marlow's. This "horror" is man's potentiality for acting as an agent who corrupts others:

> Would [the heavens] have fallen, I wonder, if I had rendered Kurtz the justice which was his due? Hadn't he said he wanted only justice? But I couldn't. I could not tell her. It would have been too dark—too dark altogether....
>
> (79)

To render Kurtz "justice," Marlow would have to tell Kurtz's Intended about her finacée's "exploits" in the Congo: Kurtz's self-centered egotism in exploiting, killing, and corrupting others. But Marlow refuses to render Kurtz his "justice" since it would necessitate corrupting the naive vision of the Intended. Through this refusal, Marlow parts company with Kurtz and lays "the ghost of [Kurtz's] gifts at last with a lie" (49).

Previous to the final interview, Marlow accepted Kurtz's dying whisper as a judgment against the corruption inherent in existence. But Marlow is not ready to deny the humanity of others as Kurtz did (emblematically indicated by the heads of the natives on stakes surrounding Kurtz's hut). Before the final interview, Marlow had interpreted Kurtz's dying repetition as representing two separate horrors: the horror of the universal triumph of corruption and the horror of "the adventures of [Kurtz's] own soul," a soul which acted as an agent in furthering corruption. In the final interview, however, Marlow realizes Kurtz's justice is without mercy because it is a justice which furthers corruption. Had Marlow followed "the nightmare of his choice" throughout the interview, the heavens would have "fallen" because Marlow would have lost his only option of resisting corruption and exercising restraint.

In refraining from telling Kurtz's Intended the truth, Marlow exercises restraint in refusing to corrupt others. Marlow's lie, however, is not an attempt to protect Kurtz's Intended from eventual corruption. Conrad gives the reader enough suggestions in the imagery of the interview to promote the feeling that she will not escape. As the interview proceeds, the images of "darkness" connected with her increase until she becomes "the whisper of a voice speaking from beyond the threshold of eternal darkness" (77). Here Conrad is making an obvious parallel between the Intended and Kurtz who has been earlier described as a "voice" who hid "the barren darkness of his heart" (69).

Both Kurtz and his Intended are described as voices speaking in darkness, as is Marlow himself aboard the Nellie. But during the course of his narrative, Marlow is able to pin-point man's sole hope of resisting inevitable corruption: it lies neither in Kurtz's "justice" nor in his Intended's naiveté. For Marlow (and Conrad), man must refrain from becoming an agent of corruption. At the end of his journey Marlow comes to accept the almost paradoxical realization that man must refrain from furthering the spread of corruption while acquiescing to its inevitability. In an action similar to Mrs. Gould's refusal to reveal the truth about Nostromo's corruption to Dr. Monygham, Marlow refrains from telling Kurtz's Intended the truth. In both novels, Conrad is advocating man's acceptance of a limited, imperfect, and corruptible existence. In Marlow's case, the compassion which leads to this acceptance must be judged morally preferable to Kurtz's form of "justice" or the Company's inhuman machinery of exploitation. Marlow's growth and final realization, in which "observer" becomes "participant," knowledge becomes wisdom, suggest the necessity of "restraint" and compassion as counterforces to man's propensity to exploit others. But "restraint" must derive from the individual in the face of the double horrors in Heart of Darkness, the inevitable outward and inward corruption of all that mankind values. This "restraint" also must continue in the certain knowledge that it is, at best, merely a gesture against overwhelming forces, and for the reader of *Heart of Darkness* this gesture is all that illuminates Conrad's vision.

BIBLIOGRAPHICAL NOTE

All quotations come from either Joseph Conrad, *Lord Jim,* ed. by Thomas C. Moser (New York, 1971) or Joseph Conrad, *Heart of Darkness,* ed. by Robert Kimbrough (New York, 1971).

Anthony Winner

LORD JIM:
IRONY AND DREAM

In leaping from the *Patna*, Jim betrays his nurture. He falls from the structured realm of public values and trust into the mystery of private reflexes and dreams. In so doing, he seems to set in motion what Guérard terms as "interior novel."[1] But for Marlow, and more extensively for Conrad, the story of this one psyche becomes a forum for the investigation of public faith. "the mystery of his attitude," Marlow insists, "got hold of me as though he had been an individual in the forefront of his kind, as if the obscure truth involved were momentous enough to affect mankind's conception of itself" (p. 93). Like Kurtz, Jim exists within the concern that preoccupies Conrad's major fiction: the authenticity and viability of the organic community to which Western civilization has sworn fidelity. Jim is a by-blow of this community: half in, half out. His father is a safe and staid clergyman; we know nothing of his mother, but may imagine her as an avatar of that veiled Eastern bride who rewards Jim's dream. Traditional value and romantic dream collide and then collude. By itself, each context is quite straightforward. But it is precisely the simplicity and direct appeal of both sides of Jim's dilemma, the near-featurelessness of his understanding of both, that make the terms of his embattled example contagious to others—as the series of doublings and identifications running from Brierly to Gentleman Brown demonstrates.[2] The values and shortcomings to Jim's upbringing and of his dream invest his example with the momentous possibility of meaning that Marlow intuits.

The first half of the novel investigates the truth of public value; the second half, the fantasy and melodrama of the misty romance of Patusan, flirts with dream. In both sections Marlow's puzzlement about Jim involves many of the questions that underlie Dowell's perplexity about sexual behavior in Ford Madox Ford's *The Good Soldier.* What one thought one knew and the stable existence one built upon the knowledge are illusions. Seeing Jim for the first time as he stands accused of deserting his trust, Marlow comments: "I liked his appearance; I knew his appear-

From *Culture and Irony: Studies in Joseph Conrad's Major Novels* (Charlottesville: University Press of Virginia, 1988), pp. 16–42.

ance; he came from the right place; he was one of us. He stood there for all the parentage of his kind, for men and women by no means clever or amusing, but whose very existence is based upon honest faith, and upon the instinct of courage" (p. 43). Jim's leap belies his appearance and the assumptions Marlow bases on his seeming decency. And on these assumptions, as we hear time and time again in *Lord Jim*, rests the faith that must order civilized endeavor. Dowell's disillusionment in Ford's novel is analogous. He has believed in a code of decency in sexual matters and implicitly connected this code with the very existence of moral civilization. When he discovers his wife's and his friend's adulteries, human behavior suddenly seems to him a maelstrom of ravening lusts. Faith topples into rending bafflement. "If for nine years I have possessed a goodly apple that is rotten at the core and discover its rottenness only in nine years . . . isn't it true to say that for nine years I possessed a goodly apple?"[3] Is all conventionally honest faith a mere facade? Is its cultural ethos merely specious? If so, is there any guide to existence? Does the "greatness" that the outcast Jim achieves in Patusan or the "goodness" of Dowell's adulterous friend contain a new knowledge or value that might offer some alternative to what has been lost?

As we shall see, the romance of Patusan and the counterpoint between Jim's monochord idealism and the cultural value Conrad comes to place in irony lead *Lord Jim* in directions far different from those Ford pursues. But the similar scope of Conrad's and Ford's novels provides a suggestive point of departure. Jim's indecent desertion and the sexual indecency of Ford's characters are comments on the values of their civilization. The ideal ethos of education, duty, and communal purpose in which earlier Victorian generations believed has become Dowell's goodly apple. The code of seamanship in Conrad and that of Tory manners in Ford embody what Marlow calls "the sheltering conception of light and order which is our refuge" (p. 313). Ford presents the violation of his code with extreme pessimism and in the rhetoric of final things. "Someone has said that the death of a mouse from cancer is the whole sack of Rome by the Goths, and I swear to you that the breaking up of our little four-square coterie was such another unthinkable event."[4] Though Conrad's perspective is more equivocal, the potential ramifications of Jim's leap are no less extreme. Marlow seeks "some convincing shadow of an excuse" for Jim's act because he hopes to lay "what is the most obstinate ghost of man's creation, . . . the uneasy doubt uprising like a mist, secret and gnawing like a worm, and more chilling than the certitude of death—the doubt of the sovereign power enthroned in a fixed standard of conduct" (p. 50).

Jim is "no mean traitor"; his betrayal of his trust is "a breach of faith with the community of mankind" (p. 157). Like adultery in Ford, infidelity in Conrad is a crime against moral civilization. But in both novels the crimes insinuate an insufficiency in traditional standards that opens the way for personal desires and dreams. In *Lord Jim*, Jim's treason is in part made comprehensible, even ambiguously made sympathetic, by the hollowness of inherited values. Marlow's initial evocation of the honest faith Jim ought to serve is markedly defensive. Our ethical nurture fosters "an unthinking and blessed stiffness before the outward and inward terrors, before

the might of nature, and the seductive corruption of men—[a stiffness] backed by
a faith invulnerable to the strength of facts, to the contagion of example, to the
solicitation of ideas" (p. 43). Marlow's comments on this faith range from his
sardonic mockery of the tourists at the hotel where he talks with Jim to respect for
the stiff courage of the French lieutenant and Bob Stanton. But both fools and
heroes live lives sequestered from the whole truth of the human situation. The
uncomfortable irony that characterizes Marlow's tone strains to mediate between
faith and fact, between the illusion that protects and the need to confront things as
they are. Jim's private stiffness is as devoid of irony as that of civilization's truest
believers. But the personal has an immediacy and an appeal that public belief has
long since lost. And Jim's story, wending its way between the simple fascination of
an individual's romantic dream and the self-protective blindness of public illusion,
engages Marlow because it appears to be a straightforward, real-life instance of the
irony inherent in the human condition.

Marlow's irony is an attempt on Conrad's part to elude the force of pessimism.
As Peter J. Glassman observes, in "*Lord Jim* . . . the universe itself seems organized
in barely surreptitious, virtually animate opposition to human expectations and
needs."[5] As a fact, Jim's leap confirms the pessimistic appraisal of nature that Royal
Roussel equates with the idea of darkness in Conrad.[6] But just as Jim's dream of
ultimate triumph refuses pessimism, so Marlow's irony complicates and tempers the
loose Schopenhauerian view that would interpret the action as an instance of
human delusion adrift in cosmic indifference. A defensive irony works as a kind of
fifth column within the bleak atmosphere of cosmic irony. Jim is a straggler from
moral order, but the flaws in this order allow Marlow to entertain the possibility
that Jim may be a harbinger of better things to come. Though Jim is simple to the
point of flatness, the fate he dreams for himself is in its way parallel to the early
modern vision of self-creation: to the idea of selfhood as art in Proust or the great
Gatsby's desire to live out a platonic idea of himself. However ingenuous Jim's
romantic heroism and his dedication to its adventure, his goals are truer—more
"sincere" in Gide's sense of the word—than the goals to which most of the other
characters attend.

This hopeful possibility is of course set starkly against the disorder Jim spawns.
The dream is quite as much a threat as an example. By desiring to go it alone, Jim
undercuts the bonds of moral community. These bonds may be illusions, but the
illusion they represent may finally be the necessary paradox inherent in the main-
tenance of moral meaning in a dark world. The pain of things makes illusion real.
Commenting on Jewel's appalling distrust of Jim in Patusan, on her plea not to "die
weeping," Marlow acknowledges that "the passive, irremediable horror of the
scene"

> "had the power to drive me out of my conception of existence, out of that
> shelter each of us makes for himself to creep under in moments of danger, as
> a tortoise withdraws within its shell. For a moment I had a view of a world that
> seemed to wear a vast and dismal aspect of disorder . . . But still—it was only

a moment: I went back into my shell directly. One *must*—don't you know?—though I seemed to have lost all my words in the chaos of dark thoughts I had contemplated for a second or two beyond the pale. These came back, too, very soon, for words also belong to the sheltering conception of light and order which is our refuge."   (p. 313)

Beyond the sheltering pale is a literally unspeakable disorder—which is why Kurtz's naming of the horror is presented as a kind of victory. Jim flies in the face of the grimly sardonic conception of the necessity of culture as refuge that is implicit in Marlow's *"must."* Marlow's strained belief in shelter is ambiguous enough to permit the off-chance of Jim's success. But the odds against such success are as vast and dismal as the fact of primal chaos.

Marlow's account of Jim is by no means the whole of Conrad's story. As Daniel R. Schwarz notes, Marlow moves toward Jim's position; "Marlow's epistemological quest culminates with the blurring of the distinction between objective and sub-jective experience."[7] Marlow is himself a character; behind his mediating irony we sense dimensions to Jim's example beyond his ken. The issues that frame *Lord Jim* involve far more than the distinction between objective and subjective: more even than the tension between Marlow's public conception of existence and Jim's private dream of heroic order. In taking Jim and Marlow as the focal points of a novel more ambitious than the dreamer could dream and more ironic than the narrator-ironist could achieve, Conrad is attempting to dramatize one of the most difficult aspects of the situation brought about by the erosion of traditional faiths. Primitive man, as E. R. Dodds reminds us in *The Greeks and the Irrational*, sought one kind of shelter in his religion and another kind in his conception of morality.[8] Religion compre-hended and tried to placate the cruel force of final things; it made possible the existence of a humanity limited in knowledge and power within a mysterious field of forces alien to man. Morality, on the other hand, grew out of the needs of man's relations to man. Religion dealt with the absolute circumstances of man's position in the universe; morality, with the relative needs of communal purposes and stabilities. A hallmark of what we regard as a mature civilization is the blending of these two functions into the single fabric of moral religion. Conrad's consistent idealization of the code of seamanship, which is maintained, as Nadjer demonstrates, against much contradictory personal experience, and the impulse behind the less convincing exemplary role he invests in figures such as Singleton stem from an impulse to believe that the traditional world of "us"—the world of unwearied efforts—had achieved a working synthesis between social ethics and cosmic circumstances. Jim's leap carries him out of this synthesis; he lands in the position of those moderns who must become mythmakers because morality no longer responds adequately or authentically to the basic questions posed by our position in the universe. Conrad is deeply doubtful about both the validity and the viability of the modern dream of which Jim's dream is the lowest common denominator. Yet he allows Marlow a greater freedom of ambivalence than his own letters and essays usually permit. Marlow's inconclusive and ironic temper leaves a certain ambiguous opening for the blurring of distinctions. But however complex, Marlow's ironies are finally contained tensely within an omniscient irony about irony itself.

This larger scope is suggested in the strategy Conrad uses to begin the novel. In J. Hillis Miller's words, the "first part of the novel is told by an 'omniscient' narrator who seems like the narrator of a novel by Trollope or by George Eliot."[9] The first four chapters introduce Jim as the kind of romantic dreamer—a descendant of Scott's Waverley—that so many Victorian novels of moral realism and education instruct in the facts of what Scott terms "real history." Jim's "thoughts would be full of valorous deeds: he loved these dreams and the success of his imaginary achievements. They were the best parts of life, its secret truth, its hidden reality" (p. 20). The implied standard treats dreams and imagination as offshoots of untested youth. Jim has the potential for all the public school virtues; he simply requires the tempering experience that yields moral character. "He was gentlemanly, steady, tractable, with a thorough knowledge of his duties; and in time, when yet very young, he became chief mate of a fine ship, without ever having been tested by those events of the sea that show in the light of day the inner worth of a man . . . that reveal the quality of his resistance and the secret truth of his pretences, not only to others but also to himself" (p. 10). Both the content and the secure, summarizing tone are familiar. Jim's imaginings are in no sense original, let alone modern; his hoped-for heroism is that enshrined in "light holiday literature" (p. 5). It is no surprise that after being forced to leave his ship because of a slow-healing minor injury, he rejects the home service "with its harder conditions, severer view of duty, and the hazard of stormy oceans" (p. 13). "The charm of vagueness" (p. 20) that pervades his secret reality leads him to an easy berth on the *Patna*. Confronted with the apparently disastrous bulging bulkhead after the mysterious collision, his imagination takes flight and he leaps after it.

The opening chapters prepare us for the kind of yarn Marlow intuits when he first sees Jim at the court of inquiry. Behind the flawed man and the cursory facts may lie what Balzac terms a "secret history": the conjunction of private and public truths that so engages the traditional novelistic mentality. Jim's story promises a compelling variation upon a time-honored structure. But the underlying and exfoliating irony of Marlow's narrative involvement in Jim's situation derives from the fact that the traditional structure implied by Conrad's omniscient opening is as misleading as Jim himself. Moral realism proposes a synthesis of individual nature, objective circumstances, and communal or ethical truth. Narrative is based upon a fluctuating but finally morally instructive relation between the subjective and the objective. Almost from the very beginning Marlow is forced to question and to attempt to reenvisage this relation. As he so often repeats, he is fascinated by the "infernal alloy" (p. 45) in Jim's seemingly trustworthy cultural metal. His initial interest is in the alloy, in Jim's individual makeup, but this investigation leads insistently into doubts about the metal itself. And these doubts reflect back onto the question of Jim's nature.

The ironic perspective in which Marlow finds himself will cast the achievement of all meaning, individual and cultural, into perplexity. The terms of moral meaning in themselves are never in doubt. What Jim has betrayed is quite clear; he has failed the code of the home service: "its saving power, the grace of its secular right to our fidelity, to our obedience" (p. 222). What is now obscure is how the individual can internalize and honestly enact the moral values in which all the decent characters believe. The central position of this ironic obscurity accounts, I believe, for the introduction of Captain Brierly so near the beginning of Marlow's narrative. Brierly, one of the judges at the inquiry, is an impeccably successful young sailor whose "self-satisfaction presented . . . a surface as hard as granite. He committed suicide very soon after" (p. 58). Like the narrative omniscience with which the novel commences. Brierly seems a firm and convincing spokesman for traditional truth. The jarring conclusion of Marlow's brief comment has the same effect on Brierly's safeness as a spokesman as Jim's story will have on our ability to accept traditional power, grace, and right. No doubt, as Schwarz argues, Brierly's sudden intuition of kinship with Jim can be understood as a subjective explanation of his offer to pay Jim to disappear, and a further empathic identification with Jim's untested faith and its result helps explain the suicide.[10] But the effect of Brierly's presence at this point in the narrative is both to generalize Jim's flaw and to show how far out of joint any conventional appraisal of appearance and reality, ethos and personality, morality and dream, may be. Jim's desertion casts him outside the pale: a man without a country. But the bewildering situation of exile now includes the bewildering possibility that there may be no viable countries and no objective standard of patriotism.

Brierly's example, of course, is part of Marlow's rhetorical strategy. His seamen listeners are, we gather, unimaginative types. Quite apart from Marlow's slowly and complexly developing bond with Jim—the ambiguous identification discussed by Guérard, Schwarz, and others—his narrative can only convey the force of his sense of Jim's story by subverting his audience's fixed standards of understanding. The fact of Brierly's untrustworthiness is one tactic. Another is Marlow's shifting of the emphasis away from the public desertion to Jim's painful private situation. Having lost name, character, and the social defenses that a company successful existence among others, Jim is naked. His pitiful state leads to his taking a reference to an offensive native pariah dog as a cur to be a personal insult. He has lost the saving power of the shell we can retreat into for safety. The pathetic view of Jim continues throughout the first half of the novel; we find it in the brief glimpses of Jim as a kind of Wandering Jew constantly in motion around Eastern ports. Yet since Marlow's concern is more with the obscurities of the truth of Jim's situation than with Jim himself, pity is employed as a permitting premise rather than as a main theme. Moreover, pity on the one hand and the subversive pessimism implicit in Brierly's suicide court a far too unambiguous reaction: the notion that we are all exiles, that the code we profess is hollow. To counter this simplistic negativism Marlow insists upon the appalling immorality of the company into which Jim has fallen—a point that will recur in full horror during the encounter with Gentleman Brown. Jim's act creates a nasty kinship with such true curs as the *Patna's* captain and other officers, the guano-mad Chester, and the senile quondam cannibal Robinson.

Against such outcasts and against the pathos of Jim's case Marlow holds up the words and example of the French lieutenant, an exemplary vicar of culture's "secular grace." He "reminded you of one of those snuffy, quiet village priests, into whose ears are poured the sins, the sufferings, the remorse of peasant generations, on whose faces the placid and simple expression is like a veil thrown over the mystery of pain and distress" (p. 139). Unlike the later references to the sunny conveniences of our sheltering code, Marlow's attitude toward the veil that the lieutenant helps hold in place seems unironic. There is even a hint that the lieutenant's blend of priestly wisdom and practical fidelity—the faith that accompanies him during his thirty hours on the unsafe *Patna*—mocks the growing entanglements of Marlow's interest in Jim. The lieutenant understands Jim's fear: we all feel it, he says. But desertion, turning tail, is another matter. "But the honour—the honour, monsieur! . . . The honour . . . that is real—that is!"; "when the honour is gone—*ah ça! par example*—I can offer no opinion—because—monsieur—I know nothing of it" (p. 148; Conrad's ellipses).

The lieutenant is the safest of all those who speak for the code of trust and decency. Yet his "stolid giblness" (p. 139) is another instance of the way in which "saving faith" has declined into "saving dullness" (p. 276). The Frenchman's idea of honor strips moral enterprise of glory; it is in its way as purblind as Jim's dream. And just before this episode Marlow complains of Jim's unawareness of the stakes his behavior involves. "I was aggrieved against him, as though he had cheated me—me!—of a splendid opportunity to keep up the illusion of my beginnings, as though he had robbed our common life of the last spark of its glamour" (p. 131). The lieutenant and those like him do not see what Marlow sees. As the exclamatory "me" suggests, Marlow's own dream is involved—is indeed the crucial narrative action—in Jim's dream. Jim's mystery broadens into the mystery of pain and distress in man's fate. Jim's situation engages the vast challenge that attends the idea of moral order as a faith, or a necessary illusion, willed into being against the odds of the human condition. Jim comes to seem the test of Marlow's hope that the work of moral shelter can repossess the heroic glamour that surrounds the dull Roman civilizers of pagan Britain in *Heart of Darkness*. For Marlow, the romance of Jim in Patusan borrows its force from the possibility of Jim's splendid opportunity: a possibility that the snuffy lieutenant and Marlow's stolid listeners cannot entertain. Both the attitude toward such dullness and the promise Jim enacts are clear in one of Marlow's several prefaces to his account of Jim in Patusan.

> "My last words about Jim shall be few. I affirm he had achieved greatness; but the thing would be dwarfed in the telling, or rather in the hearing. Frankly, it is not my words that I mistrust, but your minds. I could be eloquent were I not afraid you fellows had starved your imaginations to feed your bodies. I do not mean to be offensive; it is respectable to have no illusions—and safe—and profitable—and dull. Yet you, too, in your time must have known the intensity

of life, that light of glamour created in the shock of trifles, as amazing as the glow of sparks struck from a cold stone—and as short-lived, alas!"

(p. 225)

The last lines associate Jim with the spirit that animates "Youth"; the last word recalls the ironic retrospect that in the short novel views this spirit askance. But the dream Jim lives out is far richer in cultural and, through its relation to Marlow, psychological connotations than anything in "Youth." Marlow's ironic temper, with its self-conscious hesitation between imagination and saving dullness, between language as vital engagement and language as shelter, has itself become a subject of Conrad's treatment of the condition of Western moral order. In Marlow's dream, the intensity of meaningful action condensed into the idea of glamour offers an alternative not only to the staidness that robs civilization of force but also to his own part in such passive safety. Indeed, Marlow's account of Jim in Patusan suggests in its near-envy a story told by one of the many overcivilized, overironic early moderns—the diverse kin of J. Alfred Prufrock—who covet the unmediated splendor of "real life."

Marlow's hope, and the justification for his engagement in Jim's fate, is that the dreamer's youth may restore the stirring force and enchantment of the early days of self and culture. But simply to affirm Jim is to disallow the hard-won ironies, ambiguities, and wisdom that accompany our shelter. If Jim is true, then our compromises and hesitations are false. Moreover, as Conrad's ever-insinuated omniscient irony places in question, Jim's personal flatness may be the fatal hazard of all youthful dreams. Can youth itself and Jim's youth in particular be more trustworthy crusaders for the dream than they were defenders of the faith? When after his long evening's talk with Marlow, Jim retreats from port to port seeking to keep himself intact for the opportunity he dreams of, Marlow has strong doubts. But "what I could never make up my mind about was whether his line of conduct amounted to shirking his ghost or to facing him out" (p. 197). The force of Marlow's increasing disenchantment is equivalent to the meaning he has invested in Jim. Jim's wayward movement strikes him as "hopeless, and poor Brierly's saying recurred to me, 'Let him creep twenty feet underground and stay there'" (p. 202).

Faced with the possibility that his involvement with Jim may prove as disastrous as Brierly's empathy, Marlow goes to consult Stein. Stein will speak for all the issues that the French lieutenant ignores—indeed, Guérard views the two counselors, each with his fractured English, as "pendant."[11] The retired dreamer sees Jim as a problem in a kind of existential poetics. Unlike the Frenchman, he views Jim as a particular type of individual, not as a member of a community of faith and honor. For romantic dreamers such as Jim, "the question is not how to get cured, but how to live" (p. 212). As David Thorburn has shown,[12] Stein's answer encapsulates the general wisdom of traditional romantic idealism: "That was the way. To follow the dream, and again to follow the dream" (pp. 214–15). These words, of course, provide the standard under which Jim advances into Patusan. The direction Jim will take is that into which Stein wanders when, at the conclusion of his talk with

Marlow, he moves to the far end of his vast room. "It had an odd effect—as if these few steps had carried him out of this concrete and perplexed world.... his voice, heard in that remoteness where he could be glimpsed mysteriously busy with immaterial cares, was no longer incisive, seemed to roll voluminous and grave—mellowed by distance" (p. 213). Stein speaks out of and for the suggestive distance so dear to romantic art: "it was a charming and deceptive light, throwing the impalpable poesy of its dimness over pitfalls—over graves" (p. 215). The portals of this kind of dream close against the material cares, palpable facts, and perplexing objective challenges of the visible universe Conrad proposes to illuminate in the celebrated preface to *The Nigger of the "Narcissus."* Jim enters a spectral realm as remote from his parentage as that which awaits so many rebellious offspring of material culture in the fiction of Gide, Mann, Joyce, and others.

> "At that moment it was difficult to believe in Jim's existence—starting
> from a country parsonage, blurred by crowds of men as by clouds of dust,
> silenced by the clashing claims of life and death in a material world—but his
> imperishable reality came to me with a convincing, with an irresistible force! I
> saw it vividly, as though in our progress through [Stein's] lofty, silent rooms
> amongst fleeting gleams of light and the sudden revelations of human figures
> stealing with flickering flames within unfathomable and pellucid depths, we had
> approached nearer to absolute Truth, which, like Beauty itself, floats elusive,
> obscure, half submerged, in the silent, still waters of mystery."   (p. 216)

In Patusan, Jim will approach Truth. He will seek to realize the Beauty of his dream. His Patusan lies beyond the gates of ivory; it is a land analogous to the imaginative darkness from which Keats's nightingale sings. It exists on the far side of that Rubicon that Balzac's Eugène de Rastignac must cross if he is to challenge the real world of *Le Père Goriot.* "If there are exceptions to the Draconian laws of the Parisian code, they are to be found in solitude, in men who are never led astray by social doctrines, who live near some clear, fleeting, but ever-running brook ... happy to listen to the language of the infinite written all about them."[13] As both critics who deplore and critics who applaud the second half of *Lord Jim* agree, Patusan is a romance precinct where, in Hawthorne's words, "actualities would not be so terribly insisted upon."[14] Had "Stein arranged to send [Jim] into a star of the fifth magnitude the change could not have been greater. He left his earthly failings behind him and that sort of reputation he had, and there was a totally new set of conditions for his imaginative faculty to work upon" (p. 218). In Patusan the "straggler yearning inconsolably for his humble place in the ranks" (pp. 224–25) will recreate himself and apply his imaginative gifts to the foundation of an ideal public order. "The conquest of love, honour, men's confidence—the pride of it, the power of it, are fit materials for a heroic tale; only our minds are struck by the externals of such a success, and to Jim's successes there were no externals" (p. 226).

Romance opposes the real history to which realistic fiction is committed; it denies the force of externals. The most heroic conquest of romance would be that of the uncomfortable irony indigenous to the fallen circumstances that realism treats. And Marlow's ambivalence regarding Jim's success in Patusan follows directly from his belief in the necessary work of irony in mediating subjective and objective, ideal meaning and stern fact. Since Marlow's presentation of Jim's case in the first half of the novel opens the way for a fundamental questioning of the premises upon which moral realism rests, it offers the possibility of a new appraisal of the moral status of romance. Jim is no artist. But the compounded self-creation and public creation to which he dedicates himself involve the ideas of selfhood as art and culture as artwork so often treated in early modern fiction. Marlow's reference to the absence of external validation prefaces his divided response and rephrases a traditional realistic reaction to ideal creation. The enigma of art's truth and beauty varies the old conundrum of the cannon fired where no one can hear. Can there be real sound where there are no actual ears? What is the material, the epistemological, and the moral status of imaginative creation? Are Jim and his creation to be regarded as art, illusion, counterfeit, or simply treasonable evasion?

Marlow mistrusts his listeners' willingness and ability to imagine Jim's greatness. But he also distrusts his own willingness. Jim's treason was born in imagination. "There was imagination in that hard skull of his. . . . As to me, I have no imagination (I would be more certain about him to-day, if I had)" (p. 223). Marlow's interest in Jim, he explains, is little more than a passing sentimental curiosity; Jim's fall and his dream make "him touching, just as a man's more intense life makes his death more touching than the death of a tree. I happened to be handy, and I happened to be touched. That's all there is to it" (p. 223). Such words, uttered almost in the same breath as the affirmation of Jim's success, provide the specific terms for the ironies and ambiguities that follow. Marlow speaks with the gruff objectivity of a schoolmaster, a spokesman for the traditional education that moral realism would inculcate, whose lessons risk being compromised by weak sympathy for a wayward pupil. Visiting Jim in Patusan, he is taken aback by the young man's tone. "He was voluble like a youngster on the eve of a long holiday with a prospect of delightful scrapes, and such an attitude of mind in a grown man and in this connection had in it something phenomenal, a little mad, dangerous, unsafe" (p. 234). "This was not a proper frame of mind to approach any undertaking; an improper frame of mind not only for him, I said, but for any man" (p. 236). However, this view, which recalls the traditional generalizing omniscience of the first chapters, is countered by a sense not only of the nature but of the possible truth of youth's imaginative gift. "Youth *is* insolent; it is its right—its necessity; it has got to assert itself, and all assertion in this world of doubts is a defiance, is an insolence" (p. 236).

As the last idea indicates, Marlow's reaction involves much more than the specific case at hand. For Jim's almost lurid intensity of the youthful optimism bears on the youth that once marked the world of "us"; the subjective dream is bound up in the heroic glamour that shines in the early days of what is now a staid, profitable, safe, and perhaps hollow moral and material order. The insolence of Jim's undertaking is not so different from the brashness of the seventeenth-century pepper traders who opened up the land to the West and whose exploits Marlow exalts just a few pages earlier. The "bizarre obstinacy of [their] desire made them defy death in a thousand shapes ... wounds, captivity, hunger, pestilence, and despair. It made them great! By heavens! it made them heroic. ... It seems impossible to believe that mere greed could hold men to such steadfastness of purpose, to such a blind persistence in endeavor and sacrifice. ... To us, their less tried successors, they appear magnified, not as agents of trade, but as instruments of a recorded destiny, pushing out into the unknown in obedience to an inward voice, to an impulse beating in the blood, to a dream of the future" (pp. 226–27). Jim's motive is hardly more incredible or unworthy than pepper and greed. By connecting the youth's dream to that of the traders, Marlow includes Patusan in the history of civilization and modifies the romance of Jim's adventure by associating it with the epic enterprises upon the success of which our safe ethos rests. The association suggests a historical and moral content for the dream that Stein conceived as ideal.

Exiled by his crime, arrested in his moral development, Jim moves into an indeterminate realm. The mist that blurs him to Marlow's Western eyes is in part, as Guérard contends, "the aura of deception and self-deception that surrounds Jim's reality."[15] But since Jim's is far more than an "interior" story, the uncertain atmosphere arises from the bafflement of irony as a mature mediating vision. Jim makes romance into a political and moral possibility. His "success" bewilders the traditional ironic premise that youthful dreams must be domesticated and forced to submit to the limits that civil shelter lays down for its protection. When Marlow extols the pepper traders and affirms their greatness and Jim's, he speaks both for the early modern disenchantment with limits and for the adventurous politics spawned by this disenchantment. To the extent that, existentially and culturally, the world no longer conforms to long-established axioms, to the extent we are newly vulnerable in an inimical strangeness, Jim may be an exemplary forerunner of meaningful action. It is this possibility that underlies Marlow's wavering, anxious cogitation about the meaning of Jim's fate in Patusan. Jim looms in uncertainty much as does Kurtz before Marlow meets him. Just as Kurtz is flattered in anticipation by the falseness of the imperial enterprise, so Jim is given stature by the feebleness and hypocrisy of our traditional upbringing. Kurtz tantalizes with the hope of something better than the faithless pilgrims; Jim may be teaching truths unknown in country parsonages. Moreover, unlike Kurtz, Jim sets out to create a civil order. He wants to civilize the "brutes," not to exterminate them.

The atmosphere of Patusan, which confuses real and unreal, material and immaterial, captures uncertainty. Clearly—and it is the only clarity—there is deception. But does the deception arise from Jim, from Marlow, from the nature of things, or from an unaccountable conjunction of all of these? Are we concerned with deception or with the necessary illusion, or even the necessary faith, required by the imposition of moral order? Marlow and Jim watch

"the moon float away above the chasm between the hills like an ascending spirit out of a grave; its sheen descended, cold and pale, like the ghost of dead sunlight. There is something haunting in the light of the moon; it has all the dispassionateness of a disembodied soul, and something of its inconceivable mystery. It is to our sunshine, which—say what you like—is all we have to live by, what the echo is to the sound ... It robs all forms of matter—which, after all, is our domain—of their substance ... The houses ... vague, grey, silvery forms mingled with black masses of shadow, were like a spectral herd of shapeless creatures pressing forward to drink in a spectral and lifeless stream."

(pp. 245–46)

The equivocal, suggestive counterpoint between Patusan's echoes of ghostly epic underworlds and Marlow's insistence on the sunlit matter of the order we know creates here and throughout the Patusan narrative a shrouding climate akin to that which Tzvetan Todorov finds in fantasy as a genre. "The fantastic occupies the duration of this uncertainty." "*The reader's hesitation* is ... the first condition of the fantastic."[16] Conrad, to be sure, is not writing fantasy; at no point does he suggest that Patusan is supernatural. But the effect of the insistent ghostly imagery is to create a symbolic and moral equivalent to the hesitation that Todorov emphasizes.

This hesitation marks Conrad's ambiguous play with his characteristic association of light with order and darkness with the truths and horrors beyond civilization's pale. Amid the gloom of Patusan, "here and there a red gleam twinkled within the bamboo walls, warm, like a living spark, significant of human affections, of shelter, of repose" (p. 246). Jim's efforts fan the spark. At moments he stands as the source of light, dominating "the forest, the secular gloom, the old mankind. He was like a figure set up on a pedestal, to represent in his persistent youth the power, and perhaps the virtues, of races that never grow old, that have emerged from the "gloom" (p. 265). The archetypal brightness of youth is magnified morally by the light of the civil order Jim would impose. The beacon of Jim's dream has kindled the hopes of Doramin, the weighty chieftain, and attracted the friendship of his son Dain Waris, one of those rare natives whose virtues resemble our own: "an unobscured vision, a tenacity of purpose, a touch of altruism" (p. 262). Along with community and friendship, Jim's light compels love: the glow of Jim's Jewel. And with Jewel the ideal action and possible moral success of romance near their apogee. Two elements of Jung's triad mount into seeming splendor: the pure hero and his complementary heroine, the animal figure. Yet just as romance action includes a third figure, the bearer of evil that Jung calls shadow, so Jim's luminous endeavor takes place against Marlow's darling hesitation, against the grim limits of romance creation, and against the nature of real history. "I don't know whether it was exactly fair to him to remember the incident that had given a new direction to his life, but at that very moment I remembered very distinctly. It was like a shadow in the light" (p. 265).

Paradoxically, Jewel, the cynosure of romance, will embody as well the vulnerability that requires all the dull strengths of conventional shelter. When we first hear of her, she seems the perfect reward of dreams. Those in nearby lands, learning the girl's name, believe that Jim has obtained a fabulous gem. "But do you notice how, three hundred miles beyond the end of telegraph cables and mail-boat lines, the haggard utilitarian lies of our civilisation wither and die, to be replaced by pure exercises of imagination, that have the futility, often the charm, and sometimes the deep hidden truthfulness, of works of art? Romance had singled Jim for its own—and that was the true part of the story, which otherwise was all wrong. He did not hide his jewel. In fact, he was extremely proud of it" (p. 282). Conjoining the imaginative truth of pure art with the futility of such truth, Jewel bewilders the premises of Marlow's irony into something approaching incoherence. Women in Conrad not infrequently have this effect: a result of the unstable mixture of romantic idealization and exceptional practical weakness. But Jewel carries both elements to an exemplary extreme. Her love, romance's pure jewel, is also the tragic need that underlies the utilitarian codes and refuges that civil order can provide. She has been maltreated by life. Her stepfather, the petty demon Cornelius, had hounded her mother into death. Jewel, the only witness to her mother's misery, has been nurtured on cruelty and fear. She adores Jim, yet intruits fearfully that she does not fill his heart: that he has a past and a dream that make him unsafe. She fears that he will desert her and that, like her mother, she will "die weeping."

For Marlow, Jewel's dread strikes at the core of Jim's meaning, of his own investment in Jim, and of the irony that our culture enforces. "She should have made for herself a shelter of unexpugnable peace out of that honest affection. She had not the knowledge—not the skill perhaps" (p. 313). With his own doubts about the viability of the order Jim has violated, Marlow too wants to believe that Jim can create a truer shelter. But in Marlow's case knowledge undoes skill. Jewel demands that he affirm, not the greatness of Jim's dream, but its safety. Rhetorically and thematically, her plea intensifies the unbearable necessity for the protection of a lie, a fiction, an illusion, or a faith announced in *Heart of Darkness*.

> "Nothing easier than to say, Have no fear! Nothing more difficult. How does one kill fear, I wonder? How do you shoot a spectre through the heart, slash off its spectral head, take it by its spectral throat? It is an enterprise you rush into while you dream, and are glad to make your escape with wet hair and every limb shaking. The bullet is not run, the blade not forged, the man not born; even the winged words of truth drop at your feet like lumps of lead. You require for such a desperate encounter an enchanted and poisoned shaft dipped in a lie too subtle to be found on earth. An enterprise for a dream, my masters!"   (p. 316)

Jewel's fear condenses the dread that is the unexpugnable reality of the human situation. It contains the anxiety that brings primal religion or order into being: the "haunting fear that the unaccountable and turbulent powers may at any time bring disaster to human society."[17]

The force of such fear and its truth are the tenor behind Conrad's irony, which is more far-reaching and implacable than that contained in Marlow's ambivalent attitudes. Jim's dream-crafted shelter and the protective illusion that our culture would maintain are both vehicles that distort or conceal or disclaim the fact of fear.

Responding to Jewel's need, Marlow tells her that Jim will never leave because he is not good enough to return to the world outside Patusan. But this attempt to rescue truth from the unearthly need for deception cannot assuage the horror of Jewel's pathetic vulnerability. She cries out that Marlow is just repeating the "lie" that Jim has told her. Even Marlow's statement that "nobody, nobody is good enough" (p. 319) is not good enough. "I had only succeeded in adding to her anguish the hint of some mysterious collusion, of an inexplicable and incomprehensible conspiracy to keep her for ever in the dark" (p. 321). Because Marlow believes that our cultural refuge is no less a dream than Jim's creation, he cannot produce the golden bough of faith that might have the absolute force necessary to counter absolute fear. However historically inevitable, his irony serves Jewel no better than Jim's vision.

Yet despite the futility of his encounter with Jewel, Marlow cleaves to the subjective and objective truthfulness that he hopes to find in Jim. Jewel's fear may be the saddest confirmation of pessimism, but her almost worshipful love of Jim may confirm the dream. Hesitation of light and dark, optimism and pessimism, faith and fear continues through the short remainder of Marlow's evening narrative. About to leave the perplexing scene forever, Marlow looks back at Jim alone on the beach. "For me that white figure in the stillness of coast and sea seemed to stand at the heart of a vast enigma. The twilight was ebbing fast . . . he himself appeared no bigger than a child—then only a speck, a tiny white speck, that seemed to catch all the light in a darkened world" (p. 336). A poignant personal valediction ebbs into a suggestion of cosmic darkness and the questionable public compromises it entails. But the tone of private deprivation dominates: "And suddenly, I lost him . . ." (p. 336; Conrad's ellipsis). For a moment, empathy appears to overrule irony. At the same time, however, a larger perspective than Marlow's is contained in the puzzling echo of Cornelius's attack on Jim a few pages earlier: the intruder who has "stolen" Jewel and upset the gross rule of fear and force is "no more than a little child" (p. 329). The resonance of youthful possibility is cut off by the suggestion of Jim's childishness. And though Jewel's stepfather is a slimy, greedy outcast, he has a point. So much rhetoric, so much attention, to a child, a simple deserter, a criminal, another outcast?

Marlow's hopes for Jim and for himself through Jim have developed ever further away from the moral bearings so heavily stressed at the beginning. Gradually the account of Jim's fate in Patusan has become in itself the subject of the larger action of ironic hesitation that is Lord Jim. Jim's leap, his trial, and his banishment from trust all involve familiar standards; they can be judged against a set of values that provides a firm tenor for a stable moral irony. But the Patusan narrative flirts with an equivocal transmutation of culture's wayward child into the darkling world's only light. Marlow's attitude, to be sure, remains strongly hedged. But Jim is presented as carrying into real history the intemperate absolutism and quixotry that earlier novels of moral realism deem childish and dangerous. The crepuscular imagery comes to seem a means of distancing the implicit heresy in Marlow's view of Jim. The youth's career comes to approximate the subversive plot of the criminal, the rebel against the ranks, or the artist who creates a truer reality than his society can conceive. Jim very nearly creates an identity, a love, a commonweal, and a fate more authentic than those he has left behind. He seems poised to forge on the smithy of boys' books the uncreated conscience of his race.

At this point, however, both narratively and thematically, Marlow's perspective is fractured emphatically. With the introduction of the correspondent to whom Marlow sends the concluding fragments of his tale and the narration of Gentleman Brown within these fragments we enter a complexity that confirms Gérard Genette's comment that the narrative "entanglement reaches the bounds of general intelligibility."[18] As Jim flies in the face of common understanding and truth, and as Marlow unsteadily follows him, we are sternly brought up short by the reported reactions of Marlow's correspondent.

> "[I] remember well you would not admit he had mastered his fate. You prophesied for him the disaster of weariness and of disgust with acquired honour, with the self-appointed task, with the love sprung from pity and youth. You had said you knew so well 'that kind of thing,' its illusory satisfaction, its unavoidable deception. You said also . . . that 'giving your life up to them' (*them* meaning all of mankind with skins brown, yellow, or black, in colour) 'was like selling your soul to a brute.' You contended that 'that kind of thing' was only endurable and enduring when based on a firm conviction in the truth of ideas racially our own, in whose name are established the order, the morality of an ethical progress. . . . 'Without it the sacrifice is only forgetfulness, the way of offering is no better than the way to perdition.' In other words, you maintained that we must fight in the ranks or our lives can't count. Possibly! . . . the point, however, is that of all mankind Jim had no dealings but with himself, and the question is whether at the last he had not confessed to a faith mightier than the laws of order and progress."   (pp. 338–39)

The rigid restatement of the code places Marlow's allegiance and the question that underlies it firmly beyond the pale. Jim's faith and Marlow's willingness to entertain it involve a radical separation from the secular religion that ratifies our decency, honor, and truth.

The correspondent's conviction, Marlow's suspension of disbelief, and the near memory of Jewel's dread combine to explain the tremendous stakes involved in Jim's encounter with Gentleman Brown. The enemy Jim confronts is not a "brute" but the perfect pervasion of what Marlow calls the "European mind." In Guérard's words, Brown embodies "ruthless and cynical intelligence at the service of pure love of destruction."[19] Brown sails "into Jim's history, a blind accomplice of the Dark Powers" (p. 354). This "man-beast of folklore" (p. 372) is the enigma of evil. The little we learn about him—his possible aristocratic parentage, his fear of confinement, his elopement with a missionary's ailing wife—does nothing to clarify his "complex intention" (p. 353). the information Conrad provides serves only to connect Brown with a tradition of Gothic villains. But to be outside the pale of moral order is to be beyond interpretation; evil is as much the absence of meaning as it is the absence of caritas. Brown is all that opposes civilization. He wields a "blind belief in the righteousness of his will against all mankind, something of that feeling which could induce the leader of a horde of wandering cut-throats to call himself proudly the Scourge of God" (p. 370). Browns' diabolic self-creation opposes the self-appointed faith Jim has been living by. The two face each other as "opposite poles of that conception of life which includes all mankind" (p. 381).

The conflict, "the deadliest kind of duel on which Fate looked on with her cold-eyed knowledge of the end" (p. 385), is, as has been often observed, a brilliantly conceived psychomachia. Schwarz writes that "Gentleman Brown seems to connive with Jim's latent psychic needs to discover the latter's nature and destiny. He presents the lower, darker side that Jim has purged from the world that fulfils his fantasies. Once Jim recognises a mirror image of Gentleman Brown, the social fabric that he has woven on Patusan collapses."[20] Translated into the moral, public terms of an agon involving mankind's conception of itself, the duel has an even more darkly ramified force. For Brown is the nightmare nemesis of all that Jim's dream can represent, the vile secret sharer of Jim's great heresy. The dark "Gentleman" is the horror shadowing the bright "Lord." Brown enacts the realty behind Jewel's dread.

Brown curses Jim as a "hollow sham"; he mocks Jim's "superior soul" (p. 344). Morality, ideals, and high aspirations are lies. Because Brown speaks out of the inscrutable evil that exists in the abyss between our sheltering conception and the factual nature of an alien universe, he shares the equivocal position that Jim himself occupies. Brown's evil is the traditional blackness of melodrama; he is the most nearly perfect figure of evil in Conrad's work. And he is so because he must embody the one truth Jim's dream cannot pass beyond. The only response to Brown would be a version of the Landlady's comment on the evil Rigaud in Dickens's *Little Dorrit*: "there are people whom it is necessary to detest without compromise. . . . people who must be dealt with as enemies of the human race . . . people who have no human heart, and who must be crushed like savage beasts and cleared out of the way."[21] To Marlow, meeting Brown later, the man is a vile but shabby demon. But Jim, existing in his shadow land outside fixed meanings, is nakedly vulnerable; he cannot meet evil with the blind conventional conviction for which Dickens's landlady speaks. And Jim's inability takes us back to the conventional wisdom of Marlow's correspondent. Brown's hatred of all order, which he equates with unbearable imprisonment, perversely revises the correspondent's conservatism. Man is fallen; human nature is corruption. The correspondent, like other conservative moralists, responds to the premise by insisting on laws and limits. Those who violate the code invite perdition. But Brown, being perdition incarnate, glories in the premise itself: in our common vileness. He knows that Jim's story "is not better than mine. I've lived—and so did you though you talk as if you were one of those people that should have wings so as to go about without touching the dirty earth. Well—it is dirty. I haven't got any wings. I am here because I was afraid once in my life. . . . I won't ask you what scared you into this infernal hole" (p. 383). "And there ran through the rough talk a vein of subtle reference to their common blood, an assumption of common experience; a sickening suggestion of common guilt, of secret knowledge that was like a bond of their minds and of their hearts" (p. 387). In their opposing ways, both men do share the knowledge that "nobody is good enough." Brown glories in the fact; Jim would overleap the fact. But the fact is what necessitates the moral order of civilization's ranks; it is at the core of Jewel's dread; it is the gravest argument against Jim's dream of creating a better order out of and by himself.

The truth mightier than we know, which is the hope Marlow invests in the dream, carries with it the refusal of traditional doubts about man's ability to create order out of his weak or fallen nature. The public consequences of Jim's sanguine faith seem to reinforce the traditional worldly irony that Marlow's account has been trying to sidestep. For Jim is no longer alone in his dream. With him are Jewel, Dain Waris, and the entire "social fabric of orderly, peaceful life, when every man was sure of to-morrow, the edifice raised by Jim's hands" (p. 373). Jim advises that Brown be allowed to depart in peace. The natives are shocked, but "most of them simply said that they 'believed Tuan Jim.' "

> "In this simple form of assent to his will lies the whole gist of the situation; their creed, his truth; and the testimony to that faithfulness which made him in his own eyes the equal of the impeccable men who never fall out of the ranks. Stein's words, 'Romantic!—Romantic!' seem to ring over those distances that will never give him up now to a world indifferent to his failings and virtues, and to that ardent and clinging affection [Jewel's love] that refuses him the dole of tears in the bewilderment of a great grief and of eternal separation. From the moment the sheer truthfulness of his last three years of life carries the day against the ignorance, the fear, and the anger of men, he appears no longer to me as I saw him last—a white speck catching all the dim light left upon a sombre coast and the darkened sea—but greater and more pitiful in the loneliness of his soul, that remains even for her who loved him best a cruel and insoluble mystery." (p. 393)

Jim's last acts in Patusan sharply delimit the greatness that Marlow continues to affirm. Jim and Brown exchange promises of mutual forbearance. "It is evident that he did not mistrust Brown"; Jim could not know "the almost inconceivable egotism of the man which made him, when resisted and foiled in his will, mad with the indignant and revengeful rage of a thwarted autocrat" (p. 394). Because Jim cannot know, Dain Waris and others are killed; the social edifice collapses. "We shall have to fight," Jim's faithful servant tells him. " 'Fight! What for?' he asked. 'For our lives.' 'I have no life,' he said" (p. 409). Leaving Jewel and the others who still believe in him behind, Jim goes to stand before Dain Waris's father; he takes full responsibility for the disaster and allows himself to be shot. Neither the misjudgment nor the romantic egoism of this final gesture denies Jim's truthfulness. But if trust in the shelter his creed would raise up is the gist of the situation, then Jim's individual truth and faithfulness are beside the point. However great, however pitiful in the spotlight of his mysterious isolation, Jim has again failed. No man alone can achieve the safety that is the truth and grand illusion of our moral Realpolitik. Yet despite this strong implication, Marlow's final estimate is still hesitant.

> "And that's the end. He passes away under a cloud, inscrutable at heart, forgotten, unforgiven, and excessively romantic. Not in the wildest days of his boyish visions could he have seen the alluring shape of such an extraordinary success! For it may very well be that in the short moment of his last proud and unflinching glance, he had beheld the face of that opportunity which, like an Eastern bride, had come veiled to his side.
>
> "But we can see him, an obscure conqueror of fame, tearing himself out of the arms of a jealous love at the sign, at the call of his exalted egoism. He goes away from a living woman to celebrate his pitiless wedding with a shadowy ideal of conduct.... Now he is no more, there are days when the reality of his existence comes to me with an immense, with an overwhelming force; and yet upon my honour there are moments, too, when he passes from my eyes like a disembodied spirit astray amongst the passions of his earth, ready to surrender himself faithfully to the claims of his own world of shades."
>
> (p. 416)

To the end, Marlow is torn between the two conceptions of meaning through which he views Jim. Moving upriver into Patusan, Jim has passed beyond clear vision and through the gates of dream. For the French lieutenant or Marlow's correspondent, and often for Marlow himself, the gates are of ivory: the portal to false prophecy and deluding vision. The irony founded upon "the morality of an ethical progress" casts Jim as preposterously childish, as unreal. The issues raised by Jim's story pertain only to the world of shades. For the romantic idealist Stein and by extension for the modern tradition that would revise naive romantic individualism into the art of self-creation, the gates may be those of horn: the entry to true dreams. For the Marlow that affirms Jim's success, Jim's ideal follows the splendid will-o'-the-wisp of imaginative reality; the dream courts all the glamour, brightness, and intensity that should attend man's moral enterprise. This idea of Jim is no less shrouded in irony than the former, but the irony is of a different kind. For Marlow's imaginative empathy and the subjective allegiance that accompanies it construe Jim's endeavor, not as a delusion or a lie, but as something resembling a fiction, an artwork. And the irony here is similar to romantic irony: a moral and epistemological self-consciousness about the reality of what imagination can create: a questioning of the relation between the truths of facts and the truths of spirit.

Marlow's flickering hope that the "obscure truth" of Jim's mystery may be "momentous enough to affect mankind's conception of itself" gives life to his narrative. But Marlow is himself always at least half-aware of a larger perspective: that of the novel's irony in regard to private dreams. For in *Lord Jim* Conrad places Marlow's hope for Jim in much the same ironic distance as that Marlow himself employs to convey Jim's dedication to his ideal yet spectral success. Jim's story is paired with Marlow's empathic account of the story's momentousness; both become part of a rueful, ironic valediction to romantic aspiration. Speaking biographically, we may hazard as others have done that Conrad is turning from his romantic father's spirit to accept the lessons of necessity and futility that his practical uncle would teach. Speaking more directly to Conrad's themes as they will develop from *Lord Jim* to *Under Western Eyes*, we can say that Conrad's attitudes are already more somber and more ironic than Marlow's hesitations. That Marlow embodies much of his creator's commitment to the reality of ambiguity is evident. And part of Conrad may be as romantic as Jim and as attuned to romance as Marlow. But Conrad's own conception of romance has left the individual instance behind; the concerns evident in the nakedness of the *Patna* pilgrims adrift in a cruel universe, in Jewel's dread, and in Gentleman Brown's evil demand what is usually termed a political perspective. The individual's dreamwork, even though it involves the creation of moral order, elicits less of Conrad's interest than the necessities and ironies of the momentous illusion-making that is vested in the idea of civilization. In the progress of Conrad's concerns, the still personal scorn and duality with which Marlow regards our shelter of words will lead to the perplexing public meaning accorded the Western language teacher who narrates *Under Western Eyes*; the vulnerable pilgrims, the fearful girl, and the fact of evil will comingle in the appalling mystery that is Russia.

Jim's dream is not so much rejected as it is passed beyond. The last lines of the novel leave Jewel trailing out "a soundless, inert life in Stein's house." Stein himself, the mentor of romantic idealism, has aged markedly; he is preparing for death, and in the final words of the narrative "waves his hand sadly at his butterflies" (pp. 416–17). A page earlier, in his parting comment on Jim, Marlow seems willing to subordinate the pathos of the living woman to the glamour of the Eastern bride, the consort of Jim's dream. But the concluding scene joins Jewel to the Intended, Emilia Gould, and Winnie Verloc as a symbol, however chauvinistic on Conrad's part, of the purity, fidelity, and frailty of women: an embodiment of values and needs that demand a more responsible fiction than Jim's. And with whatever ambivalence and regret, it is to this objective fiction, to the politics of illusion, that Conrad turns in his next novel.

NOTES

With the exception of several quotations from the first edition of *Nostromo*, all quotations from Conrad's work are from the Kent Edition (New York: Doubleday, Page, 1926) and are cited by page number in the text.

[1] Albert J. Guérard, *Conrad the Novelist* (New York: Atheneum, 1967), p. 176.
[2] See Daniel R. Schwarz, *Conrad: Almayer's Folly to Under Western Eyes* (Ithaca: Cornell Univ. Press, 1980), p. 83.
[3] Ford Madox Ford, *The Good Soldier* (New York: Knopf, 1951), p. 7.
[4] Ibid., p. 5.
[5] Peter J. Glassman, *Language and Being: Joseph Conrad and the Literature of Personality* (New York: Columbia Univ. Press, 1976), p. 254.
[6] See Royal Roussel, *The Metaphysics of Darkness* (Baltimore: Johns Hopkins Univ. Press, 1971).
[7] Schwarz, p. 77.

[8] See E. R. Dodds, *The Greeks and the Irrational* (Berkeley and Los Angeles: Univ. of California Press, 1956), ch. 2.

[9] J. Hillis Miller, *Fiction and Repetition* (Cambridge: Harvard Univ. Press, 1982), p. 31.

[10] Schwarz, p. 83.

[11] Guérard, p. 157.

[12] David Thorburn, *Conrad's Romanticism* (New Haven: Yale Univ. Press, 1974). See also Ian Watt's extended discussion of Stein, *Conrad in the Nineteenth Century* (Berkeley and Los Angeles: Univ. of California Press, 1979), pp. 323–31.

[13] Honoré de Balzac, *Père Goriot*, trans. Henry Reed (New York: Signet Classics, 1962), p. 216.

[14] Nathaniel Hawthorne, *The Marble Faun* (Boston: Houghton Mifflin, 1892), [Preface], p. 15.

[15] Guérard, p. 162. See also Miller's comments on light and dark in Patusan, p. 38.

[16] Tzvetan Todorov, *The Fantastic*, trans. Richard Howard (Cleveland: Press of Case Western Reserve Univ., 1973), pp. 25, 31.

[17] H. and H. A. Frankfort, "The Emancipation of Thought from Myth," in H. and H. A. Frankfort, eds., *Before Philosophy* (Baltimore: Penguin Books, 1949), p. 240.

[18] Gérard Genette, *Narrative Discourse*, trans. Jane E. Lewin (Ithaca: Cornell Univ. Press, 1980), p. 232.

[19] Guérard, p. 149.

[20] Schwarz, p. 82.

[21] Charles Dickens, *Little Dorrit* (London: Oxford Univ. Press, 1953), p. 127 (ch. 11).

CONTRIBUTORS

HAROLD BLOOM is Sterling Professor of the Humanities at Yale University and Henry W. and Albert A. Berg Professor of English at the New York University Graduate School. He is a 1985 MacArthur Foundation Award recipient, served as the Charles Eliot Norton Professor of Poetry at Harvard University (1987–88), and is the author of nineteen books, the most recent being *The Book of J* (1990). Currently he is editing the Chelsea House series Modern Critical Views and The Critical Cosmos, and other Chelsea House series in literary criticism.

ALAN WARREN FRIEDMAN is Professor of English at the University of Texas. He has written *Lawrence Durrell and the Alexandria Quartet* (1970), *Multivalence: The Moral Quality of Form in the Modern Novel* (1978), and *William Faulkner* (1984), has edited *Forms of Modern British Fiction* (1975) and *Critical Essays on Lawrence Durrell* (1987), and has coedited *Beckett Translating/Translating Beckett* (1987); with Charles Rossman and Dina Sherzer).

JACQUES BERTHOUD is Professor of English at the University of York (York, England). He is the author of *Joseph Conrad: The Major Phase* (1978) and editor of Anthony Trollope's *Phineas Finn* (1991).

IAN WATT is Jackson Eli Reynolds Professor Emeritus of the Humanities at Stanford University. He is the author of *The Rise of the Novel* (1957), *Conrad in the Nineteenth Century* (1979), *Joseph Conrad: Nostromo* (1988), and other volumes. He has edited *Jane Austen: A Collection of Critical Essays* (1963) and *The Victorian Novel: Modern Essays in Criticism* (1971).

GARRETT STEWART is Professor of English at the University of California–Santa Barbara. He has written *Death Sentences: Styles of Dying in British Fiction* (1984) and *Reading Voices: Literature and the Phonotext* (1990).

BENITA PARRY is the author of *Delusions and Discoveries: Studies on India in the British Imagination 1880–1930* (1972) and *Conrad and Imperialism* (1983).

MARK CONROY is Professor of English at Ohio State University and has written *Modernism and Authority: Strategies of Legitimation in Flaubert and Conrad* (1985).

KENNETH SIMONS is the author of *The Ludic Imagination: A Reading of Joseph Conrad* (1985). He teaches English and writing at Syosset High School (Syossett, NY).

FRED MADDEN is Professor of English at Ithaca College (Ithaca, NY). He has written on Edgar Allan Poe and Ken Kesey.

ANTHONY WINNER is Professor of English at the University of Virginia. He is the author of *Characters in the Twilight: Hardy, Zola, and Chekhov* (1981) and *Culture and Irony: Studies in Joseph Conrad's Major Novels* (1988).

BIBLIOGRAPHY

Addison, Bill Kaler. "Marlow, Aschenbach, and We." *Conradiana* 2, No. 2 (Winter 1969–70): 79–84.

Adelman, Gary. Heart of Darkness: *Search for the Unconscious.* Boston: Twayne, 1987.

Andreach, Robert J. *The Slain and Ressurrected God: Conrad, Ford, and the Christian Myth.* New York: New York University Press, 1970.

Arneson, Richard J. "Marlow's Skepticism in *Heart of Darkness.*" *Ethics* 94 (1983–84): 420–40.

Baines, Jocelyn. *Joseph Conrad: A Critical Biography.* London: Weidenfeld & Nicolson, 1960.

Barza, Steven. "Bonds of Empathy: The Widening Audience of *Lord Jim.*" *Midwest Quarterly* 25 (1983–84): 220–32.

Batchelor, John. *Lord Jim.* London: Unwin Hyman, 1988.

Bennett, Carl D. "Tragic Awareness—Marlow." In *Joseph Conrad.* New York: Continuum, 1991, pp. 58–83.

Bevan, Ernest, Jr. "Marlow and Jim: The Reconstructed Past." *Conradiana* 15 (1983): 191–202.

Birdseye, Lewis. "*Chance:* Conrad's Modern Novel." *Studies in the Twentieth Century* No. 15 (1975): 77–94.

Bloom, Harold, ed. *Joseph Conrad.* New York: Chelsea House, 1986.

———, ed. *Joseph Conrad's* Heart of Darkness. New York: Chelsea House, 1987.

———, ed. *Joseph Conrad's* Lord Jim. New York: Chelsea House, 1987.

Bonney, William W. *Thorns and Arabesques: Contexts for Conrad's Fiction.* Baltimore: Johns Hopkins University Press, 1980.

Bouson, J. Brooks. "Storytelling as Attempted Self-Rescue in Conrad's 'The Secret Sharer' and 'Heart of Darkness.'" In *The Empathic Reader: A Study of the Narcissistic Character and the Drama of the Self.* Amherst: University of Massachusetts Press, 1989, pp. 82–104.

Boyle, Ted. "Marlow's Choice in 'Heart of Darkness.'" In *The Modernists: Studies in a Literary Phenomenon,* edited by Lawrence B. Gamache and Ian S. MacNiven. Rutherford, NJ: Fairleigh Dickinson University Press, 1987, pp. 92–102.

———. *Symbol and Meaning in the Fiction of Joseph Conrad.* The Hague: Mouton, 1965.

Bradbrook, M. C. *Joseph Conrad: Poland's English Genius.* Cambridge: Cambridge University Press, 1941.

Brashear, William R. "The Mirror of Despair: Conrad." In *The Gorgon's Head: A Study in Tragedy and Despair.* Athens: University of Georgia Press, 1977, pp. 59–87.

Brooks, Peter. "An Unreadable Report: Conrad's *Heart of Darkness.*" In *Reading for the Plot: Design and Intention in Narrative.* New York: Knopf, 1984, pp. 238–63.

Brown, E. K. "James and Conrad." *Yale Review* 35 (1945–46): 265–85.

Bruffee, Kenneth A. "The Lesser Nightmare: Marlow's Lie in *Heart of Darkness.*" *Modern Language Quarterly* 25 (1964): 322–29.

Bruss, Paul. *Conrad's Early Sea Fiction: The Novelist as Navigator.* Lewisburg, PA: Bucknell University Press, 1979.

———. "*Lord Jim* and the Metaphor of Awakening." *Studies in the Twentieth Century* No. 14 (1974): 69–84.

Cottom, Daniel. "*Lord Jim:* Destruction through Time." *Centennial Review* 27 (1983): 10–29.

Cox, C. B. *Joseph Conrad: The Modern Imagination.* London: J. M. Dent; Totowa, NJ: Rowman & Littlefield, 1974.

Crews, Frederick. "The Power of Darkness." *Partisan Review* 34 (1967): 507–25.

Curle, Richard. *Joseph Conrad and His Characters.* London: Heinemann, 1957.

Dahl, James C. "Kurtz, Marlow, Conrad and the Human Heart of Darkness." *Studies in the Literary Imagination* 1, No. 2 (October 1968): 33–40.

Daleski, H. M. *Joseph Conrad: The Way of Dispossession.* New York: Holmes & Meier, 1977.

Darras, Jacques. *Joseph Conrad and the West: Signs of Empire.* Translated by Anne Luyat and Jacques Darras. Totowa, NJ: Barnes & Noble, 1982.

Davis, Harold E. "Shifting Rents in a Thick Fog: Point of View in the Novels of Joseph Conrad." *Conradiana* 2, No. 2 (Winter 1969–70): 23–38.

Dowden, Wilfred S. *Joseph Conrad: The Imaged Style.* Nashville: Vanderbilt University Press, 1970.

Elliott, Dorice Williams. "Hearing the Darkness: The Narrative Chain in Conrad's *Heart of Darkness.*" *English Literature in Transition* 28 (1985): 162–81.

Fichter, Andrew. "Dramatic Voice in *Lord Jim* and *Nostromo.*" *Thoth* 12, No. 3 (Spring–Summer 1972): 3–19.

Fleischman, Avrom. *Conrad's Politics: Community and Anarchy in the Fiction of Joseph Conrad.* Baltimore: Johns Hopkins University Press, 1967.

Fothergill, Anthony. *Heart of Darkness.* Milton Keynes, Eng.: Open University Press, 1989.

Fowler, Doreen. "Marlow's Lie: A Terrible Truth." *CLA Journal* 23 (1979–80): 287–95.

Fraser, Gail. *Interweaving Patterns in the Works of Joseph Conrad.* Ann Arbor: MI: UMI Research Press, 1988.

Frieslich, Richard. "Marlow's Shadow Side." *London Magazine* 4, No. 11 (November 1957): 31–36.

Geddes, Gary. "The Structure of Sympathy: Conrad and the Chance That Wasn't." *English Literature in Transition* 12 (1969): 175–88.

Gekoski, R. A. *Conrad: The Moral World of the Novelist.* London: Paul Elek, 1978.

Glassman, Peter J. *Language and Being: Joseph Conrad and the Literature of Personality.* New York: Columbia University Press, 1976.

Golanka, Mary, "Mr. Kurtz, I Presume? Livingstone and Stanley as Prototypes of Kurtz and Marlow." *Studies in the Novel* 17 (1985): 194–202.

Graham, Kenneth. "Conrad's Breaking Strains." In *Indirections of the Novel: James, Conrad, and Forster.* Cambridge: Cambridge University Press, 1988, pp. 93–153.

Graver, Lawrence. *Conrad's Short Fiction.* Berkeley: University of California Press, 1969.

Guetti, James. " 'Heart of Darkness' and the Failure of the Imagination." *Sewanee Review* 73 (1965): 488–504.

———. *The Rhetoric of Joseph Conrad.* Amherst: Amherst College Press, 1960.

Gurko, Leo. *Joseph Conrad: Giant in Exile.* New York: Macmillan, 1962.

Hardy, John Edward. "*Heart of Darkness:* The Russian in Motley." In *Man in the Modern Novel.* Seattle: University of Washington Press, 1964, pp. 17–33.

Haugh, Robert F. *Joseph Conrad: Discovery in Design.* Norman: University of Oklahoma Press, 1957.

Hawkins, Hunt. "Conrad's Critique of Imperialism in *Heart of Darkness.*" *PMLA* 94 (1979): 286–99.

Hawthorn, Jeremy. *Joseph Conrad: Language and Fictional Self-Consciousness.* London: University of Nebraska Press, 1979.

——. *Joseph Conrad: Narrative Technique and Ideological Commitment*. London: Edward Arnold, 1990.

Hay, Eloise Knapp. *The Political Novels of Joseph Conrad: A Critical Study*. Chicago: University of Chicago Press, 1963.

Hodges, Robert R. "The Four Fathers of Lord Jim." *University Review* 31 (1964): 103–10.

Hough, Graham. "*Chance* and Joseph Conrad." In *Image and Experience: Studies in a Literary Revolution*. London: Duckworth, 1960, pp. 211–22.

Hubbard, Francis A. *Theories of Action in Conrad*. Ann Arbor, MI: UMI Research Press, 1984.

Johnson, Bruce. *Conrad's Models of Mind*. Minneapolis: University of Minnesota Press, 1971.

Jones, Michael P. *Conrad's Heroism: A Paradise Lost*. Ann Arbor: UMI Research Press, 1985.

Kam, Rose Sallberg. "Silverberg and Conrad: Explorers of Inner Darkness." *Extrapolation* 17 (1975–76): 18–28.

Karl, Frederick R. *Joseph Conrad: The Three Lives: A Biography*. New York: Farrar, Straus & Giroux, 1979.

——. *A Reader's Guide to Joseph Conrad*. New York: Noonday Press, 1960.

Kauvar, Gerald B. "Marlow as Liar." *Studies in Short Fiction* 5 (1967–68): 290–92.

Ketterer, David. "'Beyond the Threshold' in Conrad's *Heart of Darkness*." *Texas Studies in Literature and Language* 11 (1969–70): 1013–22.

Kirschner, Paul. *Conrad: The Psychologist as Artist*. Edinburgh: Oliver & Boyd, 1968.

Klein, Herbert G. "Charting the Unknown: Conrad, Marlow, and the World of Women." *Conradiana* 20 (1988): 147–57.

Kolenda, Konstantin. "Truth Received: Conrad's *Heart of Darkness*." In *Philosophy in Literature: Metaphysical Darkness and Ethical Light*. Totowa, NJ: Barnes & Noble, 1982, pp. 75–88.

Kramer, Dale. "Marlow, Myth, and Structure in *Lord Jim*." *Criticism* 8 (1966): 263–79.

Krieger, Murray. "From *Youth* to *Lord Jim*: The Formal-Thematic Use of Marlow." In *The Play and Place of Criticism*. Baltimore: Johns Hopkins University Press, 1967, pp. 91–104.

——. "Joseph Conrad: Action, Inaction, and Extremity." In *The Tragic Vision: Variations on a Theme in Literary Interpretation*. New York: Holt, Rinehart & Winston, 1960, pp. 154–94.

Land, Stephen K. *Paradox and Polarity in the Fiction of Joseph Conrad*. New York: St. Martin's Press, 1984.

Leavis, F. R. "Joseph Conrad." In *The Great Tradition*. London: Chatto & Windus, 1948, pp. 173–226.

Lester, John. *Conrad and Religion*. New York: St. Martin's Press, 1988.

Levin, Gerald. "The Scepticism of Marlow." *Twentieth Century Literature* 3 (1957–58): 177–84.

Lord, George deForest. "Imperial Horror: Conrad's *Heart of Darkness*." In *Trials of the Self: Heroic Ordeals in the Epic Tradition*. New York: Archon Books, 1983, pp. 192–216.

Low, Anthony. "*Heart of Darkness*: The Search for an Occupation." *English Literature in Transition* 12 (1969): 1–9.

McClure, John A. *Kipling and Conrad: The Colonial Fiction*. Cambridge, MA: Harvard University Press, 1981.

McLauchlan, Juliet. "The 'Something Human' in *Heart of Darkness*." *Conradiana* 9 (1977): 115–25.

——. "The 'Value' and 'Significance' of *Heart of Darkness*." *Conradiana* 15 (1983): 3–21.

Malbone, Raymond Gates. " 'How to Be': Marlow's Quest in *Lord Jim*." *Twentieth Century Literature* 10 (1964–65): 172–80.

Martin, David M. "The Function of the Intended in Conrad's 'Heart of Darkness.' " *Studies in Short Fiction* 11 (1974): 27–33.

Mathews, James W. "Ironic Symbolism in Conrad's 'Youth.' " *Studies in Short Fiction* 11 (1973–74): 117–23.

Meyer, Bernard C. *Joseph Conrad: A Psychoanalytic Biography*. Princeton: Princeton University Press, 1967.

Meyers, Jeffrey. *Joseph Conrad: A Biography*. New York: Scribner's, 1991.

Miller, J. Hillis. "Joseph Conrad." In *Poets of Reality: Six Twentieth-Century Writers*. Cambridge, MA: Harvard University Press, 1965, pp. 13–67.

Milne, Fred L. "Marlow's Lie and the Intended: Civilization as the Lie in *Heart of Darkness*." *Arizona Quarterly* 44 (1988): 106–12.

Moore, Carlisle. "Conrad and the Novel as Ordeal." *Philological Quarterly* 42 (1963): 55–74.

Moser, Thomas. *Joseph Conrad: Achievement and Decline*. Cambridge, MA: Harvard University Press, 1957.

Murfin, Ross C., ed. *Conrad Revisited: Essays for the Eighties*. University: University of Alabama Press, 1985.

Nalbantian, Suzanne. "Joseph Conrad and the Dissolution of an Ethical Code: The Hollow Centre." In *Seeds of Decadence in the Late Nineteenth-Century Novel: A Crisis in Values*. New York: St. Martin's Press, 1983, pp. 96–115.

Newman, Paul B. "The Drama of Conscience and Recognition in *Lord Jim*." *Midwest Quarterly* 6 (1964–65): 351–66.

O'Hanlon, Redmond. *Joseph Conrad and Charles Darwin*. Atlantic Highlands, NJ: Humanities Press, 1984.

Orange, Michael. *Joseph Conrad's* Heart of Darkness. Sydney: Sydney University Press, 1990.

Palmer, John A. *Joseph Conrad's Fiction: A Study in Literary Growth*. Ithaca, NY: Cornell University Press, 1968.

Paris, Bernard J. "The Dramatization of Interpretation: *Lord Jim*." In *A Psychological Approach to Fiction*. Bloomington: Indiana University Press, 1974, pp. 215–74.

Pecora, Vincent. "*Heart of Darkness* and the Phenomenology of Voice." *ELH* 52 (1985): 993–1015.

Price, Martin. "Conrad: The Limits of Irony." In *Forms of Life: Character and Moral Imagination in the Novel*. New Haven: Yale University Press, 1983, pp. 235–66.

Raval, Suresh. "Narrative and Authority in *Lord Jim*: Conrad's Art of Failure." *ELH* 48 (1981): 387–410.

Reeves, Charles Eric. "A Voice of Unrest: Conrad's Rhetoric of the Unspeakable." *Texas Studies in Literature and Language* 27 (1985): 284–310.

Renner, Stanley. " 'Youth' and the Sinking Ship of Faith: Conrad's Miniature Nineteenth-Century Epic." *Ball State University Forum* 28, No. 1 (Winter 1987): 57–73.

Ressler, Steve. *Joseph Conrad: Consciousness and Integrity*. New York: New York University Press, 1988.

Ridley, Florence H. "The Ultimate Meaning of 'Heart of Darkness.' " *Nineteenth-Century Fiction* 18 (1963–64): 43–53.

Rising, Catharine. *Darkness at Heart: Fathers and Sons in Conrad*. Westport, CT: Greenwood Press, 1990.

Roussel, Royal. *The Metaphysics of Darkness: A Study in the Unity and Development of Conrad's Fiction.* Baltimore: Johns Hopkins University Press, 1971.

Sagarin, Edward. "Lord Jim: In Endless Search of Redemption." In *Raskolnikof and Others: Literary Images of Crime, Punishment, Redemption, and Atonement.* New York: St. Martin's Press, 1981, pp. 77–95.

Said, Edward W. *Joseph Conrad and the Fiction of Autobiography.* Cambridge, MA: Harvard University Press, 1966.

Saveson, John E. *Joseph Conrad: The Making of a Moralist.* Amsterdam: Rodopi, 1972.

Schwarz, Daniel R. *Conrad:* Almayer's Folly *to* Under Western Eyes. Ithaca, NY: Cornell University Press, 1980.

Senn, Werner. *Conrad's Narrative Voice.* Bern: Francke Verlag, 1980.

Sexton, Mark S. "Kurtz's Sketch in Oils: Its Significance to *Heart of Darkness.*" *Studies in Short Fiction* 24 (1987): 387–92.

Sherry, Norman. *Conrad's Eastern World.* Cambridge: Cambridge University Press, 1966.

Shires, Linda M. "The 'Privileged' Reader and Narrative Methodology in *Lord Jim.*" *Conradiana* 17 (1985): 19–30.

Siegle, Robert. "Conrad, Early Modernism, and the Narrator's Relation to His Material." In *The Politics of Reflexivity: Narrative and the Constitutive Poetics of Culture.* Baltimore: Johns Hopkins University Press, 1986, pp. 66–121.

Simpson, David. "Joseph Conrad: Digging for Silver, Dreaming of Trade." In *Fetishism and Imagination: Dickens, Melville, Conrad.* Baltimore: Johns Hopkins University Press, 1982, pp. 91–116.

Singh, Frances B. "The Colonialistic Bias of *Heart of Darkness.*" *Conradiana* 10, No. 1 (1978): 41–54.

Stein, William Bysshe. "*The Heart of Darkness:* A Bodhisattva Scenario." *Conradiana* 2, No.2 (Winter 1969–70): 39–52.

Steiner, Joan A. "Modern Pharisees and False Apostles: Ironic New Testament Parallels in Conrad's 'Heart of Darkness.'" *Nineteenth-Century Fiction* 37 (1982–83): 75–96.

Stevens, R. C. "*Heart of Darkness:* Marlow's 'Spectral Moonshine.'" *Essays in Criticism* 19 (1969): 273–84.

Stewart, Garrett. "Coppola's Conrad: The Repetitions of Complicity." *Critical Inquiry* 7 (1980–81): 455–74.

Sullivan, Mary. "Conrad's Paralipses in the Narration of *Lord Jim.*" *Conradiana* 10 (1978): 123–40.

Sullivan, Zohreh T. "Enclosure, Darkness, and the Body: Conrad's Landscape." *Centennial Review* 25 (1981): 59–79.

Tanner, J. E. "The Chronology and the Enigmatic End of *Lord Jim.*" *Nineteenth-Century Fiction* 21 (1966–67): 369–80.

Thale, Jerome. "Marlow's Quest." *University of Toronto Quarterly* 24 (1954–55): 351–58.

Thorburn, David. *Conrad's Romanticism.* New Haven: Yale University Press, 1974.

Thurber, Barton. "Speaking the Unspeakable: Conrad and the Sublime." *Conradiana* 16 (1984): 41–54.

Tindall, W. Y. "Apology for Marlow." In *From Jane Austen to Joseph Conrad: Essays Collected in Memory of James T. Hillhouse,* edited by Robert C. Rathburn and Martin Steinmann, Jr. Minneapolis: University of Minnesota Press, 1958, pp. 274–85.

Todorov, Tzvetan. "Knowledge in the Void: *Heart of Darkness.*" Translated by Walter C. Putnam III. *Conradiana* 21 (1989): 161–72.

Verleun, Jan. "Conrad's *Heart of Darkness:* Marlow and the Intended." *Neophilologus* 67 (1983): 623–39.

Wasserman, Jerry. "Narrative Presence: The Illusion of Language in *Heart of Darkness.*" *Studies in the Novel* 6 (1974): 327–38.

Watt, Ian. "Impressionism and Symbolism in *Heart of Darkness.*" In *Joseph Conrad: A Commemoration,* edited by Norman Sherry. London: Macmillan Press, 1976, pp. 37–53.

Watts, Cedric. *Conrad's* Heart of Darkness: *A Critical and Contextual Discussion.* Milan: Mursia International, 1977.

———. *The Deceptive Text: An Introduction to Covert Plots.* Brighton: Harvester Press, 1984.

Weston, John Howard. "'Youth': Conrad's Irony and Time's Darkness." *Studies in Short Fiction* 11 (1974): 399–407.

Whiteley, Patrick J. "Joseph Conrad." In *Knowledge and Experimental Realism in Conrad, Lawrence, and Woolf.* Baton Rouge: Louisiana State University Press, 1987, pp. 27–76.

Wilcox, Stewart C. "Conrad's 'Complicated Presentations' of Symbolic Meaning in *Heart of Darkness.*" *Philological Quarterly* 39 (1960): 1–17.

Wiley, Paul L. *Conrad's Measure of Man.* Madison: University of Wisconsin Press, 1954.

Wills, John Howard. "A Neglected Masterpiece: Conrad's *Youth.*" *Texas Studies in Literature and Language* 4 (1962–63): 591–601.

Willy, Todd G. "The Call to Imperialism in Conrad's 'Youth': An Historical Reconstruction." *Journal of Modern Literature* 8 (1980): 39–50.

Wilson, Robert. *Conrad's Mythology.* Troy, NY: Whitston, 1987.

Wright, Walter F. *Romance and Tragedy in Joseph Conrad.* Norman: University of Oklahoma Press, 1949.

ACKNOWLEDGMENTS

"The Journey Within" by Albert J. Guérard from *Conrad the Novelist* by Albert J. Guérard, © 1958 by the President and Fellows of Harvard College. Reprinted by permission of the author.

"Character as Reality: Joseph Conrad" by Harold Kaplan from *The Passive Voice: An Approach to Modern Fiction* by Harold Kaplan, © 1966 by Harold Kaplan. Reprinted by permission of Ohio University Press and the author.

"Conclusion" by Norman Sherry from *Conrad's Western World* by Norman Sherry, © 1971 by Cambridge University Press. Reprinted by permission of Cambridge University Press.

"Joseph Conrad's Discontinuous Point of View" by William W. Bonney from *Journal of Narrative Technique* 2, No. 2 (May 1972), © 1972 by The Eastern Michigan University Press. Reprinted by permission.

"Conrad's *Lord Jim:* Meditations on the Other Hemisphere" by Stephen Zelnick from *Minnesota Review* NS No. 11 (Fall 1978), © 1978 by *The Minnesota Review.* Reprinted by permission of *The Minnesota Review.*

"*Chance:* The Sympathetic Structure" by Gary Geddes from *Conrad's Later Novels* by Gary Geddes, © 1980 by McGill-Queen's University Press. Reprinted by permission.

"*Heart of Darkness* and the Process of *Apocalypse Now*" by William M. Hagen from *Conradiana* 13, No. 1 (1981), © 1981 by the Textual Studies Institute, Department of English, Texas Tech University. Reprinted by permission of Texas Tech University Press and the author.

"*Chance:* Manners as Psychosexual Drama" by Daniel R. Schwarz from *Conrad: The Later Fiction* by Daniel R. Schwarz, © 1982 by Daniel R. Schwarz. Reprinted by permission of The Macmillan Press Ltd.

"The Truth about Marlow" by Jerome Meckier from *Studies in Short Fiction* 19, No. 4 (Fall 1982), © 1982 by Newberry College. Reprinted by permission of *Studies in Short Fiction.*

"Ideas of Forced Dialogue and Conrad's Forced Dialogue" by Aaron Fogel from *Coercion to Speak: Conrad's Poetics of Dialogue* by Aaron Fogel, © 1985 by the President and Fellows of Harvard College. Reprinted by permission of Harvard University Press.

"The Divided Protagonist: Reading as Repetition and Discovery" by Donald M. Kartiganer from *Texas Studies in Literature and Language* 30, No. 2 (Summer 1988), © 1988 by the University of Texas Press. Reprinted by permission of the University of Texas Press and the author.

"Conrad's Picaresque Narrator" (originally titled "Conrad's Picaresque Narrator: Marlow's Journey from 'Youth' through *Chance*") by Alan Warren Friedman from *Joseph Conrad: Theory and World Fiction,* edited by Wolodymyr T. Zyla and Wendell M. Aycock, © 1974 by the Interdepartmental Committee on Comparative Literature, Texas Tech University. Reprinted by permission of Texas Tech University Press.

"'Heart of Darkness'" by Jacques Berthoud from *Joseph Conrad: The Major Phase* by Jacques Berthoud, © 1978 by Cambridge University Press. Reprinted by permission of Cambridge University Press.

"Marlow and Henry James" by Ian Watt from *Conrad in the Nineteenth Century* by Ian Watt, © 1979 by The Regents of the University of California. Reprinted by permission of University of California Press.

"Lying as Dying in *Heart of Darkness*" by Garrett Stewart from *PMLA* 95, No. 3 (May 1980), © 1980 by The Modern Language Association of America. Reprinted by permission of The Modern Language Association of America.

"Lord Jim" by Benita Parry from *Conrad and Imperialism: Ideological Boundaries and Visionary Frontiers* by Benita Parry, © 1983 by Benita Parry. Reprinted by permission of The Macmillan Press Ltd.

"Paragon and Enigma: The Hero in *Lord Jim*" by Mark Conroy from *Modernism and Authority: Strategies of Legitimation in Flaubert and Conrad* by Mark Conroy, © 1985 by The Johns Hopkins University Press. Reprinted by permission of The Johns Hopkins University Press.

"The Ludic Imagination: 'Youth'" by Kenneth Simons from *The Ludic Imagination: A Reading of Joseph Conrad* by Kenneth Simons, © 1980, 1985 by Kenneth Joseph Simons. Reprinted by permission of the author.

"Marlow and the Double Horror of *Heart of Darkness*" by Fred Madden from *Midwest Quarterly* 27, No. 4 (Summer 1986), © 1986 by Pittsburg State University. Reprinted by permission of *Midwest Quarterly.*

"Lord Jim: Irony and Dream" by Anthony Winner from *Culture and Irony: Studies in Joseph Conrad's Major Novels* by Anthony Winner, © 1988 by the Rector and Visitors of the University of Virginia. Reprinted by permission of The University Press of Virginia.

INDEX

A Rebours (Huysmans), 99
Adventures of Huckleberry Finn
    (Twain), 63
Adventures of Tom Sawyer, The
    (Twain), 63
Alistoun, Captain (The Nigger of the
    "Narcissus"), 73, 87, 91
Althusser, Louis, 161n.4
Ambassadors, The (James), 100, 104
Anderson, Sherwood, 73
Anthony, Captain (Chance), 14, 38–40,
    43, 68, 76
Apocalypse Now (film), 40–42
"Apparition of Mrs. Veal, The" (Defoe),
    15
Awkward Age, The (James), 101, 104

Balzac, Honoré de, 62, 186, 190
Beach, Joseph Warren, 101
"Bear, The" (Faulkner), 19
Beard, Captain ("Youth"), 33, 164–69,
    171
Blackwood's Edinburgh Magazine, 7,
    107–8
Booth, Wayne C., 63, 73, 78
Braddon, Mary Elizabeth, 10
Brando, Marlon, 41
Brierly, Captain Montague (Lord Jim),
    7, 16, 36, 62, 71, 133, 148–49,
    157, 160, 182, 187, 189
Brown, E. K., 102
Brown, Gentleman (Lord Jim), 25, 35,
    62, 66, 69, 137, 140, 142, 154–56,
    158–59, 182, 187, 196–98, 200
Buddha, 33, 50, 67, 122
Byron, George Gordon, Lord, 1–3

Canterbury Tales, The (Chaucer), 62
Carlyle, Thomas, 66
Castorp, Hans (The Magic Mountain),
    113
Céline, Ferdinand, 125
Chance: 1, 3, 5–6, 13–14, 24, 37–40,
    42–46, 62–63, 68, 73–78, 108
Chaucer, Geoffrey, 62
Chester (Lord Jim), 35, 137, 154–56,
    188
Christianity, 2, 26, 58

Chuzzlewit, Martin (Martin Chuzzlewit),
    47
Clarissa (Richardson), 44
Coleridge, Samuel Taylor, 2
Congo, the, 16–17, 21, 24–31, 34, 47–
    51, 63–67, 83–87, 112, 121, 173–
    75, 177–78
Conrad, Joseph: on art, 39–40; on
    Chance, 38; and colonialism, 47,
    153, 161; ethics of, 40, 47, 107,
    164; on fiction, 37, 105–6; as im-
    pressionist, 1, 102; and language,
    10, 21; life of, 1, 17, 25–32; on
    Marlow, 2, 7–9, 32, 77; politics of,
    152–53; on his short stories, 33;
    on symbolism, 98–99
Conrad's Politics (Fleishman), 152
Coppola, Francis Ford, 41–42
Cornelius (Lord Jim), 156, 158, 194–95
Crankshaw, Edward, 107
Cummings, Mr., 10–11

Daleski, H. M., 123
Dante Alighieri, 42, 83
de Barral, Flora (Chance), 10, 14, 24,
    37–40, 43–45, 62–63, 75–78
de Barral, Mr. (Chance), 38–39, 75
Defoe, Daniel, 15
Dickens, Charles, 47, 75, 117, 197
Dodds, E. R., 185
Don Juan (Byron), 2
Don Quixote (Cervantes), 54
Donkin (The Nigger of the "Narcis-
    sus"), 91
Dostoevsky, Fyodor, 116
Double, The (Dostoevsky), 116
Dowell, John (The Good Soldier), 183
Dupee, F. W., 99–100

Eliot, George, 117, 170, 186
Eliot, T. S., 73
Ellmann, Richard, 117
"End of the Tether, The," 33–34

Farange, Maisie (What Maisie Knew),
    101
Faulkner, William, 2, 19, 65
Faust, 22, 27, 120